TREATMENT OF ADULT SURVIVORS OF CHILDHOOD ABUSE

Eliana Gil

Launch Press

Second Edition, 1990

97 96 95   9 8 7 6

Library of Congress Cataloging-in-Publicaton Data

Gil, Eliana.
   Treatment of adult survivors of childhood abuse.

   Bibliography: p.
   1. Adult child abuse victims—Mental health. 2. Psychotherapy.
I. Title.
   RC569.5.C55G56 1988   616.85'82   88-80275
   ISBN 0-9613205-6-7

Launch Press
P.O. Box 5629
Rockville, MD 20855
(800) 321-9167)

To TANYA whose spirit was never broken
and whose heart is on the mend

To MARIAN who allowed me
to stand by her side
as she awakened

Memories have been created
and mutual hope has surfaced.

Contents

Preface

Thousands of children have survived childhood abuse and faced a myriad of emotional and psychological problems as adults. This book discusses treatment of adult survivors of childhood abuse.

There has been a great deal of recent media attention to the topic of child abuse. The increased awareness of the problem has encouraged adult survivors to break their silence and seek help. Mental health professionals are being asked to treat these clients and may lack necessary understanding of the underlying therapeutic issues or techniques. This book offers guidelines for creating an effective therapeutic plan based on known problems encountered by adults who were abused as children. The most critical advice I give therapists is to empathize with and help the small abused child who remains trapped in the adult client.

I have written this book out of respect and concern for the pain and perseverance of hundreds of adult survivors I have seen in therapy.

Many clients allowed me to share partial transcripts of their actual therapy sessions and I thank them. All names used in the text are fictitious.

Acknowledgements

Writing a book is a challenge, an opportunity, a struggle, and an all-consuming experience. You are either at the computer, thinking about being at the computer, preparing to get on the computer, or avoiding the little box.

Although my name is on the front of this book, the project has been completed with the help of many.

I first thank my clients. They have been a source of inspiration and awe. They have survived horrendous experiences, and they are striving to become healthy and happy. I have learned from each and every client because they were willing to trust me.

My colleagues encourage and support my work. In particular, I thank my immediate support group at Gil and Associates: Kathy Sinsheimer, Enid Sanders, and Bill Barron. Jeffrey Bodmer-Turner and I started G & A, and I am filled with respect for his dedication and high standards. He is always available, honest, and caring. Teresa Davi is my best friend; she creates an environment that keeps me sane and allows me to do my job and look forward to coming to work. I also thank Teresa for allowing me to be "Aunt Eliana" to her charming and lovable daughters Melissa and Melinda Brown. (I also act as a sister in law to Tony Davi, a brilliant glass artist). My friends have been incredibly supportive during this project, and I want to thank Mary Herget, Robert Green, Don Wilson, Kathy Baxter-Stern, Lou Fox, and Steve Santini for listening to my occasional woes and self-doubts and giving me unconditional love and encouragement.

A special thanks to Karen Saeger for her valuable contribution as a reader-editor. She helped me become clear and focused. Karen continues to be an inspirational role model and a great friend. I also am greatly indebted to Irene Elmer, my editor, who organized this book and offered suggestions and directives in a succinct, masterful way and Dr. Karen Trocki for the data analysis.

A note of thanks to Dr. Eric Greenleaf, Dr. Arthur O'Keefe and my friends in the Tuesday night group, and Lori Zickerman, for contributing to my sense of well-being.

Last but not least, I want to thank my family. Eric, my sweet and sensitive son, has sat by my side as I worked. He has been patient as I spent full days at the computer, and he is consistently proud of my accomplishments. He is one of my great joys. I also thank my daughter, Teresa Gene, who is always supportive of my work and my life. I am grateful to my step-daughter Christy Lynch for her encouragement and I thank my mother and father in law, Eilleen and Norm Lynch, my mother Eugenia Valero, and my brother, Peter Gil. My family cheers me on in my personal and professional endeavors.

This was a joint project with my husband John. I could not have done this without you. You give me strength when I need it; you make me laugh when I'm down; you give me love when I doubt any exists. I thank you for being who you are and for the feelings you inspire in me.

Part 1

What Was . . .

The Child's Inner World

1.

Behavioral Indicators of Abuse

To understand the adult, we must understand the child within the adult. This is especially true in the case of adults who were abused as children. Let us begin, then, by reviewing some research findings on, and clinical impressions of, children who are the victims of abuse. In this chapter, we shall examine behavioral indicators of abuse. In the next chapter, we shall explore the internal thoughts and perceptions of the abused child.

Abused children are frequently reluctant to talk about their victimization. They may have been told to keep it a secret. They may have been threatened with worse harm if they tell. They may not know that what is happening in their family is not happening in every other family. They may keep quiet simply out of family loyalty.

How, then, are we to recognize the child who is being abused? Physical indicators of abuse are usually apparent only in extreme or chronic cases. In cases of sexual abuse for example, they will be revealed only by a detailed medical examinations. (I should add that the procedures for conducting such an examination have been highly refined in recent years. See Hager, 1987.)

Mental health professionals usually come into contact with abused children because someone is concerned about the child's problem behavior and has sought a professional evaluation. It then becomes the mental health professional's task to collect data, formulate hypotheses, and make appropriate, age-sensitive inquiries to determine the nature of the problem.

Research Findings

There are numerous studies on the impact of abuse on children. Unfortunately, many of these studies are fraught with methodological weaknesses. It is to be hoped that current and future research will yield more reliable data. Meanwhile, in this section I shall summarize the most consistent findings on behavioral indicators of abuse.

Behavioral Indicators of Sexual Abuse

Finkelhor (1986) analyzes the empirical data on short-term effects of sexual abuse. He concludes that abused children regularly exhibit:

- Fear or anxiety

- Depression

- Difficulties in school

- Anger or hostility

- Inappropriate sexualized behavior

- Running away or delinquency

Behavioral Indicators of Physical Abuse

In a ground breaking book, Martin (1976) finds that physically abused children exhibit:

- Impaired capacity to enjoy life

- Psychiatric symptoms, enuresis, tantrums, hyperactivity, bizarre behavior

- Low self-esteem

- Learning problems in school

- Withdrawal

- Opposition

- Hypervigilance

- Compulsivity

- Pseudomature behavior

Martin and Rodeheffer (1980) state that:

> Physical abuse may result in a number of biological consequences, including death, brain damage, mental retardation, cerebral palsy, learning disabilities and sensory deficits. The neurological handicaps of physical abuse are of particular interest because of their chronicity and significance to the long-range functioning of the individual. It is estimated that between 25 and 30% of abused children who survive the attack have brain damage or neurological dysfunction resulting directly from physical trauma about the head (207).

> Martin and Rodeheffer also quote a study conducted by the National Center for Prevention of Child Abuse and Neglect in Denver in 1976 that found that physically abused children have deficits in gross motor development, speech, and language (210).

Martin and Rodeheffer go on to say that physically abused children exhibit:

- Interpersonal ambivalence

- Hypervigilant preoccupation with the behavior of others

- Constant mobilization of defenses in anticipation of danger

- Inability to perceive and act on the environment in pursuit of mastery

- Impaired socialization skills with peers

- Frustration from inability to meet expectations of others

- Defensiveness in social contacts

- "Chameleon nature" (shifting behavior to accommodate to others)

- Learned helplessness ("To try a task and fail is more dangerous than not to try at all")

- Tendency to care for their parents physically and emotionally

- Lack of object permanence or object constancy (distortion of normal object relations)

Reidy (1982) summarizing traits of physically abused children found that they exhibit:

- Aggression and hatred

- Uncontrollable, negativistic behavior, severe temper tantrums

- Lack of impulse control

- Emotionally disturbed behavior both at home and at school

- Withdrawn or inhibited behavior

In his own study (1982), Reidy finds that:

- Abused children express significantly more fantasy aggression on the Thematic Apperception Test (TAT) than other children

- Abused children exhibit aggressive behavior more frequently than other children

- Abused children in their natural homes expressed significantly more fantasy aggression than abused children in foster homes

Kent (1982) finds that physically abused children:

- Tend to have more problems managing aggressive behavior than other children

- Tend to have more problems establishing peer relationships than other children

Martin (1976) makes an important point:

> The child's personality is affected and shaped by the total environment in which [the child] lives. The specific incidents of physical assault are a psychic trauma. However, the broader picture, which may include rejection, chaos, deprivation, distorted parental perceptions, unrealistic expectations as well as hospitalization,separation, foster placement and frequent home changes, is in the long run more significant to the child's development (107).

Behavioral Indicators of Neglect

The dynamics of child neglect differ significantly from the dynamics of physical and sexual abuse. The greatest single difference is that physically and sexually abused children receive attention from their parents. The attention is inappropriate, excessive, harsh, and damaging, but the parent is definitely <u>aware</u> of the child's existence. Energy is directed towards the child.

Neglectful parents do the opposite. Overwhelmed, lethargic, and incapacitated, they feel no interest in the child. They <u>withhold attention.</u> They do not stimulate the child; they rarely make physical or emotional contact. In extreme cases, the neglectful parent seems to be unaware that the child exists.

Polansky (1981) finds that neglected children exhibit:

- "Deprivation-detachment"

- Massive repression of feelings (affect inhibition)

- Impaired ability to empathize with others

- Violence

- Delinquency

- Decrease in general intellectual ability (due to lack of cognitive stimulation on the part of the parent)

Kent (1982) finds:

- Developmental delays

Behavioral Indicators of Emotional Abuse:

Garbarino (1987) describes emotionally abused children as "showing evidence of psychosocial harm." He finds:

- Behavioral problems (anxiety, aggression, hostility)

- Emotional disturbance (feelings of being unloved, unwanted, unworthy)

- Inappropriate social disturbance (negative view of the world)

- In infants, irritability and in some cases non-organic failure to thrive

- Anxious attachment to parents

- Fear or distrust

- Low self-esteem

- Feelings of inferiority; withdrawal; lack of communication

- Self-destructive behavior (self-mutilation, depression, suicidal tendencies)

- Tendency to act as caretaker to parents

- Delinquency or truancy

Garbarino summarizes his findings as follows:

> The psychologically maltreated child is often identi-
> fied by personal characteristics, perceptions, and behav-
> iors that convey low self-esteem, a negative view of the
> world, and internalized or externalized anxieties and
> aggressions. Whether the child clings to adults or avoids
> them, his or her social behavior and responses are
> inappropriate and exceptional.(63)

It should be noted that some victims of child abuse seem to
emerge unscathed. Garbarino (1987) discusses these "stress-resis-
tant" children, who become prosocial and competent, in spite of
their harsh, or even hostile, upbringing. He concludes that these
children receive "compensatory doses of psychological nurtur-
ance and sustenance [that] enable them to develop social competence, that fortify self-esteem, and [that] offer a positive social
definition of self" (9). In the next section, I shall offer some clinical
observations based on my own experience of providing therapy
to abused children. I shall not attempt to categorize behavioral
indicators by type of abuse because they frequently overlap.

Clinical Observations

The problem behaviors of abused children are manifested internally or externally. The following behaviors are ones that are
regularly observed by myself and by those of my colleagues who
specialize in the treatment of abused children. I consider them to
be indicators of abuse. However, they are not conclusive of abuse.
Children who are not abused but who live in dysfunctional
families, may also exhibit these behaviors.

Internalized Behavior

Children who exhibit internalized behavior tend to be isolated
and withdrawn. They attempt to negotiate the abuse by themselves; they do not interact with others. These children frequently:

- Appear withdrawn and unmotivated to seek
  interactions

- Exhibit clinical signs of depression

- Lack spontaneity and playfulness

- Are overcompliant

- Develop phobias with unspecified precipitants

- Appear hypervigilant and anxious

- Experience sleep disorders or night terrors

- Demonstrate regressed behavior

- Have somatic complaints (headaches, stomachaches)

- Develop eating disorders

- Engage in substance and drug abuse

- Make suicide gestures

- Engage in self-mutilation

- Dissociate

Externalized Behavior

Conversely, children with externalized manifestations engage in behavior directed towards others. They exhibit outward expression of their emotions. They are:

- Aggressive, hostile, and destructive

- Provocative (eliciting abuse)

- Violent, and may kill or torture animals

- Sexualized

These children are often more readily identified, because their behavior creates a problem for other people.

Internalized and externalized behaviors can overlap. In my experience, a child may present with internalized behaviors and develop externalized behaviors during treatment. My own hypothesis is that as these children learn to trust the therapist, and are encouraged to express their hidden emotions, they become more able to show feelings such as anger and hostility.

Special Issues

Abused children can develop a couple of special behaviors: dissociation and sexualization. Both are important to assess and treat and seem to be frequently misunderstood, remaining undiagnosed and untreated.

Dissociative Phenomena

The Diagnostic and Statistical Manual of Mental Disorders defines dissociative phenomena as "a disturbance or alteration in the normally integrative functions of identity, memory, or consciousness." (1987) The DSM-III-R categorizes three types of dissociative phenomena: 1) multiple personality disorder (disturbance in identity); 2) depersonalization disorder (disturbance in identity); and 3) psychogenic amnesia or fugue (disturbance in memory). Dissociative phenomena is clearly linked to trauma. There seems to be a tendency towards speedier identification of dissociation in adults.

According to Eth and Pynoos (1985), psychic trauma occurs "when an individual is exposed to an overwhelming event resulting in helplessness in the face of intolerable danger, anxiety, and instinctual arousal" (38). Clearly, child abuse is a psychic trauma to children, the more so by virtue of their size, dependency, and vulnerability.

In addition, emerging empirical data indicate a high correlation between early, severe childhood abuse, and multiple-personality disorder (Kluft 1985).

Clinicians seeking to assess or treat victims of abuse must familiarize themselves with the dissociative phenomena. This subject is discussed in chapters 11 and 12.

Sexualized Behavior

Finkelhor (1986) developed a conceptual model for understanding the impact of sexual abuse. One of the areas cited is "traumatic sexualization." He presents the following information regarding the sexualization of victims:

Dynamics:

- Child rewarded for sexual behavior inappropriate to developmental level

- Offender exchanges attention and affection for sex

- Sexual parts of child fetishized

- Offender transmits misconceptions about sexual behavior and morality

- Conditioning of sexual activity with negative memories and emotions

Psychological Impact:

- Increased salience of sexual issues

- Confusion about sexual identity

- Confusion about sexual norms

- Confusion of sex with love and care getting or care giving

- Negative associations to sexual activities and arousal sensations

- Aversion to sex or intimacy

Behavioral Manifestations:

- Sexual preoccupations and compulsive sexual behaviors

- Precocious sexual activity

- Aggressive sexual behaviors

- Promiscuity

- Prostitution

- Sexual dysfunctions

My own clinical observations of these children are consistent with Finkelhor's concept of traumatic sexualization. Sexually abused children develop an excessive and abnormal interest in sex, an interest that is frequently expressed in precocious sexual activity. One of the difficulties that arise in assessing children's sexual behaviors is that there are very few contemporary normative data on the development of children's sexuality. Sgroi, Bunk, and Wabrek (1988) have organized their combined clinical experience working with normal and troubled children to offer a developmental framework for children's sexuality. I have found this framework helpful in determining whether a child's sexual behavior indicates a need to intervene or a history of abuse:

Age Range: Preschool (0-5 years)
Patterns of Activity: Intense curiosity; taking advantage of opportunities to explore the universe
Sexual Behaviors: Masturbation; looking at others' bodies

Age Range: Primary school (6-10 years)
Patterns of Activity: Game playing with peers and with younger children; creating opportunities to explore the universe
Sexual Behaviors: Masturbation; looking at others' bodies; sexual exposure of self to others; sexual fondling of peers or younger children in play or gamelike atmosphere

Age Range: Preadolescence (10-12 years); Adolescence (13-18 years)
Patterns of Activity: Individuation; separation from family; distancing from parents; developing relationships with peers; practicing intimacy with peers of both sexes; "falling in love"
Sexual Behaviors: Masturbation; sexual exposure; voyeurism; open-mouth kissing; sexual fondling; simulated intercourse; sexual penetration behaviors and intercourse

As Sgroi's framework clearly illustrates, children's sexual behaviors tend to be progressive over time. Premature sexual activity in children always suggests two possible stimulants: experience and exposure. The child may have experienced sexual contact with an adult or older child and may be mimicking the learned behavior. Or the child may have been overstimulated by exposure to explicit sexual activity and may be acting this activity out. Many young children have access to soft or hard core pornography on their television sets.

An additional factor in many sexualized children is a disinhibition of behavior. A child who has not been sexually abused will abruptly stop masturbating when someone enters the room. Sexually abused children, possibly having learned the sexual behavior with another person, will not be inhibited and may continue to masturbate.

Clinicians have reported very sophisticated and focused sexual behavior on the part of these children. This behavior is always unusual and alarming. Children may enter a room and remove their underwear, masturbate, hump, or attempt to engage the clinician in sexual activity. This is understandable; they have been conditioned to behave this way. Nevertheless, the behavior must be extinguished. The therapist must set and enforce speedy, consistent, and directive limits and must suggest alternative behaviors. Thus the therapist might set verbal limits as follows: "It's not OK for you to touch private parts of my body, or to kiss my mouth." "It's not OK for you to take off your underwear in my office." These limits must be followed immediately by offering an alternative behavior: "I can see you're trying to get my attention . . . to do that, you can touch my hand and call my name." "I can see you're trying to show me how you feel. To do that, you can draw me a picture, write me a card, tell me a story, or talk to me about your feelings."

Behavioral indicators show the child's distress. They are red flags which indicate a problem. They are symptomatic of underlying concerns in the child. The next chapter discusses the underlying concerns of the abused child.

2.

The Inner World of the Child

The Child Stuck

In the last chapter, we reviewed research and clinical data on behavioral indicators of abuse in children. In this chapter, we shall examine the child's perceptions and feelings regarding the abuse.

Summit (1983) defines and discusses the Child Sexual Abuse Accommodation Syndrome. This syndrome comprises five categories of responses, two of which are preconditions to, and three which are the results of, sexual abuse. "Each category reflects a compelling reality for the victim and each category represents also a contradiction to the most common assumptions of adults" (181). While this syndrome refers specifically to victims of child sexual abuse, I believe that the five underlying concepts apply to children in any abusive environment. These five concepts are secrecy, helplessness, entrapment and accommodation, conflicted disclosure and retraction.

Secrecy

Abused children tend to keep the abuse a secret. They do so for a variety of reasons. They may be afraid of the abuser. The abuser may have promised safety to the child or child's loved ones. The abuser may have threatened the child or someone whom the child loves. Physically abused children may be afraid of being beaten again. Neglected or emotionally abused children long for their parents' approval and affection; they may keep silent for fear of losing the parents' love.

Helplessness

Children are inherently helpless and subordinate. They are small, dependent, inexperienced, and cognitively and emotionally immature. For all of these reasons, they cannot escape from a dangerous situation. Children who try to protect themselves are usually overridden by more powerful adults. When their attempts to protect themselves fail, these children develop learned helplessness. Eventually they stop trying to protect themselves overtly. Instead they may withdraw, go physically limp, or dissociate.

Entrapment and Accommodation

Children who keep their abuse a secret and continue to feel helpless inevitably feel trapped. However, they learn to accept the situation and survive. Summit contends that "the child faced with continuing helpless victimization must learn to somehow achieve a sense of power and control" (184). The acceptable alternative is for the child to blame himself or herself for provoking the abuse. Physically abused children may refer to their bad behaviors as reasons why their parents must punish them. Emotionally abused or neglected children may conceptualize unacceptable traits in themselves. Physically, sexually and emotionally abused children may also employ defensive mechanisms in an attempt to accommodate to the abuse.

Delayed,Conflicted, and Unconvincing Dislosure

Adults who ask to disclose abuse must recognize that this request may precipitate an acute crisis for the child. For reasons that I have just indicated, the initial disclosures may be fraught with anxiety, retractions, and inconsistencies. Therefore it may sound unconvincing. Because the child has used various defensive mechanisms to cope with the abuse, memory may be fragmentary, perceptions may be altered, and information may be scattered and sparse.

Retraction

Children who do disclose abuse may be flooded with guilt, fear, and feelings of betrayal or confusion. The adults' immediate responses may frighten them further. For example, the child may be removed into foster care; the parent may be put into prison; and members of the child's family may suffer. All this may make the child recant. Children gravitate towards the safety of a familiar situation, no matter how painful it is. Most abused or neglected children remain loyal to their families and if given a choice, frequently want to stay with their abusive parents.

It is important to understand the child's inner world so a treatment plan can be designed to address the underlying issues. Untreated, these perceptions can become belief systems which will sabotage the development of a realistic self-image and resultant self-esteem and motivation.

The Child Copes and Survives

Now let us take a look at the abused child's coping mechanisms. Children may employ one or several of these, and they may also proceed from one coping mechanism to another as they mature.

Intrapsychic Defenses

Intrapsychic defenses are defenses that exist within the self. The most common intrapsychic defenses are denial, dissociation, physiologic defenses, and cognitive defenses.

Denial

Many child victims suffer from chronic abuse. It is difficult for these children to deny the abuse itself, because it keeps on happening. But is possible for them to deny the importance of the abuse. They do this by giving themselves internal messages: "It really isn't that bad." "They don't mean anything by it."

"It doesn't bother me." Unfortunately, when reality is denied, it cannot be negotiated or resolved.

Dissociation

Another type of denial occurs when the child separates body from mind. This child says, "I am not here. This is happening to someone else. I'm leaving. I'll be back when this is over." The child who dissociates has found a way to be absent during the abuse.

There are many forms of dissociation. One of them is the ability to have out-of-body experiences. Physically abused children, for example, have described leaning against a wall, touching the wall, and then moving inside the wall, where they are cold and hard and cannot feel pain. Sexually abused children describe "leaving their bodies" and observing the abuse from a safe place on the ceiling or the window sill. Dissociation is discussed in chapter 9.

Physiologic Defenses

Child abuse always affects the body. In cases of physical abuse, the body experiences pain. In cases of sexual abuse, the body experiences intrusion, sometimes accompanied by physical pain. In cases of neglect or emotional abuse, the child's body experiences a lack of physical affection and nurturing. Severe cases of neglect seriously impair the child's physical and emotional development.

Abused children often develop idiosyncratic responses to pain. These responses are dysfunctional and may be dangerous. For example, a child may view pain as comforting, being compelled to self-mutilate.

Some children who are physically and sexually abused learn to anesthetize the parts of the body that cause them emotional or physical pain. These children may develop a high tolerance for pain, enabling them to survive physical beatings. If dissociation is employed, the child's identity may become confused or blurred. Since these children are observing themselves from the outside, they may view themselves as robot-like or inhuman. Michael, a chronically physically abused child of nine, who had been placed in foster care, was referred to treatment for self-mutilation. Here is a brief excerpt from a session with Michael:

Dr.G. *Michael, it is very important to me that you listen to what I have to say. You must stop cutting up your arms. I don't want you hurting yourself.*

Michael. *But I like doing it.*

Dr.G. *Tell me why.*

Michael. *I don't know. It makes me feel . . .*

Dr.G. *It makes you feel what?*

Michael. *Nothing special.*

Dr.G. *What do you think about when you cut yourself up?*

Michael. *I think that there's red blood inside me.*

Dr.G. *And what does that mean to you, having red blood?*

Michael. *It means that I'm normal.*

Dr.G. *Normal?*

Michael. *Yeah. Like everybody else.*

Dr.G. *Do you doubt that you're a real person sometimes?*

Michael. *Yeah. Sometimes I think . . . (<u>pause</u>)*

Dr.G. *Is this hard for you to talk about?*

Michael. *I only told one person about this.*

Dr.G. *How did that person react?*

Michael. *He thought I was crazy.*

Dr.G. *I'm sure it's hard for you to talk about. Tell me – do you doubt you're real sometimes?*

Michael. *Yeah. I think I'm some kind of space thing . . . with green guk instead of blood.*

Dr.G. *And when you see your red blood, what do you think?*

Michael. *I think, Wow, I'm really a human. And . . . (<u>pause</u>)*

Dr.G. *You think you're really human, and what else?*

Michael. *I'm really alive.*

Dr.G. *Yes Michael, you are alive, and I want you to stay that way. We need to figure out how you can make sure you're human and alive without cutting yourself and bleeding. Let's talk now about times when you feel very alive . . .*

In addition to depersonalizing and inflicting pain, abused children may also develop hyperalertness to the slightest physical discomfort. This may trigger an anxiety response, including tension, adrenalin rush, rapid pulse, restricted breathing, hyperventilation, and so forth. The fear of activating these physiologic responses may severely restrict the child's social life. It may also prevent the child from experimenting with new behaviors.

Cognitive Defenses

Abused children frequently integrate perceived or received messages about themselves, and they repeat those messages over and over. In so doing, they shape their own beliefs about who they are. The child forms a self-concept based on information given by trusted others. This information, particularly if it is provided by parents or by parent figures, takes on a monumental importance. If it is negative and erroneous, the child's self-concept suffers accordingly.

Interactional (Defense) Patterns

The abused child frequently copes by developing negative or unrewarding interactional patterns. The commonest of these coping mechanisms are aggression, avoidance, acting out, protective behavior and sexualized behavior.

Aggression

Abused children often feel frustrated and angry at their inability to stop the abuse. They may feel hostile towards the abuser and yet be unable to express their hostility directly. As their inner rage grows, they may direct it towards others, most frequently towards a smaller child. Not only is it safer to do this, but it represents the integration of one of the dynamics between aggressor and victim—namely, the power differential. Abused children may also direct their pent-up hostility against other scapegoats—usually strangers, pets, or property.

Avoidant Behavior

The older abused child sometimes avoids the abuse by running away. This child may also run away in an effort to escape unresolved conflicts at home. Younger children may become withdrawn, or overly-compliant.

Acting-out Behavior

Abused children may see themselves as bad or unworthy. They may then inadvertently set up situations that reinforce this belief. They may become a behavior problem to teachers at school, shoplift, seek out undesirable friends and can end up in juvenile hall, classified as delinquents or incorrigibles.

Provocative Behavior

Abused children sometimes provoke others to abuse them. These children are not usually masochists, seeking the physical sensation of pain. Rather, they usually see the abuse as a sign of love; or they are seeking negative attention (as opposed to no attention at all); or they believe that they deserve to be punished. This may partly explain why some abused children are revictimized, even when they are placed in an institutional setting, designed to protect them and to help them. These children have an uncanny ability to provoke other people to hurt them. Unfortunately, every time they succeed, it reinforces their belief that they deserve to be hurt.

Sexualized Behavior

Sexually abused children are taught to interact sexually with others. They are shown explicit sexual behaviors, and they are reinforced for engaging in them. These children are frequently labelled "seductive." The use of this term is ludicrous. According to Webster's dictionary, seduce is "to entice into wrongful conduct, to induce to have sexual intercourse." Children who are sexually abused are rarely the initiators of that abuse. When, after they have been taught to interact sexually, they do initiate sexual behavior, they are usually seeking guidance about sexuality, love, approval or safety, which they may have been taught to associate with sexual abuse.

Affective/Expressive Disorders

Abused children may develop self-monitoring behaviors in order to cope. Some children believe that if only they alter their behavior, the abuse will cease. They may imagine that they are being abused because, for example, they look a certain way. This causes them to inhibit their facial expressions.

Sometimes children actually are abused if their faces register certain emotional expressions. The abuser may interpret the look as defiance, pleasure, fear, or anger—any of which may elicit further abuse. It can therefore be in these children's best interest to learn, not merely to establish a neutral expression, but actually to control affect—to show nothing, so as not to be punished for their feelings. This may become a habit that is difficult to break. The constriction of affective expression can hinder the child's ability to engage in full, rewarding interactions.

The Lessons of Abuse

There are certain lessons to be learned from abuse.

People Who Love You Hurt You

When children are abused by someone who claims to love them, they learn that abuse is inherent in intimate relationships. These children therefore expect abuse when they establish intimate relationships of their own. People who expect abuse will tolerate abuse. Adults who were abused as children tolerate abuse longer than adults who were not abused. Frannie, a four-year-old-child I had worked with for six months came into the session carrying a paddle:

> Dr.G.   *What's that?*
> Frannie. *A paddle.*
> Dr.G.   *What's it for?*
> Frannie. *For you to hit me.*
> Dr.G.   *Why would I want to hit you?*
> Frannie. *You like me, don't you?*

Clearly, Frannie surmised that my interest and affection for her would be accompanied by abuse. So strong was this conviction that she brought in the instrument with which I would abuse her. When I did not hit her, she tried everything she knew to make me see her as bad—to make me hurt her. I had constantly to set limits and convey the concept <u>I will show you that I care in other ways. I will not hit you or hurt you.</u>

People are Either Victims or Abusers

Another lesson conveyed by abuse is that human interaction is painful. It includes a victim and an abuser, it entails a power differential; and it is usually accompanied by threat, force, or emotional coercion. One person has more power (be it physical or emotional), and one person has less power. Physical inequality is based on size or strength. Emotional inequality depends on the nature of the relationship; it is based on dependency, perceived authority or fear. The child may view the victim-abuser role inherent in every interaction, and may seek to take one or the other role.

The World Is a Dangerous Place.

Children who are abused or neglected see the world as dangerous and inconsistent, and human interactions as unrewarding. These children believe that they must protect themselves from others, and limit contact in order to survive.

The lessons of abuse are insidious. The child develops perceptions of the world based on these lessons. Consequently, protective behaviors are developed which initially help the child, but later interfere with the adult's ability to engage with others or secure a rewarding life.

Part 2

What Is...

The Adult's Experience

3.

Review of The Literature and Clinical Sample

The Literature

A history of childhood abuse affects each adult survivor differently. To date, there have been relatively few studies that document these effects. Controlled studies are currently under way that may be expected to yield more data in the future. In this section, I shall review the literature on adult survivors emphasizing common effects across studies.

No prospective studies of abused children have been done to determine what percentage of these children develop symptoms, what percentage of them do not, and what the differentiating variables are. Most of the studies on adult survivors have been retrospective. That is, they first identify a symptom, and then correlate it to early childhood abuse. Friedrick (1987) and Powell (1987) both found it almost impossible to establish a linear relationship between childhood abuse and a specific outcome in adulthood.

Browne and Finkelhor (1986) summarized the major studies on the known correlations between childhood sexual abuse and adult problems. They found many methodological weaknesses in past research, including small or biased samples, inadequate measuring procedures, and the absence of control groups. However, the majority of published studies on childhood sexual abuse do provide a consistent picture of psychological problems in adulthood. These studies include Sgroi (1975); Meiselman (1978); Herman (1981); Peters (1984); Tsai and Wagner (1978); Fritz, Stoll, and Wagner (1981); Brown (1979); Gelinas (1983); Browne & Finkelhor (1986); Briere & Runtz (1986); Finkelhor (1979); Wyatt (1985); and Russell (1986). The most consistent of these problems include depression, self-destructive behaviors (suicide attempts and self-mutilation), anxiety and tension (anxiety attacks, nightmares, difficulty sleeping), isolation, alienation and distrust, poor self-esteem and feelings of stigmatization, transient or negative relationships, sexual dysfunctions, anger, and dependence on alcohol and drugs.

Briere and Runtz (1987) designed a study of a random clinical sample comparing self-reported abused women with nonabused women, and evaluated their respective medical or psychological symptomatology. They found that the abused women had considerably more symptoms than the nonabused women. They were also more likely to be using psychoactive medication, and to have a history of suicide attempts and substance addiction. Finally they were more likely than the nonabused women to have suffered battery as adults.

Briere (1985) notes that clinicians often diagnose as personality disorders the problems of adult survivors who experienced extended or severe sexual abuse. In a later study (1987) Briere questions the use of psychiatric labels. He suggests instead that the psychological disturbances experienced by survivors of sexual abuse be considered post-sexual-abuse trauma. This term refers to symptomatic behaviors that were initially adaptive, but that over time have become "contextually inappropriate components of the victim's adult personality" (374).

Finkelhor (1984), Conte (1984), and Powell (1987) have provided guidelines and directives for future research on the effects of childhood abuse.

I agree there is a critical need to structure research to meet the highest methodological standards. I would like especially to see larger samples, and both prospective and longitudinal studies. In addition, I suggest that research be undertaken on random and clinical samples of adult survivors to determine if there are differences between types of problems experienced by survivors based on the type of abuse they experienced and the ages they were when their abuse occurred.

The Sample

I prepared to write this book by reviewing the records of clients I saw between 1978 and 1986 in my clinical practice. I was interested in documenting patterns of symptomatology; differences in symptoms by type of abuse and gender; average age of client at onset of abuse; duration of abuse and other factors. This review led to the compilation of data that is presented below.

Limitations

There are obvious limitations to the sample. It consists of individuals who sought counseling voluntarily, because they were aware they had a problem or had been identified by another professional as needing therapy. Some clients came to therapy knowing that they had been abused in childhood"they sought specifically to resolve the issue of abuse. Other clients presented with a variety of symptoms, and the abuse surfaced only when I took the childhood history. A few clients came to therapy because they could not remember their childhoods. These clients spoke of having "gaps in memory," and apparently feared that these gaps were caused by the repression of traumatic experiences.

I am known as a specialist who works with child and adult victims of abuse. Some clients chose me as a therapist on the basis of my reputation. However, for three years (from 1982-1985), I worked at the Redwood Center in Berkeley, California. This is a family therapy program serving a wide range of clients; it is not primarily identified for work in child abuse. Some of the sample, therefore, sought therapy for marital, sexual, or parenting problems. Only after the initial symptoms were relieved did the clients abusive childhoods surface.

All of the clients in the sample were able to pay for weekly counseling services at a rate of ten to fifty dollars per session. All of the clients were residents of the San Francisco Bay Area. This is an area known for its acceptance of counseling. It is also an area where the issue of child abuse is widely and publicly discussed. Therefore clients may be more willing to seek and find therapy services.

Description of the Sample

There were ninety-nine cases in the sample. Of these, 86 percent were female and 14 percent were male. In my experience, this is representative of adult survivors—many more women seek therapy than men—although in the past year the number of self referrals to my agency by men abused as children has doubled. This increase may represent a change in men's willingness to seek help. If so, that change, in turn, may be due to recent increased awareness and open discussion about the fact that men too, can be victimized.

Ethnic Breakdown

The sample was 66 percent Caucasian; 18 percent Hispanic; 11 percent Black; and 4 percent Asian.

Age

The mean current age of the sample was nearly thirty-three years old. Members ranged in age from eighteen to fifty. Of these, 34 percent were under the age of thirty; 49 percent were between the ages of thirty and thirty-nine; and 17 percent were over the age of 40.

Marital Status

Forty-one percent of the people in the sample were married, 30 percent were divorced, and 31 percent had never married.

Children

Seventy percent of the people in the sample were childless. Eighteen percent had one child, 8 percent had two, 2 percent had three, and 2 percent had four children.

Occupation

The largest occupational category was clerical-sales (36 percent), followed by professional-managerial (25 percent). Blue-collar or service occupations accounted for another 20 percent and the final 20 percent were housewives, students or unemployed.

Types of Abuse

Three types of abuse were represented in this group. Thirty-seven percent of the cases had suffered physical abuse, 48 percent sexual abuse and 15 percent emotional abuse. There were no cases of neglect per se. However, emotional abuse included neglectful attitudes or behaviors towards the child. Fourteen percent of the group had suffered two types of abuse concurrently. In all but one of the cases where the primary abuse was physical, the secondary abuse was sexual. The exception was a case in which the secondary abuse was emotional. In all cases where the primary abuse was sexual, the secondary abuse was physical. I should add that I consider all forms of child abuse to be emotionally abusive. For the purposes of this summary, I have categorized the cases according to the client's self-report. This may also explain why there were no reported cases of neglect. It may be that adults are less likely to describe themselves as having been neglected than as having been abused.

The cases chosen for the sample were cases in which the client clearly remembered and described specific behaviors that are defined as abuse under current law. Cases in which the client had memory gaps, feared that abuse might have occurred, but could not actually recall abuse were not included in the sample.

The term physical abuse refers to hitting, punching, biting, or shoving that resulted in internal or external physical injuries to the child. Sexual Abuse refers to sexual contact, including oral sex, anal sex, vaginal sex, digital penetration, and penetration of an orifice with a foreign object for sexual gratification (bottle, candle, enema, or dildo). Sexual contact also includes fondling or masturbating the child or forcing the child to fondle or masturbate the abuser. Noncontact sexual abuse, such as seductive or suggestive behaviors, or exposure is not included in the study. For the purposes of this study, sexual abuse is considered to have occurred when the child was at least three years younger than the abuser, even when the victim describes the event as non-traumatic. Emotional abuse refers to verbal assault or to lack of verbal or physical affection. It also refers to lack of eye contact, lack of positive feedback, or a general lack of positive attention. Behavior categorized as emotional abuse did not cause physical injury to the child.

These data are self-reported. I have no reason to disbelieve these reports, and the reports were consistent over time.

Age at Onset of Abuse

For 38 percent of the sample, the abuse started between the ages of six and nine. For another 33 percent, it started before age six, and for 29 percent, it started after age nine.

Duration of Abuse

The duration of abuse ranges from one or two days up to eighteen years. Thirty-two percent of the sample experienced two years or less of abuse; 38 percent experienced three to five years of abuse; and 31 percent experienced six or more years of abuse.

Perpetrators

In the vast majority of cases (78 percent), the perpetrator was a member of the client's immediate family. In 70 percent of these cases, the perpetrator was male. In 26 percent, the perpetrator was female, and in 3 percent there were both a male and a female perpetrator.

Referral to Therapy

Clients were referred to therapy in many ways. Twenty percent were referred; 20 percent were self-referred; 9 percent were probation referrals; and 15 percent were medical referrals.

Previous therapy

Forty-five percent of the clients in the sample had been in therapy before. Of these, 27 percent reported that they had had sexual relations with their previous therapist.

The sample of ninety-nine clients were mostly middle-aged Caucasian women. Less than half were married and seventy percent were childless. There were three types of abuse represented in this group, physical, sexual and emotional abuse. Members of the sample had clear memories of being abused and abuse was defined using current legal definitions. For thirty-eight percent of the sample, abuse began between the ages of six and nine. For another thirty-three percent it started before age six. The abuse lasted from one or two days to eighteen years. Most clients were abused by male members of the immediate family. An alarming revelation was that twelve clients had been sexually abused by therapists.

4.

Findings - Correlations and Trends

Variables by Type of Abuse

The material which follows looks at differences in a number of factors (age, duration of abuse, sex of subject, marital status, etc.) based on the type of abuse experienced.

Current Age by Type of Abuse

There appears to be a mild cohort effect for types of abuse (see table 1). Disproportionately more of the older people have been physically abused (53 percent of those over age 40 reported physical abuse and only 12 percent reported emotional abuse). The younger clients report mostly sexual abuse (47 percent of those under 29 were sexually abused and only 33 percent were physically abused).

TABLE 1

Current Age by Type of Abuse

Age	Physical Abuse		Sexual Abuse		Emotional Abuse		Total	
	%	N	%	N	%	N	%	N
Up to age 29	30%	(11)	34%	(16)	47%	(7)	34%	(34)
Age 30 to 39	46%	(17)	53%	(25)	40%	(6)	48%	(48)
40 or older	24%	(9)	13%	(6)	13%	(2)	17%	(17)

Age at Onset of Abuse by Type of Abuse

The age at which abuse begins differs for specific types of abuse (see table 2). More than 70 percent of subjects who were emotionally abused reported that the abuse began before the age of five. By contrast, 51 percent of subjects who were physically abused reported that the abuse began at age ten or later. Sexual abuse falls somewhere in between. For 47 percent of subjects, it began between the ages of six and nine, and for 40 percent before the age of five. This relationship between type of abuse and age of onset is statistically significant (chi square = 27.18, 4df, p <.001).

The sexual abuse of subjects in this sample began considerably earlier than it did for the women interviewed in Russell's study (1986). Russell found that sexual abuse began before age ten for 31 percent of the cases in her study. In this sample, it began before age ten for 86 percent of cases. This difference may perhaps be explained by the fact that Russell's sample was drawn from the general population while in this study, the sample consists of clients who were seeking treatment.

TABLE 2

Age at Onset of Abuse by Type of Abuse

Age	Physical Abuse		Sexual Abuse		Emotional Abuse		Total	
	%	N	%	N	%	N	%	N
Up to age 5	11%	(4)	40%	(18)	71%	(10)	33%	(32)
Age 6 to 9	38%	(14)	47%	(21)	7%	(1)	38%	(36)
10 or older	51%	(19)	13%	(6)	21%	(3)	29%	(28)

Duration of Abuse by Type of Abuse

There is a clear relationship between the type of abuse and the duration of the abuse (see table 3). Emotional abuse lasted the longest. Nearly 80 percent of subjects who were emotionally abused reported having been abused for six years or more, and for three years or more, the figure was 93 percent. Physical abuse lasted the second longest; of these subjects, 70 percent were abused for three years or more. Of subjects who reported sexual abuse 41 percent were abused for less than two years and only 18 percent for six years or more. Again, the chi square for this table is statistically significant (x2 = 19.28, 4df, p <.001).

TABLE 3
Duration of Abuse by Type of Abuse

Duration	Physical Abuse %	N	Sexual Abuse %	N	Emotional Abuse %	N	Total %	N
2 years or less	30%	(11)	41%	(18)	7%	(1)	32%	(30)
3 to 5 years	43%	(16)	41%	(18)	14%	(2)	38%	(36)
6 years or more	27%	(10)	18%	(8)	79%	(11)	31%	(29)

Perpetrators by Type of Abuse

There is also a clear relationship between the type of abuse and the perpetrator of the abuse (see table 4). Both physical and emotional abuse are almost entirely within the immediate family (see table 4). Both physical and emotional abuse occurred entirely within the family, and almost entirely within the immediate family. Only in cases of sexual abuse was the perpetrator ever unrelated to the subject.

TABLE 4
Perpetrator by Type of Abuse

Perpetrator	Physical Abuse %	N	Sexual Abuse %	N	Emotional Abuse %	N	Total %	N
Immediate family	97%	(36)	62%	(29)	80%	(12)	78%	(77)
Extended family	3%	(1)	13%	(6)	20%	(3)	10%	(10)
Unrelated	"	"	26%	(12)	"	"	12%	(12)

Sex of Subject by Type of Abuse

The type of abuse varied with the sex of the subject (see table 5). Of the subjects who were physically abused, 27 percent were male. Of those who were sexually abused, only 9 percent were male. All cases of emotional abuse were reported by females.

TABLE 5

Sex of Subject by Type of Abuse

Sex	Physical Abuse %	N	Sexual Abuse %	N	Emotional Abuse %	N	Total %	N
Male	27%	(10)	9%	(4)	0%	(0)	14%	(14)
Female	73%	(27)	91%	(43)	100%	(15)	86%	(85)

Marital Status by Type of Abuse

There is an interesting correlation between type of abuse and marital status (see table 6). Subjects who were physically abused were evenly distributed among the married, divorced, and never married. Slightly more than 50 percent of subjects who were sexually abused were married, while 33 percent had never married. Of the emotionally abused subjects, 53 percent were divorced, 25 percent were married, and 20 percent had never married.

TABLE 6

Marital Status by Type of Abuse

Marital Status	Physical Abuse %	N	Sexual Abuse %	N	Emotional Abuse %	N	Total %	N
Married	33%	(12)	52%	(24)	27%	(4)	41%	(40)
Divorced	33%	(12)	15%	(7)	53%	(8)	28%	(27)
Never married	33%	(12)	33%	(15)	20%	(3)	31%	(30)

Alcoholic Family by Type of Abuse

Nearly half of all subjects came from alcoholic families (see table 7). The correlation varies with the type of abuse, but it is high for emotional abuse. Of the subjects in this category, 87 percent came from an alcoholic family.

TABLE 7

Alcoholic Family by Type of Abuse

Alcoholic Family	Physical Abuse %	N	Sexual Abuse %	N	Emotional Abuse %	N	Total %	N
Not indicated	57%	(21)	64%	(30)	13%	(2)	54%	(53)
Yes	43%	(16)	36%	(17)	87%	(13)	46%	(46)

Age of Onset of Abuse by Duration of Abuse

There are some significant associations between the duration of the abuse and other variables. The first of these variables is age of onset (see table 8). The abuse that lasted the longest (six years or more) started the earliest (before age six).

TABLE 8

Age at Onset of Abuse by Duration of Abuse

Age	2 Years or Less %	N	3 to 5 Years %	N	6 Years or More %	N	Total %	N
Up to age 5	20%	(6)	22%	(8)	61%	(17)	33%	(31)
Age 6 to 9	37%	(11)	42%	(15)	32%	(9)	37%	(35)
10 or older	43%	(13)	36%	(13)	7%	(2)	30%	(28)

Perpetrator by Duration of Abuse

Duration of abuse also correlated with the identity of the perpetrator (see table 9). Again as one would expect, the abuse lasted the longest when the perpetrator was a member of the subject's immediate family.

TABLE 9

Perpetrator by Duration of Abuse

Perpetrator	2 Years or Less %	N	3 to 5 Years %	N	6 Years or More %	N	Total %	N
Immediate family	57%	(17)	92%	(33)	83%	(24)	78%	(74)
Extended family	20%	(6)	0%	(0)	14%	(4)	11%	(10)
Unrelated	23%	(7)	8%	(3)	3%	(1)	12%	(11)

Marital Status by Duration of Abuse

There is also a significant association between the duration of the abuse and marital status (see table 10). Of subjects who were abused for six years or more, 78 percent were currently unmarried - half of these having never married and the other half being divorced. Of subjects who were abused for less than two years, 62 percent were married

TABLE 10

Marital Status by Duration of Abuse

Marital Status	2 Years or Less		3 to 5 Years		6 Years or More		Total	
	%	N	%	N	%	N	%	N
Married	62%	(18)	42%	(15)	21%	(6)	42%	(39)
Divorced	14%	(4)	28%	(10)	39%	(11)	27%	(25)
Never married	24%	(7)	31%	(11)	39%	(11)	31%	(29)

Consequences Of Abuse

The following section provides an overview of the types of clinical problems most frequently reported by the sample.

The most common problem was depression which was reported by nearly 75 percent of the sample. The second most common problem, reported by 45 percent of the sample, was low self-esteem. Alcohol abuse and lack of motivation were each reported by about 25 percent of the sample.

Tables 11 through 25 illustrate the frequency of specific types of clinical symptoms or complaints by the type of abuse. Each abuse group seems to have experienced a somewhat different set of presenting problems. However, these problems do not fall into clear-cut clusters. Tables 11 through 17 illustrate the association between type of abuse and various problems.

Low Self-Esteem by Type of Abuse

Low self-esteem is clearly correlated with type of abuse (see table 11). Of subjects who were emotionally abused, 67 percent reported problems with self-esteem. For subjects who were physically and sexually abused, the corresponding figures were 30 percent and 49 percent respectively.

TABLE 11

Low Self-Esteem by Type of Abuse

Low Self-Esteem	Physical Abuse		Sexual Abuse		Emotional Abuse		Total	
	%	N	%	N	%	N	%	N
Not indicated	70%	(26)	51%	(24)	33%	(5)	56%	(55)
Yes	30%	(11)	49%	(23)	67%	(10)	44%	(44)

Violent Relationships by Type of Abuse

Violent relationships are also clearly correlated with type of abuse (see table 12). Of subjects who were physically abused, 38 percent reported having this problem as compared to 20 percent of those who were emotionally abused and 13 percent of those who were sexually abused.

TABLE 12

Violent Relationships by Type of Abuse

Violent Relationships	Physical Abuse		Sexual Abuse		Emotional Abuse		Total	
	%	N	%	N	%	N	%	N
Not indicated	62%	(23)	87%	(41)	80%	(12)	77%	(76)
Yes	38%	(14)	13%	(6)	20%	(3)	23%	(23)

Orgasmic Disorders by Type of Abuse

About 30 percent of both sexually and emotionally abused subjects reported having orgasmic disorders (see table 13). This problem was reported by only 8 percent of those who were physically abused.

TABLE 13

Orgasmic Disorders by Type of Abuse

Orgasmic Disorders	Physical Abuse		Sexual Abuse		Emotional Abuse		Total	
	%	N	%	N	%	N	%	N
Not indicated	92%	(34)	70%	(33)	73%	(11)	79%	(78)
Yes	8%	(3)	30%	(14)	27%	(4)	21%	(21)

Desire Disorders by Type of Abuse

More emotionally abused subjects reported having desire disorders - 60 percent as compared to less than 30 percent in each of the other two groups (see table 14).

TABLE 14

Desire Disorders by Type of Abuse

Desire Disorders	Physical Abuse		Sexual Abuse		Emotional Abuse		Total	
	%	N	%	N	%	N	%	N
Not indicated	70%	(26)	77%	(36)	40%	(6)	69%	(68)
Yes	30%	(11)	23%	(11)	60%	(9)	31%	(31)

Alcohol Problems by Type of Abuse

Physically abused subjects had more problems with alcohol than other subjects (see table 15). This is particularly interesting in view of the fact that, as we have seen, it was the emotionally abused subjects who most often came from alcoholic families.

TABLE 15

Alchohol Problems by Type of Abuse

Alchohol Problems	Physical Abuse		Sexual Abuse		Emotional Abuse		Total	
	%	N	%	N	%	N	%	N
Not indicated	59%	(22)	81%	(38)	73%	(11)	72%	(71)
Yes	41%	(15)	19%	(9)	27%	(4)	28%	(28)

Dissociative Experience by Type of Abuse

Dissociative experience was most common for sexually abused and physically abused subjects; the incidence was 30 percent and 16 percent respectively. None of the emotionally abused subjects presented with this problem.

TABLE 16

Dissociative Experience by Type of Abuse

Dissociative Experience	Physical Abuse		Sexual Abuse		Emotional Abuse		Total	
	%	N	%	N	%	N	%	N
Not indicated	84%	(31)	70%	(33)	100%	(15)	80%	(79)
Yes	16%	(6)	30%	(14)	0%	(0)	20%	(20)

Tables 17 through 21 illustrate the association between duration of abuse and various problems.

Depression by Duration of Abuse

There is a curvilinear relationship between duration of abuse and depression (see table 17). Subjects who were abused for the shortest and the longest periods of time were the most likely to experience depression. For these two groups, the incidence of depression was 83 percent and 79 percent respectively. Only 58 percent of subjects who were abused for three to five years experienced depression.

TABLE 17

Depression by Duration of Abuse

Depression	2 Years or Less		3 to 5 Years		6 Years or More		Total	
	%	N	%	N	%	N	%	N
Not indicated	17%	(5)	42%	(15)	21%	(6)	27%	(26)
Yes	83%	(25)	58%	(21)	79%	(23)	73%	(69)

Low Self-Esteem by Duration of Abuse

Longer periods of abuse are also associated with lower self-esteem (see table 18).

TABLE 18
Low Self-Esteem by Duration of Abuse

Low Self-Esteem	2 Years or Less		3 to 5 Years		6 Years or More		Total	
	%	N	%	N	%	N	%	N
Not indicated	73%	(22)	56%	(20)	45%	(13)	58%	(55)
Yes	27%	(8)	44%	(16)	55%	(16)	42%	(40)

Stomachaches by Duration of Abuse

An increased incidence of stomachaches is associated with longer periods of abuse (see table 19).

TABLE 19
Stomach Aches by Duration of Abuse

Stomachaches	2 Years or Less		3 to 5 Years		6 Years or More		Total	
	%	N	%	N	%	N	%	N
Not indicated	83%	(25)	89%	(32)	69%	(20)	81%	(77)
Yes	17%	(5)	11%	(4)	31%	(9)	19%	(18)

Sadomasochistic Practices by Duration of Abuse

Longer periods of abuse are also associated with an increased incidence of sadomasochistic practices (see table 20).

TABLE 20
S and M Practices by Duration of Abuse

S/M Practices	2 Years or Less		3 to 5 Years		6 Years or More		Total	
	%	N	%	N	%	N	%	N
Not indicated	97%	(29)	97%	(35)	79%	(23)	92%	(87)
Yes	3%	(1)	3%	(1)	21%	(6)	8%	(8)

Self-Mutilation by Duration of Abuse

An increased incidence of self-mutilation is associated with longer periods of abuse (see table 21).

TABLE 21

Self-Mutilation by Duration of Abuse

Self Mutilation	2 years or Less		3 to 5 Years		6 Years or More		Total	
	%	N	%	N	%	N	%	N
Not indicated	93%	(28)	86%	(31)	66%	(19)	82%	(78)
Yes	7%	(2)	14%	(5)	34%	(10)	18%	(17)

Tables 22 through 25 illustrate the association between the onset of abuse and various problems.

Obesity by Age of Onset of Abuse

There is again a curvilinear relationship between obesity and onset of abuse (see table 22). Subjects whose abuse began between the ages of six and nine are likeliest to have problems with obesity.

TABLE 22

Obesity by Age of Onset of Abuse

Obesity	Up to Age 5		Age 6 to 9		10 or Older		Total	
	%	N	%	N	%	N	%	N
Not indicated	81%	(26)	69%	(25)	96%	(27)	81%	(78)
Yes	19%	(6)	31%	(11)	4%	(1)	19%	(18)

Suicide Attempts by Age of Onset of Abuse

The earliest onset of abuse is associated with the highest incidence of suicide attempts (see table 23).

TABLE 23

Suicide attempts by Age of Onset of Abuse

	Up to Age 5		Age 6 to 9		10 or Older		Total	
Suicide Attempts	%	N	%	N	%	N	%	N
Not indicated	78%	(25)	97%	(35)	93%	(26)	90%	(86)
Yes	22%	(7)	3%	(1)	7%	(2)	10%	(10)

Self-Mutilation by Age of Onset of Abuse

The earlier the onset of abuse, the greater the incidence of self-mutilation (see table 24).

TABLE 24

Self Mutilation by Age of Onset of Abuse

	Up to Age 5		Age 6 to 9		10 or Older		Total	
Self Mutilation	%	N	%	N	%	N	%	N
Not indicated	69%	(22)	81%	(29)	100%	(28)	82%	(79)
Yes	31%	(10)	19%	(7)	0%	(0)	18%	(17)

Dissociative Experience by Age of Onset of Abuse

Onset of abuse before the age of ten is associated with the highest incidence of dissociative experiences (see table 25).

TABLE 25

Dissociative Experience by Age of Onset of Abuse

	Up to Age 5		Age 6 to 9		10 or Older		Total	
Dissociative Experience	%	N	%	N	%	N	%	N
Not indicated	75%	(24)	69%	(25)	96%	(27)	79%	(76)
Yes	25%	(8)	31%	(11)	4%	(1)	21%	(20)

This material was presented to give mental health professionals a general overview of the type of clinical issues which may be relevant as presenting problems or underlying concerns when treating adult survivors. The data have implications for assessment areas during the early phase of therapy, particularly since adult survivors are often reluctant to self-report problems or concerns.

This information, coupled with the literature on adult survivors (see Suggested Readings), provide a comprehensive review of the types of psychological problems most commonly encountered by adults abused as children.

5.

Summary of Common Therapeutic Issues

Based on the clinical sample presented in Chapter 3, symptomatology can be categorized as follows:

Psychosocial Problems

The first category of symptoms consists of psychosocial problems. These include intrapsychic problems (depression, dissatisfaction, low self-esteem, lack of motivation, control issues, and dissociative phenomena); self-destructive problems (addictive behaviors—drug abuse, alcohol abuse, gambling, compulsive spending—suicide attempts, and self-mutilation); and interactional problems such as parenting difficulties.

The client presented the symptom as a primary or secondary concern. Symptoms that were either undefined by client or undetected by me, were not included in the study.

Intrapsychic

Depression was the commonest of the intrapsychic problems. Depression was usually identified by the presence of clinical symptoms such as lethargy, emotionality, eating or sleeping disorders, or general sadness.

Dissatisfaction was defined as a general feeling on the part of the client that "nothing is working; nothing turns out the way I want it to; I can't seem to change things; they always turn out the same shitty way."

Low Self-Esteem was defined as an inability to identify positive aspects of the self in realistic terms. Low self-esteem is a problem to many adults abused as children. This is easily understood, given the fact that most children get a sense of who they are from their parents. If the parents' messages are negative, critical, or even neutral, the child's self-esteem is bound to suffer. These clients may not have said, "I feel bad about myself" in so many words, but they consistently made self-deprecating statements, and when asked to list their own strengths, could not identify any. They often referred to themselves in harsh terms: "Well, I was never too smart." "I don't really have anything to say or I wouldn't want to spend time with me either."

Lack of Motivation was defined as the inability to generate the energy to go after what the client wanted. Clients who lack motivation may say, "I'd like to make more friends" or "I'd like to hear more live music," but they feel stymied when it comes to taking action. These clients often say, "I wish I could get myself out there and do things."

Control Issues were defined as situations where the client described feeling out of control. Typically, these clients can identify and even describe what they want, but they are prevented from going after it by feelings of anxiety, helplessness, and emotional paralysis. These clients may say "Sometimes I don't know whose running things" or "Something seems to take over before I know it." They say they are dissatisfied with their lives yet they feel impotent to change them. This is an important area for the therapist to address, since feeling out of control is remarkably like feeling victimized—in both cases, one sees the control as being outside of one's self.

Dissociative Phenomena were defined as a splitting between the body and the mind in which the client does not feel present during an experience. Dissociation is linked to trauma. Many adults abused as children have experienced dissociation, and yet are unable to identify it. Most often these clients will say that they "space out," and they can be guided to give a behavioral description. Dissociation is discussed in Chapter 9.

Self-Destructive

The self destructive problems were defined as physically or socially self-destructive behaviors, including addictions to alcohol, over-the-counter, prescription or illegal drugs, spending, or gambling. The client felt controlled by the addiction, and the addiction appeared to be ego-dystonic. These were clients who were beyond denial; their focus was on altering the self-destructive behaviors.

The clinical sample included two other types of self-destructive behavior. These were a history of suicide attempts and a history of self-mutilation. All clients who exhibited the first type of behavior had attempted suicide more than once. The average number of attempts was six, but one client had attempted to kill herself forty-nine times, and her arms, neck, and legs were covered with old scars. (This client was not included when the average was drawn in order to avoid the obvious skew.) Self-mutilating behaviors ranged in severity from overt cutting and slashing to picking at scabs (which sometimes resulted in infections), scratching, and generating skin disorders.

Interactional Problems

Most of the interactional problems involved parenting. Parenting problems were defined as difficulties in caring for children. Most adults abused as children have not had appropriate modeling regarding discipline and communication with children. They feel at a loss when they themselves become parents. Some of the clients in the sample were keenly cognizant of the so-called cycle of child abuse. These clients asked for specific help to avoid hurting their own children. They asked to be taught how to show love and affection, while at the same time setting limits.

Physical and Eating Disorder Problems

The second category of symptoms consists of physical or health-related problems and eating disorders.

Physical

There was a wide variety of physical problems, including headaches, stomachaches, skin problems, pelvic inflammatory disease, bladder infections, cramping, and sore throats.

Headaches were in all cases, migraine headaches. They were severe and debilitating and they grew progressively worse. In every case, the migraine headaches had commenced shortly after the abuse began. Thus they appeared to be post-traumatic head-aches, which became more severe over time.

Stomachaches included "nervous stomachs," "acid stomachs," nausea, and vomiting. These symptoms were usually directly related to anxiety and fear.

Skin problems included rashes, blemishes, and scabs. These did not seem to be the result of self-mutilation. Rather, they seemed to be created by anxious scratching and picking at the skin.

Pelvic inflammatory disease without gonorrhea, was present in a few clients. The PID had surfaced suddenly and had become chronic. The medical etiology was unknown.

Bladder infections were nonspecific and chronic. They were unresponsive to most medications.

Cramping was in some clients was so painful that it impaired functioning. Cramping was either menstrual, or general muscle cramping.

Sore throats occurred mostly in clients who had been forced to engage in oral copulation. The sore throats were chronic and stress related. When these clients were discussing the childhood abuse, their throats usually responded with tightness and pain.

Eating Disorders

The eating disorders in this sample included anorexia, bulimia, and obesity, although obesity was the only class of disorder that was seen in the male clients. This is another symptom that I believe warrants an evaluation of abuse, given the the informal clinical information available from eating disorder programs.[1]

Relationship and Sexual Problems

The third category of symptoms consists of problems concerning relationships and sexual problems. Problems concerning relationships involve length of relationship, fear of commitment, poor choice of partner, and violence. Sexual problems include problems regarding sexual preference, sexual dysfunctions, sadomasochistic practices, desire disorder, and promiscuity.

Relationship

Most clients who presented with problems involving the length of the relationship had a history of short relationships, abruptly broken off. These people could not maintain a long-term relationship, and they wanted to find out why and change.

Fear of commitment was another common problem. Clients who presented with this symptom expressed a desire to commit to a relationship but found themselves bailing out prematurely, even when they felt that the relationship was perfect for them.

Poor choice of partner was a problem for clients who found themselves strongly attracted to the wrong person, even though they knew intellectually that this person was not right for them. These clients felt frustrated by their persistent attraction to these inadequate partners. At the same time, most of them felt either that the wrong partner was really what they deserved, or else that they couldn't do better—that is, that the right partner was "out of my reach."

Violent relationships were those in which one partner was physically abusing the other. The violence was seen as a problem or concern to one or the other partner and help was being sought to stop the violence. The adult survivor was always the victim of abuse in this sample.

Sexual

Problems of sexual preference were experienced by homosexual clients who were not comfortable with their homosexuality. These clients felt stigmatized by society, isolated, and self-conscious. They usually entered treatment to investigate their reactions to people of the same sex and opposite sex.

Dysfunctions were defined as disorders of sexual function that caused problems for the clients. The most common dysfunctions were orgasmic disorders and vaginismus for women and impotence for men. The men who experienced impotence in this sample were men who had been sexually abused and had learned to suppress their erections in an effort to dissuade the abuser from continuing the abuse. Orgasmic disorders in women occurred when women were unable to reach orgasm, or could not reach orgasm with a partner. Vaginismus is the collapsing of the vaginal walls, preventing penetration. Clients with vaginismus felt highly threatened by the act of penetration. In these cases women felt heightened anxiety during foreplay and clearly for them sex had become associated with negative, painful memories. Sadomasochistic practices were defined as violent or humiliating practices necessary to obtain desire, arousal or orgasm.[2] These behaviors further reinforced an association between sex and degradation or pain.

Desire Disorders was defined as a general apathy towards sexual activity. Clients with this disorder talk about "spacing out" during sex and express little motivation to engage in it. Usually this has become a problem to them only because it is a problem to their partner.

Promiscuity was defined as a compulsion to engage in sexual activity. This activity sometimes provides physical satisfaction, but little emotional comfort or connection for the client. Many of these clients believe sex is all anyone wants from them or all they have to offer others. Some clients have also discussed promiscuity in terms of control, that is, having the decision-making power of who to have sex with, what kind of sex to have, and when to leave.

Special Issues

There are two special problems which can appear in adult survivors. These are Multiple Personality Disorder and Post-Traumatic Stress Disorder (see Chapters 10 and 11 respectively for further discussion of these issues).

Post-Traumatic Stress Disorder was a presenting problem for some clients and developed during treatment in others. When this diagnosis is used, at least three of the DSM-III-R criteria were present. All clients in this sample experienced painful physical sensations as one of the symptoms of the disorder.

Several adult survivors presented symptoms of Multiple Personality Disorder. These clients shared a history of chronic, severe childhood abuse.[3]

Part 3

What Will Be ...

The Adult In Process

6.

Goals of Treatment

Therapists who work with adults abused as children have one overriding goal. That is to repair the client's self-image. Once the client's self-image is repaired, he or she is on the road to full recovery.

This goal can be accomplished through both abstract and concrete strategies. On an abstract level, the therapist enables the client to experience a healthy human interaction. People cannot learn how something feels by being told—they must experience the feeling. Once these clients have learned how a healthy interaction feels, the strength of that feeling can lead them to seek out other healthy interactions, if they can learn to tolerate the anxiety generated by new, unfamiliar feelings. In short, clients may seek to repeat the pleasant experience. On a concrete level, the therapist must teach the client new skills. Clients must learn to recognize and express their own feelings, to communicate, to take controlled risks, to solve problems, to identify and negotiate personal needs. Teaching clients to use these skills instead of using outworn defense mechanisms will help these clients to break old patterns of victimization. The client with the aid of the therapist rehearses and masters his or her new skills.

In pursuing these strategies, the therapist should focus on the following issues:

Self-image

Abuse severely damages the child's sense of self. Self-image is acquired in childhood. It is heavily influenced by the conveyed or perceived, attitudes of the parents or primary caretakers. The child seeks the parent's acceptance and love, and if these are withheld, inconsistent or inadequately expressed, the child will remain emotionally under-developed. Abused children, then, are at a serious disadvantage if they must attempt to construct a positive self-image on their own.

The parents can deny the child in a variety of ways. Some parents are unable to bond, to interact physically or emotionally, with their child. These parents do not exhibit bonding behaviors such as cooing, rocking, holding, touching, primping, or maintaining eye contact. They tend to ignore the child when it demands attention or cries. Children who are neglected in this way may long for attention and affection, yet may act passive and withdrawn as if they want or need nothing. Sometimes these children stop growing; this is known as <u>nonorganic failure to thrive.</u> The lack of nurturing and physical attention actually causes the child's system to shut down. As these children grow older, they may believe that their parents rejected them because there was something unacceptable about them. Most abused children personalize this rejection and develop negative introjects.

This type of neglect occurs when the parents withdraw. In cases of physical and sexual abuse, the parents do not withdraw. Instead, they interact inappropriately, punitively, or harshly with the child. These parents expect too much of their children, often they treat them like small adults.

Children who are victims of chronic physical abuse may develop a range of problem behaviors. They have seen violence used as a problem-solving technique. Often this teaches them to be violent, and they become abusive in their turn when they establish their own intimate relationships. These children grow up thinking that violence is an inherent part of personal interactions.

Some abused children have within them a seemingly bottomless reservoir of rage towards the abusive parent. Their feelings of helplessness and pain have accumulated over the years. This resentment may be expressed in a generalized way, or it may be directed at specific family members, or at people who symbolize them to the child. Physically abused children often receive periodic affection and love from one or both abusive parents. In some families, one parent hits, while the other parent does not hit, but cannot (or does not) stop the first parent from hitting. Abused children will react differently to each parent. Children who are physically abused may also be afraid to express or receive anger, and they may be more sensitive to deprivation and pain. They may also see themselves as worthless and undeserving, and they may feel responsible for having caused their parents to disapprove of them or to beat them.

Children who are sexually abused react in a variety of ways. They may experience pain, confusion, pleasure, disgust, or fear. For some children, sexual abuse can be a life-threatening event.

For example, a young child who is forced to engage in oral copulation may be unable to breathe, and may have to struggle to stay alive.

Sexually abused children may develop an aversion to or a compulsion for sexual activity (Finkelhor 1987). They may gain self-esteem through manipulation of their sexuality ("I can get anybody to jump in bed with me"), or they may question their self-worth ("that's all anyone wants from me").

Some children punish their bodies for attracting sexual attention. They may work hard to make themselves unattractive, or they may mutilate themselves.

Children whose parents never approved of them, or rejected them outright, or engaged in improper parenting practices, have trouble accepting praise or approval from others. Although such praise or approval is frequently helpful since it provides the child with alternative perceptions, these children will usually sustain long-lasting self-doubts or self-recriminations.

If these children's self-image is negative, or even undefined, negative or neutral exchanges will seem familiar to them, but positive exchanges will seem untrustworthy and provoke anxiety.

Empowerment

It is the therapist's job to combat the client's sense of entrapment, despair, helplessness, isolation, and self-blame. Adult survivors must be convinced that they are in control of and that they can change their own lives. They must identify those situations which they wish to change, and develop realistic plans for changing them.

This is not easy. Many adult survivors are emotionally paralyzed. They believe that they cannot move and they must be inspired or guided to self-activate. One way to do this is to contrast these client's current self image with their envisioned self image, in an effort to get them to act <u>on behalf of the envisioned self.</u> While the therapist can serve as a role model by acting in the client's best interest, success will depend on the client eventually acting in his or her own best interest.

Hope

Because childhood abuse can distort the child's view of what life has to offer, the therapist must help the adult survivor motivate towards a rewarding future. The client must learn what is realistic and possible. Hope will motivate and comfort the individual. We must have hope if we are to survive; without it, we cannot grow. With hope, the future can be envisioned and action taken, and the past can be seen as an influence rather than as an obstacle.

Trauma Resolution

The therapist must also ascertain how much trauma resolution has occurred in the client. What is trauma resolution? "In 'Moses and Monotheism,' Sigmund Freud (1939) distinguished positive from negative effects of trauma. Positive effects consist of attempts to bring the trauma into operation again by remembering, repeating, and reexperiencing. Negative effects serve to keep the forgotten event from being repeated, and as such are defensive reactions of avoidance, inhibition, and phobia" (Eth and Pynoos 1985).

The trauma of adult survivors is resolved when they cease to feel victimized and instead feel self-fulfilled and whole. Trauma resolution is a kind of repair process that parallels the process of child development. In adult survivors, development has been blocked. These clients must be helped to complete the developmental process. The therapist acts in some respects as a parent, providing a corrective experience.

Grieving

Clients who confront childhood abuse experience a dilemma. If they acknowledge that the abuse was real, they give up their idealized image of childhood. The idealized image of childhood can be created by the child to protect from a harsh reality. The child and adult survivor may wish to view their parents as non-abusive and nurturing, to defend against the pain associated with the reality. Giving up this idealized image of childhood is painful. These clients will go through a period of grieving, following the usual sequence of denial, sadness, anger, and finally, acceptance. Acceptance can provide relief and healing, open the door to change and control, and enable the adult to face reality rather than continuing to live with illusion.

Affiliation

Adult survivors are often isolated. The therapist must help them to break their isolation. The therapeutic relationship itself is a first step. This relationship teaches the client to recognize the rewards of interaction: He or she begins to feel heard, seen, understood, and validated for the first time. For the first time, he or she is able to trust, confide in, reach out for assistance, and feel safe. The client is then directed to seek these same rewards by engaging in healthy interactions with other people. This hastens the healing process. Clients often feel threatened by this stage of their healing, first, because it obliges them to take active risks, and second, because it signals the approaching end of therapy. These issues must all be considered in analyzing the recovery process. They are summarized here to serve as a guide for setting goals of treatment.

7.

Treatment Phasing: The Beginning Phase

Treatment phasing is important with any client; with adult survivors it is critical. Adults abused as children have grave fears and doubts about themselves and others. The very nature of their problem stems from a severely restricted emotional development. They have only a very limited ability to interact and respond, and their lives are constricted by fear, shame, guilt, longing and isolation.

Therapy often represents these clients first adult relationship. Their expectations may be vast but so are their initial fears.

The therapeutic relationship mimics an intimate relationship. The focus is on the client. He or she is asked highly personal questions. The client scans the therapist's office, and his or her behavior for clues as to what the therapist thinks or expects. This is a high-risk situation for the client, whose own behavior is constricted by anxiety. The therapist must proceed cautiously, with tremendous sensitivity and purposefulness.

One client mustered up a great deal of strength to relate (for the first time) a history of horrendous childhood abuse. The therapist remarked, "That sounds so Sybil-like!" The therapist meant no harm but the client was mortally wounded. It took her another four months to work up the courage to venture out again. Venturing out is essential to survival, but it feels like risking death. This client's instinct to survive was stronger than her pain at feeling disbelieved. Another client might not have had the courage to go on.

Other seemingly benign remarks, "That's so hard to believe!" "Do you think some of this might be unconscious fears?", might be perceived as attacks. Many clients cannot overcome the sense of betrayal and accusation that these remarks inspire. Think before you speak. Often you will have to guess how the client perceives you and your therapeutic interventions. Many clients will not volunteer this information. Some may not dare to disclose their real feelings even when they are asked. Maintain a constant open dialogue, and encourage these clients to discuss anything at all. This will help them feel safe as time goes by.

In working with adult survivors, I have found that there are three distinct treatment phases. These are the beginning phase (assessment, and alliance); the middle phase (rebuilding); and the termination phase (empowerment). It is important to proceed purposefully and cautiously. To pose a necessary challenge prior to establishment of trust may cause the client to flee from treatment.

The length of each phase is determined by the individual client, who should be permitted to progress at his or her own pace. Thus one client may remain in the beginning phase for months, while another for only a week or two. The middle phase may last for months or years; so may the third phase.

I am frequently asked how long this type of therapy takes. That depends on how much trauma resolution has occurred prior to treatment. I have had clients complete therapy in as little as nine months. The average is about one and one-half years, and I have had clients who stayed in treatment as long as five years. Treatment in the different phases can include individual therapy, marital therapy, family therapy and group therapy. I may also make referrals to hypnotherapy, body therapy, movement therapy or workshops using the creative arts (writing, art, clay) in the healing process.

Some clients with prior trauma resolution come into treatment to do periodic short-term work on specific issues. For example, they may be visiting their parents, or entering into a new relationship, or having trouble parenting their own children. These clients wish to use therapy to examine their reactions or explore their options.

The following information on the three treatment phases is intended as a general guideline—a blueprint for the work. It is not intended to be a rigid or restricted process. I have had the privilege of consulting with hundreds of clinicians, all of whom have creative and compassionate techniques. You are encouraged to experiment with, and expand on, my ideas.

The Beginning Phase

The beginning phase of treatment consists of two essential goals: a comprehensive assessment and the development of a therapeutic alliance.

A Comprehensive Assessment

Telephone Contact

As we have seen, adult survivors can be terrified of coming to therapy. They may fear being rejected, being humiliated, being disbelieved, being abused, or being called crazy. Their ability to trust is usually fragile at best, and they are almost incapable of taking risks.

During the initial telephone contact, you should listen to, and validate, any fears that the client expresses about coming to therapy. Be prepared to spend some time on this appointment-setting call; and do it yourself—don't ask your secretary to handle it. Let the client know that you understand how difficult it is to decide to seek therapy, to find a therapist, to set an appointment and to keep it.

Here is a transcript of an initial contact with Marcy, a twenty-eight year old waitress who attends junior college:

Marcy

    Dr.G   . *Hello, this is Dr. Gil*

    Marcy.   *Hello. My friend Annie Chang referred me to you.*

    Dr.G.   *And what is your first name?*

    Marcy.   *Marcy.*

    Dr.G.   *Marcy, thank you for calling. How can I help you?*

    Marcy.   *Well . . . I think I need to come in and see you.*

    Dr.G.   *OK. How are you feeling about coming in to see me?*

Marcy.   *It's very scary. I'm really not sure what I want, or need. My friends keep telling me it's important for me to talk to somebody.*

Dr.G.   *What do you think about what your friends say?*

Marcy.   *They're probably right.*

Dr.G.   *Still, it's sometimes hard to come and talk to a stranger about personal things.*

Marcy.   *Really.*

Dr.G.   *Is there anything you would like to know about me, or the type of therapy I do?*

Marcy.   *Well, I'm really not wanting to talk about everything now. You won't make me will you?*

Dr.G.   *Absolutely not, Marcy. You are in charge of what happens in therapy. You can say as much or as little as you want.*

Marcy.   *I do want to talk about things. Just not right away.*

Dr.G.   *Of course. That makes absolute sense. You want to get to know me a little so you feel as comfortable as you can talking about personal things.*

Marcy.   *That's right. Also, someone told me you've worked with people who were abused as children. Is that all kinds of abuse?*

Marcy.   *Yes Marcy. There are so many different kinds of abuse that children go through. I work with people who have been sexually abused, physically abused, neglected, abandoned or emotionally abused.*

Marcy.   *Well for me . . . I was just physically abused a little. So I'm really not sure how I feel about things. I know it wasn't really that bad.*

Dr.G.   *You know, a lot of people tend to talk that way about their abuse"it wasn't really that bad, it was just a little bit of abuse. Even a little abuse can feel real bad. Especially when you're a little person.*

Marcy.   *Yeah, I know.*

Dr.G.   *Marcy this is what I'd like to do. I have a couple of openings right now, and I'd like to set an appointment. Getting a therapist is like anything else, you need to see how you feel about me, and if you think we can work together. What's your schedule like?*

Marcy.   *I've got free time on Thursdays.*

Dr.G.   *That's good. My openings are both on Thursdays. One time in the morning, one time in the afternoon. What's best?*

Marcy.   *The morning. What time?*

Dr.G.   *Ten o'clock.*

Marcy.   *OK*

Dr.G.   *Well, Marcy. This is a big step for you. How do you feel?*

Marcy.   *OK so far.*

Dr.G.   *What's your worst fear about coming in to see me?*

Marcy.   *That I won't want to tell you anything.*

Dr.G.   *Well, that happens. It's hard to just start talking to a complete stranger. Anything I can do to make it easier for you?*

Marcy.   *No. I think it'll be OK.*

Dr.G.   *OK. And remember, when you feel ready or comfortable, I'm sure the important things will start coming out. I'll do what I can to make you feel comfortable.*

Marcy.   *It's been nice talking to you. I'm sorry I took up so much of your time.*

Dr.G.   *You didn't take up my time. I made time to talk with you and I'm glad I was able to reach you. See you on Thursday.*

Marcy.   *OK*

In this interview, I took the time to address the client's major fears. Many survivors tend to minimize themselves, their experiences, their perceptions, and their fears. They compare themselves to other survivors and imagine that their own experiences were less serious.

They also have problems with the issue of control. They are very much afraid of being manipulated, of being forced to behave in certain ways, of being forced to reveal information that they may not feel ready to reveal. It is an interesting paradox. On the one hand, they believe that others have the power to make them do things. On the other hand, they struggle to establish some semblance of control. Colleagues have often commented to me how simultaneously needy and demanding these clients can be. This dichotomy is characteristic of survivors.

The first face-to-face contact is very important. You-the therapist-represent both the (longed-for) nurturing and the (feared) rejecting, abusive parent. Your client will be struggling desperately to feel safe, monitoring everything you say or do.

The First Appointment

When you greet your client, he or she may experience massive anxiety. Some clients actually experience an altered state of consciousness. Simply being seen may constitute a major threat to many adult survivors. If you are late, these clients experience intolerable anxiety.

Since so many survivors are afraid of physical contact, it is best not to offer to shake your client's hand. Don't stand too close, offer a simple greeting using the client's first name, and your own:

> **Dr.G.**   *Hello Marcy. My name is Eliana. I'm glad to see you. Did you have any trouble finding the place?*
>
> **Marcy.**   *No.*
>
> **Dr.G.**   *Good. Sometimes people have trouble finding the address.*
>
> **Marcy.**   *I grew up in this area.*
>
> **Dr.G.**   *I see–Marcy, I'd like you to fill out these papers for me. If there are any questions that are not clear* [not "any questions you do not understand"] *I'll be happy to go over them with you later. Write down as much or as little as you want. Here's a pen, and I'll be back in just a few minutes.*

Most clients do not feel comfortable writing down a whole lot about their problems. A few, however, would rather have the therapist read about their problems so that they won't have to describe what happened. If you get reams of information, I think it's best to thank the client, and ask him or her to summarize it for you explaining that you will read it as soon as you get a chance.

When you come back out to the waiting room to escort your client to your room, be sure not to ask, "Are you finished yet?" These clients are acutely sensitive to performance clues, and may feel stupid or inadequate if they in fact have not finished. It is best just to simply say, "Marcy, come on in." If the client says, "I'm not finished filling out the form," you can say, "That's OK; we'll finish it together."

Your clients may ask you where you want them to sit. Always offer a choice: "Clients sit here or here, whatever seems more comfortable for you."

Your clients may ask you where you want them to sit. Always offer a choice: "Clients sit here or here, whatever seems more comfortable for you."

Once your clients are seated, help them to feel less anxious by reviewing the information they have written down. Review only the nonthreatening information: where they live, whom they live with, where they are from, whether they have children. Once you have done this you can ask the client what it's like for them to be answering these questions and how they feel. By asking these nonthreatening questions and immediately attending to their current experience, you are demonstrating that you will be careful and safe. By being directive, you are also creating a structure. Anxious clients usually find this reassuring. (This behavior would be inappropriate, or infantalizing, in dealing with clients who are confident about entering therapy, who have more practice with personal interactions, and who do not experience regressive tendencies due to fear.)

> Dr.G.   *Marcy, what was it like for you to come here today?*
>
> Marcy.   *I was really nervous.*
>
> Dr.G.   *What do you do when you feel nervous?*
>
> Marcy.   *Well, I ate a lot. I couldn't decide what to wear. I left my house really early. I was downstairs an hour ago.*
>
> Dr.G.   *What was going through your mind?*
>
> Marcy.   *Just that I do the right things, you know.*
>
> Dr.G.   *I know how it can feel to want to do the right thing. How have you done so far?*
>
> Marcy.   (<u>Nervous laugh</u>) *OK I guess.*
>
> Dr.G.   *I'll say. You found the place. You were on time. You filled out this form.*
>
> Marcy.   *Yeah . . . I didn't really say that much about Why I'm here now.*
>
> Dr.G.   *Maybe we can talk about that now.*
>
> Marcy.   *I feel really stupid. I keep thinking I probably don't have any real problems.*
>
> Dr.G.   *Tell me a little about your problems.*

A couple of things in this passage are worth noting. The therapist validates all the tasks the client has completed. This reinforces the client's sense of competence. However, it would be premature at this point to comment on how the client looks, since she says she had difficulty choosing what to wear. If the therapist compliments the client on her appearance, she may scare the client away by being positive when the client has no context yet within which to believe the therapist. The compliment would be premature for other reasons as well. First, it would make the client feel painfully visible. Second, the therapist sets a model of approval, which carries the implied threat of disapproval. And third, the therapist who compliments too much encourages the client to seek gratification from the outside. This can prevent the client from seeking change from within.

The therapist has also made the client feel safe by not reading back what the client wrote down. Rather, she gives the client an opportunity to explain her problems herself. If the therapist reads the client's statements out loud, the client may feel intruded upon or betrayed, even though it is her own words that are being read back to her.

This concludes the first, rapport-building, stage of the interview. Let us go on to the second, information-gathering, stage. This stage is more structured; it provides an opportunity to gather information about the client's primary defenses, coping strategies, and self-image, as well as his or her interactive skills. The client may not be able to address the issue of abuse directly. But you can describe what you observe in the session, and comment on any defense mechanisms that you recognize.

> Dr.G.   *Well, Marcy, you've given me a lot of important information about yourself so far. I know that you were one of two sisters in your family; your dad worked the graveyard shift on an automobile assembly line at night; and he would sleep during the day. Your mom had a job during the day and wasn't around much that you remember. You were born in New York, grew up in New Jersey, and you moved here to California when your dad got transferred. Let's see—you were about twelve.*
>
> Marcy.   *That's right.*
>
> Dr.G.   *One other thing I've noticed is that you seem more comfortable talking about your sister and mother than you do about your dad. When you talk about your dad your voice gets low, and you hold your hands together.*
>
> Marcy.   *You noticed all that?*
>
> Dr.G.   *Yes I did.*

Marcy.   *I guess I didn't know it was so obvious. I hardly ever talk about my dad.*

Dr.G.   *And when you do, does it feel uncomfortable?*

Marcy.   *Sometimes I even shake.*

Dr.G.   *Well, we'll go very slowly. There must be some strong feelings there about your dad.*

Marcy.   *Yeah.*

Gathering Information

The client may be unwilling or unable to be specific about problems at this stage of the interview. It is advisable to allow your client to bring up or avoid whatever they wish. Document what is volunteered and what is not, and point out any glaring gaps in the information.

Clients may start out by saying vaguely that things "aren't going well," or expressing general dissatisfaction with the quality of their lives. They may play down their problems, and at times even question their right to be in therapy, "taking up your valuable time." It is important to reassure the client that the problems he or she is raising are indeed serious and well worth exploring.

When the client has given you some basic information about the nature of the presenting problem, you should ask questions that will help you to fill in the gaps. Ask how long the problem has been going on, when it first surfaced, what the client thinks may have caused it, and how the client has tried to cope with it in the past.

Marcy.   *You know, suddenly I don't know what to say.*

Dr.G.   *Just take your time and think about what was going on right before you called to set up an appointment with me.*

Marcy.   *Well, I know I was feeling really lousy.*

Dr.G.   *In what way?*

Marcy.   *I was feeling depressed. I've been crying a lot lately, without any real reason.*

Dr.G.   *When you say you've been depressed, describe how you are when you are depressed.*

Marcy.   *Well, I've been down. I don't feel like going to work or school. I've been sleeping a lot. Mostly, I've been crying a lot.*

Dr.G.   *When did these feelings start?*

Marcy.   *About two months ago.*

Dr.G.   *Did anything specific happen then?*

Marcy.   *Well, I went to a funeral back home.*

Dr.G.   *New York or New Jersey?*

Marcy.   *Oh, New Jersey– Cherry Hill.*

Dr.G.   *Whose funeral was it?*

Marcy.   *A distant cousin. No one I knew real well. The whole family was there.*

Dr.G.   *Who is the whole family?*

Marcy.   *My mom, aunts, grandparents. My dad too. My sister and her kids.*

Dr.G.   *What's it like to be around them?*

Marcy.   *Well. . .* (Tears begin to well up. Dr. Gil waits) *I feel so . . .* (crying) *so . . . different when I'm with them.*

Dr.G.   *How so?*

Marcy.   *I can't be myself.*

Dr.G.   *How are you when you're not yourself?*

Marcy.   *I get . . . you know . . . quiet.*

Dr.G.   *So you don't say much when you're around them.*

Marcy.   *No. I kind of fade into the woodwork.*

Dr..G.   *What's it like to fade into the woodwork?*

Marcy.   *I don't mind it really . . . but I do, you know . . . 'cause I don't feel like I decide; it just happens.*

Dr.G.   *What would happen if you didn't fade into the woodwork?*

Marcy.   *Then I'd have to be there . . .* (crying)

Dr.G.   *So you're used to disappearing around your family.* (Pause: Marcy nods her head) *Anyone in particular you disappear from?*

Marcy.   *Mostly Mom, I guess.*

Dr.G.   *Any particular reason?*

Marcy.   *I just can't face her. I don't even like to look at her.*

Dr.G.   *What would you see if you looked at her?*

Marcy.   *I'd see how old and tired she looks.*

Dr.G.   *And what would she see in your eyes or face?*

Marcy.   *How ashamed I feel . . .* (suddenly shifting her weight and blowing her nose) *Look, I don't want to get into this right now. I don't know how we got off into that.*

Dr.G. *We can stop talking about that for now. We were talking about your going to the funeral back home, and how when you came back home, the feelings of depression began.*

Marcy. *I remember now.*

Dr.G. *It sounds like going back to New Jersey and seeing your family may have something to do with your feeling depressed these past few months. Does that sound right to you?*

Marcy. *I guess so.*

Dr.G. *Of course, knowing that may not help you to feel better right away. Let's talk about what you've tried so far to get you to feel less depressed.*

Marcy. *Well, usually I try to get out . . . but it's been so cold and wet lately.*

Dr.G. *So getting out of the house lifts your spirits sometimes.*

Marcy. *Well, it's not so much being away from the house as being with friends.*

Dr.G. *Any special friends you can call on?*

Marcy. *I have just a couple.*

Dr.G. *Two friends is a lot.*

Marcy. *Michelle is away on holiday. Claire is around, but she's got a new job and so she's been real busy lately.*

Dr.G. *You might be able to call Claire and set up a time to see her.*

Marcy. *Yeah, that would be nice.*

Dr.G. *What else seems to work for you when you're depressed?*

Marcy. *Well, I'm not really sure.*

Notice how much information the therapist has gathered so far. The client presented with moderate depression. However, some of the things she says in the phone contact and the first interview make it clear that unresolved childhood problems are interfering with her adult life. Specifically, she refers to early physical abuse. She says that she cannot be herself with her family. She identifies a coping mechanism by which she "disappears." She does not want to face her mother, and does not want her mother to look in her eyes and see that she feels ashamed. She is able to speak very distinctly about her father, although she says that she shakes when she discusses him. He worked at night and spent the days at home sleeping, and the mother worked during the day.

Closure

At the end of the initial interview, you must do three things. First, you must validate the client for taking the risk of making the appointment, keeping it, and sharing his or her feelings with you. Second, you must summarize the content of the interview, so the client knows he or she has been understood. Third, you must set a context for ongoing therapy.

> **Dr.G.**   *Marcy, our time is almost up for today, and I'd like to say a few things before we stop. First, I want to support your decision to call and make an appointment. I know it was hard for you to keep the appointment, and I think you took a big step coming here, and sharing the information you told me about today.*
>
> *I'm glad that you were able to tell me a little about how depressed you're feeling, and about going home for the funeral. I think your going home and feeling depressed might be connected. Later on, I'd like to talk to you about you and your family. It seems it's hard for you to be yourself with them, and you have feelings of shame around your mom. And it sounds like you have some pretty strong feelings about your dad. These feelings and reactions are painful.*
>
> *I'm also glad you were able to stop when you felt you had gone as far as you wanted to for today. I want you to know that you always have that option. I'm going to be bringing these things up again, because I believe they need to be discussed. I think they're connected to some of the feelings you have about yourself and your life today. My guess is that you may be able to talk more about them as we get to know each other better.*
>
> *Don't forget to call your friend and make a date with her, and I'd like you to try that TV exercise show at least two times before I see you again. Is there anything you'd like to ask me, Marcy?*

Marcy.   *I don't know. (*<u>pause</u>*) Do you think what's going on is serious enough to take up your time?*

Dr.G.   *Yes. You are clearly depressed and unhappy. These are serious problems. There seem to be some childhood experiences that are painful for you. You need to, and deserve to, talk about how these experiences affect you today, and what role they play in your depression. I think it might be important for you to think about why you are uncertain whether you really deserve to speak and to be heard.*

Marcy.   *Yeah. I always wonder if I have the right.*

Dr.G.   *You have every right to talk to someone about your life and take the time to sort things through. How do you feel about your first session?*

Marcy.   *I'm glad it's over.*

Dr.G.   *Was it better or worse than you expected?*

Marcy.   *Oh, a whole lot better. I'm just surprised that I cried in here. It's usually hard for me to cry in front of people. It was hard, but I did it anyway.*

Dr.G.   *That's another important step you took towards feeling better. I'll see you again next week. You have my number if you need to call before our next session.*

Marcy.   *Don't worry. When things get real bad, I do have friends I can call.*

Dr.G.   *See you next week.*

In this exchange, the therapist summarizes the salient points of the interview; she lets the client know that she understands her coping strategy; and she also lets her know that they are going to discuss these issues in the future. The therapist validates the client for making and keeping the appointment. She reassures the client that she—the client—will be able to control what she discusses and when. Because the client has had the experience of setting limits in this first session, she probably feels that she can control what she discusses in the future.

It is critical to make early assessments of suicide risk in adult survivors, particularly when they present with depression. Potentially suicidal clients must be protected and stabilized.

The Motivated Client

The client in the previous clinical example will be somewhat reluctant to talk about childhood abuse. She will have difficulty tolerating the painful memories and feelings. Some clients however, are more motivated to address the issue. These clients tend to have specific expectations. The following clinical example illustrates the motivated client. Grace is a thirty-eight year-old Mexican-American woman. She is unmarried and works as an electrician:

Grace

    Grace.   *I came to see you because I understand that you specialize in these kinds of situations, and I want to work this thing through and get on with my life.*

    Dr.G.   *Tell me a little about your particular situation.*

    Grace.   *My father raped me from the time I was three until I was about twelve.*

    Dr.G.   *Have you always been aware of this or did you remember it recently?*

    Grace.   *I always knew it on some level, but I remembered all the gory details about four years ago.*

    Dr.G.   *Was there anything in particular four years ago that triggered the memory?*

    Grace.   *I went in for a hysterectomy. Something about the whole process . . . going under the anesthetic, having these cold doctors probing and grasping at my insides. It all felt reminiscent.*

    Dr.G.   *What was it like for you to remember?*

    Grace.   *I have no basis for comparison. I don't know how most people react. I just felt cold–numb, almost. Thought about what kind of animal would do that to a child. And then I felt angrier than hell.*

    Dr.G.   *So at first you went numb. I assume that means you felt nothing.* (Grace nods affirmatively) *And then you felt angry.*

    Grace.   *That's right. And I haven't been able to move beyond that.*

    Dr.G.   *Has your anger increased over the years?*

    Grace.   *Nope. Doesn't get stronger. Doesn't let up.*

Dr.G.   *How does it affect you to feel this anger a lot of the time?*

Grace.   *That's why I'm here. I'm getting an ulcer. I get into fights at work with people over nothing, everything, nothing. My friends keep telling me to go get help; they think I'm all screwed up.*

Dr.G.   *So you find yourself getting angry a lot of the time, and your friends think you should get help. What do you think?*

Grace.   *As much as I hate to admit it, I think this anger thing has got control of me. I just can't relax. I can't get this thing out of my mind.*

Dr.G.   *When you're thinking about it, what kinds of things go through your mind?*

Grace.   *Mostly, I see this one picture.*

Dr.G.   *Tell me about the picture.*

Grace.   *It's pretty gross.*

Dr.G.   *Tell me what you can about this picture, since it seems to especially bother you.*

Grace.   *Well, it's about me in a little bed, with side rails, and my dad scrunched up, holding my head to his dick. (*<u>Very uncomfortably</u>*) God, it's so disgusting. It makes me sick.*

Dr.G.   *That is a very disturbing picture for you to see. It is difficult to believe adults force children to have sex with them, and it's also painful to imagine what the child is feeling at the time. (*<u>Grace looks down at the floor</u>*) At some point I'd like to talk more about the little child and her pain.*

Grace.   *I swear I get so furious.*

Dr.G.   *I know you do. You have every right to feel angry. (*<u>Pause</u>*) And it sounds like that anger also gets in your way.*

Grace.   *What do you mean?*

Dr.G.   *Well, it sounds like the anger is not going where it's intended, but it's going other places.*

Grace.   *Like where?*

Dr.G.   *You tell me. Where do you think it goes?*

Grace.   (<u>Pensive</u>)   *I guess it goes to my friends, and people I work with.*

Dr.G.   *And who else? (*<u>Grace looks bewildered</u>*)*

Grace.   *I don't get it.*

Dr.G.   *Don't you sometimes get mad at yourself for feeling so mad at your dad and at others?*

Grace. *I guess you're right. That son of a bitch. And I thought I'd gotten him out of my system.*

Dr.G. *It doesn't sound like it. To get him out of your system, you'll probably have to get the anger out completely and direct it at him in some way.*

Grace. *The asshole died already.*

Dr.G. *That's part of it too.*

Grace. *What does that mean?*

Dr.G. *In my mind, people feel most angry when they feel helpless about something. It's almost like two sides of the same coin. You feel helpless because your dad is gone; and you think there's nothing you can do about the abuse now; and the more helpless you feel, the angrier you get. Make sense?*

Grace. *Yeah. I can't believe this. I used to think when he died I was rid of him. I didn't shed one tear. I didn't go to the funeral. I got my revenge, I thought. Everyone in the family wondered what the wonderful Mr. Sanchez could have done that made his first-born daughter stay away.*

Dr.G. *I'm sure you felt strong not going to the funeral and not crying for a dad you have such mixed feelings about.*

Grace. *Damn right.*

Dr.G. *I'll tell you what I think.*

Grace. *That's what I'm paying you for.*

Dr.G. *There is no excuse for the abuse that happened to you. Most children feel confused, hurt, and angry about being abused. For you, angry feelings are the most prominent right now, and they need to be expressed directly.*

Grace. *But–*

Dr.G. *I know; he's dead. But you're the one who needs to express the feelings. You and I will talk about ways to do that–like letter writing, pretending you're talking to him in a chair, or to his picture. The work to be done is for you, not for him.*

Grace. *OK, I get it.*

Dr.G. *And there's one more thing.*

Grace. *What's that?*

Dr.G. *In addition to angry feelings, I wouldn't be surprised if there were other feelings as well.*

Grace. *If you're implying I have love for that asshole you're dead wrong.*

> **Dr.G.** *I'm saying you may have some other feelings buried deep inside, way under the anger. I'd like to talk about that possibility as well.*
>
> **Grace.** *When do we start?*
>
> **Dr.G.** *We started today. I hear how anxious you are to put this behind you. But you know, to say goodbye, you first have to say hello, and some of this work may take a while.*
>
> **Grace.** *Well I'm not one to stay in therapy for years.*
>
> **Dr.G.** *That may not be necessary for you– want to take the rest of the time today, and work on expressing some of the anger you have very ready to come forward.*

This client works at a much faster pace than Marcy. That fast pace is her defense: she talks fast, affirmatively, almost clinically about her self and the fact that she was abused. She is angry and volatile. She is giving the message <u>Be direct with me</u>, and I am very direct with her. She functions at an intellectual level and responds to interpretations and directives. The goal with this client will be to help her acknowledge and express the other feelings she has about her father, about the abuse she has suffered, and about her mother.

During this first session, I gave Grace the opportunity to express a lot of angry feelings. I asked her to tell her father all the things she had always wanted to say to him, and she went into a fifteen-minute tirade. At last she burst into tears, and I concluded the therapy session with a period of guided imagery and deep relaxation. Once she was calm, I set the next appointment. I also asked her during the coming week to write down any specific memories she had. I asked her to note the details of each memory, the time of day at which the memory occurred, and what was happening before and after the memory surfaced. This cognitive task is designed to prevent panic by providing an immediate structure for responding to intrusive memories, if any occurred.

Other Common Presentations

The following excerpts from transcripts of initial interviews illustrate other common presentations by adult survivors.

Charlene is a single woman of thirty-six. She has had numerous failed relationships. She reports that when men are nice to her, she backs away; but when they treat her like dirt, she falls for them. She puts up with everything these men dish out, yet inevitably they dump her. Charlene wants to understand why she can't like, as she says, "nice guys." She wants to find a good, permanent relationship. Charlene believes that she is her own worst enemy.

When I take her family history, Charlene avoids saying anything about her father, but she expounds on all of her mother's fine qualities. She was mother's favorite, and she has tried to emulate her all her life. She tries especially to emulate her mother's patience, her good humor and her unfailing optimism. Her mother is in good health, and Charlene visits her frequently. Charlene was the only girl in the family. She has two older brothers.

When I ask her to tell me about her father, her lively chatter ceases abruptly. She is almost speechless. During the third session, I manage to get her to respond:

Charlene.

Charlene. *Well, there's really not much to say. He was a . . . difficult sort of person.*

Dr.G. *In what way?*

Charlene. *Well . . . he was kind of loud.*

Dr.G. *How did you respond to his loudness?*

Charlene. *I usually went into my room.*

Dr.G. *How did you feel when you were in your room, and your dad was being loud outside?*

Charlene. *I didn't like it. I would put cotton in my ears.*

Dr.G. *What would you have heard if the cotton wasn't there?*

Charlene. *Just yelling.*

Dr.G. *What did he yell about?*

Charlene. *Oh, different things.*

Dr.G. *Like what, for example?*

Charlene. *Well . . . he mostly complained.*

Dr.G. *About anything specific?*

Charlene. *No, not really.*

Dr.G. *What did your mom do when he yelled?*

Charlene. *Oh, not much. Mostly, she would try to take care of whatever it was he was upset about. Mom was incredibly intuitive. She seemed to know what other people wanted.*

Dr.G. *And what did your father usually want?*

Charlene. *Oh, different things.*

Dr.G.   *Hmm. I'm having a hard time picturing what was going on.*

Charlene.   *Well, that's because he was so hard to explain.*

Dr.G.   *Was he ever complaining about you or your brothers?*

Charlene.   *Oh, all the time, but mostly it was about me.*

Dr.G.   *OK. What specific things about you did he complain about?*

Charlene.   *Mostly that I was dirty.*

Dr.G.   *Dirty?*

Charlene.   *Yeah.* (Client becomes visibly uncomfortable, shifts her weight from side to side, and looks at her watch)

Dr.G.   *Tell me a little about the dirtiness he would complain about.*

Charlene.   *Well, I don't know.*

Dr.G.   *This seems hard for you to talk about.*

Charlene.   *Yeah.*

Dr.G.   *What do you think will happen if you talk about it?*

Charlene.   *Well, nothing.*

Dr.G.   *How do you imagine I will react to what you say?*

Charlene.   *I'm sure you've heard worse.*

Dr.G.   *How do you imagine I'll react?*

Charlene.   *I don't know.*

Dr.G.   *How do you feel right now?*

Charlene.   *Just embarrassed.*

Dr.G.   *Can you say a little about what embarrasses you?*

Charlene.   *It's a funny thing. All my life I've felt embarrassed about my father.*

Dr.G.   *Embarrassed?*

Charlene.   *Yeah. I would feel embarrassed because he was so . . . different.*

Dr.G.   *What one thing did he say or do that embarrassed you the most?*

Charlene.   *Well . . . I guess when he had had too much to drink.*

Dr.G.   *Did that happen a lot?*

Charlene.   *Most days.*

Dr.G.   *And when he had had too much to drink, what was he like?*

Charlene.   *He got loud.*

Dr.G.   *This is when he yelled and complained?*

Charlene.   *Yeah.*

Dr.G.   *And what specifically did he complain about that had to do with you?*

Charlene.   *He really didn't like me too much.*

Dr.G.   *What gave you that feeling?*

Charlene.   *He would say I smelled a lot.*

Dr.G.   *And he said you were dirty?*

Charlene.   *Yeah.*

Dr.G.   *What did you think about what he said?*

Charlene.   *Well, I just tried to smell better.*

Dr.G.   *Did you ever understand what he was talking about?*

Charlene.   *He kept screaming that my mother didn't bathe me . . . that I had a horrible smell on my body. He didn't want anyone to come to the house, because he said they would vomit if they smelled me.*

Dr.G.   *How did you react to the things he said?*

Charlene.   *I felt . . . you know . . . bad.*

Dr.G.   *Like you were doing something bad? Or you just were bad?*

Charlene.   *I thought I was just bad. There was something wrong with me.*

Dr.G.   *And did you ever ask your mom about the smell that your dad kept talking about?*

Charlene.   *She just said that Dad was wrong and I shouldn't listen to him . . . especially when he was drinking.*

Dr.G.   *What did she say about the smell?*

Charlene.   *She said I didn't smell.*

Dr.G.   *What did you think?*

Charlene.   *I thought I did smell, but my mom was too nice to tell me.*

Dr.G.   *Did anyone else ever mention the smell?*

Charlene.   *No one talked about it. But I always thought they were being polite.*

Dr.G. *How old were you when your father first started complaining about your smell?*

Charlene. *I don't know.*

Dr.G. *When's the first time you remember hearing about it?*

Charlene. *I think I was in kindergarten, because I was afraid to go to school and have people notice it.*

Dr.G. *How long did your dad complain about it?*

Charlene. *He still does.*

Dr.G. *He still mentions this smell?*

Charlene. *Yeah.*

Dr.G. *What do you think about it now?*

Charlene. *Well, I think I know I don't smell.*

Dr.G. *You* think *you know. Sounds like you're not sure.*

Charlene. *No, I'm not sure.*

Dr.G. *When you visit your mom and dad now, what do you do when he complains about your smell?*

Charlene. *Oh, he doesn't complain now.*

Dr.G. *How do you know he still thinks about the smell?*

Charlene. *Because when I visit he opens the windows. He also asks anyone who is visiting to leave. He also has Mom put out the paper towels so I don't dirty anything.*

Dr.G. *How do you feel when you visit your father?*

Charlene. *Well, I don't visit him.*

Dr.G. *How do you feel when you visit your mother and your father implies that you have an unpleasant smell?*

Charlene. *He doesn't mean any harm.*

Dr.G. *He may not. But how do you feel?*

Charlene. (Tears up a little) *I don't know.*

Dr.G. *Think a little bit now. You go to visit your mom, and your dad opens the windows when you come over, so your bad smell doesn't bother him. How do you feel when he does that?*

Charlene. *Usually I don't feel anything. I just walk over to my mom's room and kind of stay out of his way.*

Dr.G. *Supposing you went over to him and kissed him and put your arms around him instead?*

Charlene. (Looking alarmed) *Oh, I would never do that.*

Dr.G. *What would happen?*

Charlene. *I can't imagine.*

Dr.G. *Let's imagine it together. You go over and give him a hug. What happens next?*

Charlene. (<u>Teary-eyed</u>) *This is really hard.*

Dr.G. *I know it is. I think it hurts to think about you and your dad.*

Charlene. *Me and my dad?*

Dr.G. *Do you talk about you and your dad frequently?*

Charlene. *Never.*

Dr.G. *I can see how it's hard for you.*

Charlene. *Did you ask something?*

Dr.G. *What would happen if you hugged him?*

Charlene. *He would push me away.*

Dr.G. *How would he do that?*

Charlene. *Just push me away . . . with his arms.*

Dr.G. *Would he say anything?*

Charlene. *Just make a grunt.*

Dr.G. *A grunt?*

Charlene. *Yeah, . . . like "yuk."*

Dr.G. *And what would you do?*

Charlene. *Go to Mom's room.*

Dr.G. *And would you tell her what happened?*

Charlene. *Oh no. Poor Mom. She hates the way he treats me.*

Dr.G. *Has she ever said anything to your dad about how she feels.*

Charlene. *She says it's useless.*

Dr.G. *Has your dad ever pushed you away when you want to hug him?*

Charlene. *Well, I've never tried to hug him.*

Dr.G. *Never?*

Charlene. *No.*

Dr.G. *Even when you were very little?*

Charlene. *I just don't remember.*

Dr.G. *How did you know not to hug him?*

Charlene. *Well, he would always tell me, "Go away. You smell something terrible."*

Dr.G. *And would you go away?*

Charlene. *Oh, yes. Right away.*

Dr.G. *It must have been very hard to have your parent push you away, with his words or his actions.*

Charlene. *I don't really care anymore.*

Dr.G. *Well, you probably have cared sometime in your life.*

Charlene. *Oh, yeah. There were times . . .*

Dr.G. *What times?*

Charlene. *When my dates came to get me, he would . . .* (pause) *I don't know why I still remember these things.*

Dr.G. *Well, when important things happen to us, whether they are full of joy or pain, we tend to remember them.*

Charlene. *With the boys. He would tell them not to get too close because I had this problem.*

Dr.G. *Did the boys tell you that, or did you overhear it?*

Charlene. *Both.*

Dr.G. *Were you embarrassed he did that?*

Charlene. *Oh God, yes.*

Dr.G. *What did the boys say?*

Charlene. *They asked if my dad was always drunk.*

Dr.G. *Did that embarrass you?*

Charlene. *A lot.*

Dr.G. *How did you respond to them?*

Charlene. *I said he wasn't drunk.*

Dr.G. *Was he?*

Charlene. *Yeah . . . but my mom and I never let on.*

Dr.G. *I see.*

Charlene. (Looking at her watch again) *I'd like to tell you about a new guy I met at the office.*

Dr.G. *So you'd like to change the subject.*

Charlene. *Yeah.*

Dr.G. *Charlene, I'm willing to change the subject now, but I think it's important to talk about your dad some more, maybe at a later time. Your problems these days are with men and relationships, and your first relationship with a man was your dad. I'm sure this has had an impact on how you view men.*

Charlene. *There's nothing more to say.*

Dr.G. *You don't have to talk about it anymore today. How did you feel talking about it though?*

Charlene. *I don't like it. I don't like thinking about him.*

Dr.G. *How does it make you feel to think about him?*

Charlene.   *It upsets me somehow. Makes me feel bad. I just try to not let it get to me anymore.*

Dr.G.   *And do you succeed?*

Charlene.   *Sometimes.*

Dr.G.   *And other times?*

Charlene.   *Other times it gets to me . . . you know . . . makes me feel like it's hopeless.*

Dr.G.   *What's hopeless?*

Charlene.   *My life . . .* (Sighs)

Dr.G.   *In what specific way?*

Charlene.   *I'll never find someone who will love me or treat me well, and I'll never convince myself I'm OK.*

Dr.G.   *It sounds to me like there are some very deep doubts inside of you about whether you are good, or worthy of love. I think that has something to do with how you felt as a child, and the messages you got from your father. That's why I think it's important to talk about what was happening back then.*

Charlene.   *It hurts to do that.*

Dr.G.   *I can see it hurts you, and we'll take it slowly . . . These painful memories are interfering with your current life. It sounds like you've learned ways to avoid pain, but in order to feel better, we'll need to discuss the source of the pain.*

Charlene.   *I really would like to talk about this new guy I met.*

Dr.G.   *Please do.*

This client has developed a major avoidance response to thinking or speaking about her relationship with her father. She does not understand why he behaved towards her as he did, and she is not really consciously aware of the many ways she may have reacted. This is clearly a case of emotional abuse, and the impact on this client has been enormous. It is probable that the way her father treated her as a child is directly related to her inability to allow men to be nice to her today. Charlene and her mother both used denial to cope with living with an alcoholic, who may have been seriously emotionally disturbed. Since her mother was unable to model a protective and appropriate response to the father, Charlene never learned how to deal with inappropriate, excessive, or abusive behavior directed towards her.

It will be difficult to overcome Charlene's resistance and get her to fully remember and discuss her childhood. Her tendency to avoid pain by changing the subject must be pointed out to her repeatedly. This defense has served her well in the past, but it is counterproductive at present. She must be made to understand how the defense has worked, and why it is no longer working. I will have to let her know that while I respect her ability to avoid, she and I will have to confront the avoidance at a later time. All of these strategies will help to create an atmosphere of safety and trust.

Timing is always a delicate issue. Don't be too quick to label parental behavior abusive. To do so may elicit defensiveness or denial. I prefer simply to accept the client's description of what the parent did, and how the client responded. Midway in therapy, when the client describes an abusive behavior, I label the behavior as abuse. By then, the client has a context within which to understand what happened. When you label parental behavior abusive, you help your clients to shift from seeing themselves as responsible or bad, to seeing their parents as inadequate or abusive. When your clients can acknowledge that they were abused, old, buried feelings will surface. You and the client can then explore these feelings and resolve them. That is what I did in the following case:

David, a forty-five year-old executive, was referred to therapy from an employee assistance program because he lacked motivation. David's employers wanted to promote him to a higher management position, but they felt that he lacked the necessary motivation for a leadership position. David was apathetic about coming to therapy. He seemed willing enough to participate if the company wanted him to, but he said he didn't see how he could change his basic personality to suit them. He was skeptical about his ability, and his motivation, to become a leader.

At first glance, David appeared to have no serious problems. He and his wife seemed to be content. Money was not a big issue. During history taking, he told me that he had had a "happy, normal childhood." On the surface everything seemed to be fine.

The only recent event that seemed at all related to David's general apathy (or as he said, "fatigue") was the birth of his second child, a boy. His first child was a four-year-old girl.

<u>David.</u>

> **Dr.G.** *David, tell me a little about when you were a kid. How many brothers and sisters did you have?*
>
> **David.** *Just one sister.*
>
> **Dr.G.** *Older or younger?*
>
> **David.** *She was five years older.*
>
> **Dr.G.** *So you were the little baby that Mom brought home to the big sister, eh?*
>
> **David.** *Yeah.*
>
> **Dr.G.** *And it sounds like your kids have just about the same age spread as you and your sister*
>
> **David.** *Just about.*
>
> **Dr.G.** *How were things with you and your sister?*
>
> **David.** *We got along OK.*
>
> **Dr.G.** *No sibling rivalry?*
>
> **David.** *Just the usual.*
>
> **Dr.G.** *Did you share the same room?*
>
> **David.** *Why do you ask?*
>
> **Dr.G.** *Just wondering.*
>
> **David.** *I really don't see how this relates to my leadership skills at work.*

David became extremely resistant at this point and canceled the next two appointments. It was clear that there was something that needed discussion; that David was anxious about it; and that he was using an avoidance response to deal with his anxiety.

He did keep the following appointment, saying that unavoidable circumstances had prevented him from keeping the two previous ones. I returned to the issues of leadership and of his stress-related work long enough to re-engage his trust. At this point, David spontaneously brought up his concerns about his children, specifically his concern that his daughter might hurt his son.

> **Dr.G.** *David, I'd like you to tell me what your greatest fear is about what Melissa might do to Scott.*
>
> **David.** *Well, you know. Hurt him in some way.*
>
> **Dr.G.** *How, specifically?*
>
> **David.** *Well, any of a number of ways.*
>
> **Dr.G.** *So I assume you might mean physically?*

David.   *Yes.*

Dr.G.   *Or not be able to protect himself from some harm?*

David.   *Yes.*

Dr.G.   *Anything else?*

David.   *Well, you know. Make him do things or touch him in the wrong places.*

Dr.G.   *So you're also concerned about inappropriate touching.*

David.   *Well, it does happen.*

Dr.G.   *Yes, sometimes brothers and sisters can touch each other in inappropriate ways.*

David.   *That's right. I just want to spare Scott.*

Dr.G.   *David, when you were growing up, did your sister ever touch you inappropriately?*

David.   *Why do you ask?*

Dr.G.   *Because I'm interested in you, and if something caused you pain or confusion as a child, I believe that's important.*

David.   *My sister was sick.*

Dr.G.   *What do you mean, sick?*

David.   *She did sick things.*

Dr.G.   *Can you give me an example?*

David.   *I've never told a living human being about this.*

Dr.G.   *I appreciate your trusting me with it.*

David.   *She would urinate in my mouth.*

Dr.G.   *What was your reaction to that?*

David.   *What do you think?*

Dr.G.   *I can imagine it must have been upsetting and scary.*

David.   *To say the least.*

Dr.G.   *Did it happen more than once?*

David.   *That's a joke. We slept in the same room. Every night, when the lights went out, she would get really weird. She did all kinds of things. A nice little angel during the day, a monster by night.*

Dr.G.   *How long did this go on?*

David.   *For about two years.*

Dr.G.   *How old were you?*

David.   *About six or seven.*

Dr.G.   *So you were six or seven and your sister about eleven or twelve. Quite an age difference. Was she a lot bigger as well?*

David.   *By a lot. I didn't have my growth spurt until I was about thirteen. She had hers very early.*

Dr.G.   *Well, I can see why you'd be worried about Scott being safe.*

David.   *I swore nothing like that would ever happen if I had kids.*

Dr.G.   *I can understand why Scott's safety has been so important to you. You know David, you mentioned that you'd never talked to anyone else about this. I'm wondering what it's like to talk about it now.*

David.   *It feels strange. Like I'm wondering what you think about all this.*

Dr.G.   *What's your guess about what I might think?*

David.   *I assume you've heard this kind of stuff before.*

Dr.G.   *So how would I react if I've heard it all before?*

David.   *Well, you're probably not shocked.*

Dr.G.   *How might I react towards you?*

David.   *You probably aren't blaming me for it.*

Dr.G.   *Is that your worst fear about how others might react?*

David.   *Oh, yeah. I guess most people would say, Why didn't you fight back or say no or something? You were the boy.*

Dr.G.   *Yeah, some people might not understand how a little boy of six or seven might feel trapped or scared enough and be unable to fight back.*

David.   *I wasn't so much scared as I felt trapped. My sister had me convinced that I was just as bad as she was, and that if I told on her we would both get punished, because we were doing this stuff together.*

Dr.G.   *Was there other stuff you didn't tell me about?*

David.   *Oh, yeah. But I'm not sure the details are important for anyone to know. The main thing is, we did some stupid stuff together and we shouldn't have.*

Dr.G.   *I'm really glad you were able to talk about this, David, because I'm sure it's been a burden to keep it a secret all these years. I think it's sometimes especially hard for men, because these kinds of bad things are supposed to happen mostly to women, not to men.*

David.   *Yeah . . . as a matter of fact . . . I know you work with abused women; I just didn't know if you've ever heard of a guy having stuff happen to him?*

Dr.G.   *It happens more than you imagine. It's very often more difficult for men to bring it out than for women. There are groups now for men who were abused.*

David.   *Well, I'm not even sure it would be called abuse. I mean, it wasn't my father or anything.*

Dr.G.   *Well, abuse does happen between siblings, and the effects on the victim are just the same.*

David.   *I hate that word* <u>victim</u>.

Dr.G.   *I know. No one likes to think of themselves as helpless in any situation.*

David.   *Listen, I've got to leave ten minutes early today because I have a dentist appointment. I forgot to tell you at the start.*

Dr.G.   *I wish you'd told me early on. What we're discussing right now is really important, and it's hard for me to stop abruptly.*

David.   *Well, I've got to run.*

Dr.G.   *Is there a possibility you can be late to your dentist?*

David.   *No. I can't. I missed the last appointment, and as it is I probably will be a little late . . . I'm sorry . . . Are we on for the same time next week?*

Dr.G.   *Yes, your appointment is set for the same time. Please make sure you're able to stay the full session.*

David.   *No problem.*

Dr.G.   *OK, David. I'll see you again next week.*

This client had a very difficult time talking about his abuse, and would probably still resist using that label to describe what his sister did to him. But he began to feel relieved as the therapy progressed, to be able to talk about it. Slowly, he began to recognize that he really hadn't been able to fight back, and that his silence had not been compliance. The most difficult aspect of the abuse for him was not the sexual activity itself, but the sadistic acts that had accompanied it. David's sister had forced him to drink urine, and had frequently tied him up and hit him if he could not get an erection fast enough. This had caused him excruciating humiliation and degradation, and had made him feel helpless and enraged. The whole experience had also caused him to question his masculinity, and he remembers a period in young adulthood when he mistreated a couple of sexual partners. This further reinforced his sense of being an inadequate, confused man. But once he met his future wife, he believed that all these issues had been resolved.

David eventually chose to confront his sister, from whom he had been estranged for many years. While they did not become close friends, David felt much better about himself once he had expressed to her his anger and disgust. He also learned that what he had suspected—that is that she was emotionally unstable—was true. It turned out that she had frequent "breakdowns" requiring hospitalization, and that she was on medication.

David terminated therapy and turned down the promotion, saying that he felt unwilling to take on more responsibilities that might infringe on his time with his family. He told his employer that he would like to consider a promotion in a few years, when his children were older.

In this particular case, although David's presenting problem had little about it to suggest childhood abuse, taking a family history, and assessing his extreme responses about his infant son, led me to inquire further. Although David was clearly uncomfortable discussing his childhood abuse, the relief he felt when he finally did so was immediate and self-reinforcing. Dealing with his sense of victimization and his guilt about being unable to protect himself, enhanced his self-esteem and gave him a renewed sense of control. In addition, therapy enabled David to view his daughter more realistically. He no longer assumed that she wanted to abuse her brother and he no longer saw his son as a potential victim. This made it much easier for David to see the children for who they were, and it helped him to establish a closer relationship with them both.

Had David continued to avoid the issue of abuse, saying that it wasn't important or refusing to talk about it, I might have provided him with a rationale for doing so. I would have done this by relating the abuse to his current problems with his children:

> *Dr.G.   David, it seems it is very difficult for you to talk about what happened between you and your sister. I don't want to push. I want to tell you that I'm here to listen any time that you want to talk about it. I also want to say that I think it*

*would be important for you to talk about you and your sister
at some point, because most people find that these secrets become
a burden, and they feel much better when they can talk about
them. I also think that in your life this comes up concerning
your own kids and their safety. So even though you are keeping
these memories bottled up, they are coming out in other ways,
and they're causing you to worry about the safety of your son.*

Taking a Detailed History

After your clients have had an opportunity to discuss their presenting problems, and you have taken steps to address their
presenting problems, I recommend taking a detailed history.

Tell the client that you will be taking a history for the next two
or three sessions, and that after that, you will be going back to the
less structured therapy style that you used in the beginning. This
discourages the client from expecting to follow passively wherever
you lead. Once you have collected the information, you can
decide whether specific guidance or follow-up is required. For
example, if by taking a history, you discover that the client has
self-mutilated in the past, and is currently self-mutilating, you
should spend time discussing how the client can stop this dangerous behavior.

The reason you need to take a <u>detailed</u> history is that adult
survivors tend to provide sketchy information about themselves.
Usually they will minimize their problems. It is easier for them, at
this early stage in treatment, to describe their behaviors than their
feelings. Therefore, you will want to focus on obtaining descriptions of problems behaviors. Thus, for example, the client may
not respond to general questions about health issues, but may
respond to specific questions about everyday aches and pains.
These are relevant if they are stress-related or established coping
mechanisms. One client responded: "I've learned to live with this
pain. I hardly notice it anymore. It's a lot easier than the other
kind of pain—I figured everyone had it."

The following sample questions may be used to detect the
psychological problems that are most common among adult
survivors.

The first group of questions concerns <u>behavioral symptoms</u>.
These include sleeping disorders, eating disorders, self-destructive behaviors, physiologic problems, and interactional problems.

Introduce <u>sleeping disorders</u> by saying: "I'd like to ask you a few questions about sleeping, and what sleeping habits you may have." (Ask about the specific symptom, and ask at what time in the client's life—childhood, adolescence, young adulthood, adulthood, the present—it occurred.)

Is it hard for you to fall asleep? How much sleep do you usually get? What helps you to fall asleep?

Do you think you sleep too much? How much?

Do you find it hard to wake up?

Do you have unpleasant, scary, or confusing dreams?

Do you sleepwalk? Where do you go? How do you feel about being a sleepwalker?

Do you sleep with your eyes open or shut?

Is it hard for you to sleep in a bed?

Is it hard for you to sleep alone? With someone else?

Introduce <u>eating disorders</u> by saying: "Now I'm going to ask some questions about food and eating in your life."

Are there times when you eat too much?

Are there times when you do not eat enough?

Do you feel uncomfortable or afraid of eating in front of others?

Are you afraid of eating alone?

Do you ever eat things rather than food?

Are there times when you eat a lot and then throw up?

Do you sometimes hoard food?

Are there times when you're hungry but you refuse to eat?

Do you often gag or choke on food?

Are you able to stop eating when you want to stop?

Are there times when you aren't able to start eating?

Introduce <u>self-destructive behaviors</u> by saying: "This part of the interview has to with situations that end up hurting you."

Do you find yourself hurting parts of your body?

Do you find yourself cutting parts of your body?

Do some kinds of pain feel good to you?

Are you too sensitive to pain? Do you react to pain in what you see as extreme ways?

Do you drink alcohol? How much? How often?

Do you take any drugs? What kind? How often?

Do you buy over-the-counter medication? For what?

Do you take diuretics? How often?

Do you give yourself enemas? How many? For what?

Do you eat a lot of sugar? How much? How do you react?

Do you drink a lot of caffeine? How much? How do you react?

Do you shoplift? Do you get caught?

Do you commit other kinds of petty crimes? Have you been caught?

Have you ever been arrested? For what?

Have you done jail time? For what? How long were you in?

Introduce <u>Physiologic problems</u> by saying: "This next section has to do with pain, and what role pain has played, or is playing, in your life?"

Do parts of your body hurt you?

Are there kinds of pain that you're used to, or don't even notice anymore?

How often do you go to see doctors?

Do most medications work or not work for you?

Introduce <u>interactional problems</u> by saying: "These questions are about your relationships with people."

Do you stay away from people?

Do you avoid social activities ?

Do you spend most of your time alone?

Would you want to spend more time with others?

Do you feel afraid to talk with others, or approach others?

Do you back away from people who show an interest in you?

Are you afraid of people getting physically close?

Do you believe if people really knew you they wouldn't like you?

When people express love or affection, do you back off?

Do others hurt you physically?

Do others force you to have physical contact with them?

Is sexual intimacy scary to you?

Do you feel you can say no to people's sexual advances?

Do you find yourself taking care of other people a lot?

Do you wish someone would take care of you the way you take care of others?

Do you feel angry and hostile towards others?

Do you feel that your anger just pops up unexpectedly?

Are you afraid of how angry you can feel or behave?

What do you do or say when you feel angry?

How do you react when others express anger towards you?

Do you feel afraid to depend on others?

Do you believe others will always let you down?

Do you feel comfortable trusting others?

Do you feel you are trustworthy?

Do you have periods of time when you space out?

Are there periods of time that you can't remember?

Do you sometimes wake up somewhere and not know how you got there? Do people recognize you who you don't remember meeting?

The second group of questions concern eating:

What were meals like during your childhood?

How were your meals prepared? Who prepared them?

What usually went on during meals?

The third group concerns sleeping:

How did the children in your family know that it was time to go to sleep?

Were there any nighttime rituals, such as storytelling? What (if anything) happened once people went to sleep?

The fourth group concerns the expression of <u>anger:</u>

> How did you know when other people in the family were angry? What did they say or do?

> What kinds of things did you do that caused others to be angry?

> What were the family rules about anger?

Ask these questions about <u>religion:</u>

> Did your family practice any religion?

> Were the children expected to adhere to religious practices? Do you practice any religion now? Do you attend a church or temple or mosque?

Ask these questions about <u>cultural differences</u>:

> Were there any special childrearing practices unique to your culture?

> Are cultural practices incorporated into your life now?

Ask these questions about <u>discipline</u>:

> How were children disciplined in your family?

> How do you view those disciplinary practices now?

> Were different kinds of discipline used for different children?

Ask these questions about the expression of <u>affection</u>:

> How was affection shown in your family?

> How did the adults show affection to each other?

> How did the adults show affection to the children?

> Who was the most affectionate person in the family? Who was next?

> Who was the least affectionate person in the family?

Ask these questions about <u>family activities</u>:

> Were there any activities that your family did together?

> Did family members feel close to each other?

> Who were you the closest to? Who next?

Ask these questions about <u>mental illness</u>:

> Was anyone in your family hospitalized for mental illness? Who? What were you told about this person's mental illness?

Ask these questions about <u>suicide</u>:
> Did anyone in your family kill him/herself? Who? How old were you and what were you told about it?

Ask these questions about <u>drug abuse</u>:
> Was anyone in your family alcoholic? Who?
>
> Was anyone in your family addicted to other drugs? Who?

This list of questions is not intended to be exhaustive. But discussing these subjects with your clients can evoke childhood memories and set the stage for them to think and talk about their experiences. Bear in mind that your clients will vary in their ability to recall, disclose, and discuss what they remember.

An Alternative Model for Assessing Survivors

McCann et al (1988) present a "schema framework" for assessing and treating survivors of childhood sexual abuse. The basic tenet of this model is that "individuals hold certain beliefs and expectations (schemata) about the self and others, which both shape and are shaped by their experience in the world" (78). The authors add that "the main implication of this notion for understanding childhood sexual abuse victims is that a victim's unique interpretation of the trauma determines his or her reactions (emotional, cognitive, behavioral) to that trauma, which in turn affect his or her subsequent interactions with others" (78).

Based on this model, McCann et al recommend that the therapist assess the client's functioning in the five areas of <u>Safety</u>, <u>Trust</u>, <u>Power</u>, <u>Esteem</u>, and <u>Intimacy</u>. Once the initial assessment is complete, the therapist designs an individualized treatment plan based upon the client's own particular schemata. I believe that the McCann et al model is a valuable theoretical framework for assessing and treating survivors. I am especially impressed by the way in which it respects the client's individual experience.

Forming a Therapeutic Alliance

You must form a therapeutic alliance with your client if therapy is to succeed. This must be done slowly and deliberately. One thing that will help you to form an alliance is to explain the parameters of therapy. Many clients have had questionable therapeutic experiences, which may have frightened or confused them or they have absolutely no idea of what to expect, which may make them apprehensive. You will decrease your client's anxiety if you describe your own orientation and techniques. For example:

> "I'd like to tell you what to expect from therapy with me. I will ask you to tell me about yourself, your thoughts, perceptions and feelings, and you can say as much or as little as you want. I will listen to anything you may want to discuss . . . I expect there are some things you will feel more comfortable discussing as you get to know me better . . . I do verbal therapy, that is, we will mostly talk when we meet. From time to time I may ask you to do some homework, like write down some thoughts, or draw something. I will always explain why it is helpful to do a certain task, and you certainly can say no."

If your client asks questions, answer them honestly and directly, remembering that you are trying to create a safe environment. To do this, you must respond clearly to your client's concerns.

One of these concerns may well be how long therapy will last. It is impossible to answer this question exactly, especially without knowing the extent of the problem. "I can't say right this minute. I'd like to meet with you about six times. At the end of that time, I'll be able to give you an <u>estimate</u> of how long I think therapy might last."

Setting a Safe Structure

Most clients find it helpful if you initially structure the therapeutic sessions. I usually say something like this:

"I want to say a few things about therapy, particularly the rules that I work under. I like to tell all my clients these rules. I will not hit you or allow you to hit me. I will not be sexual with you or allow you to be sexual with me. I will not hurt you in any way on purpose, and if your feelings are accidentally hurt, I hope you will be able to tell me so. As I have already mentioned, you can say as much or as little as you want in here. There may be times when I will keep asking, if I feel the topic is important for you to discuss. If you have any questions about anything I say or do, I want you to feel free to ask. I know that at the moment you have no reason to trust me, since you don't know me. I hope to earn your trust over time by saying what I mean, and doing what I say. Eventually, I hope you will feel able to count on my being honest and trustworthy."

Becoming Trustworthy

The new client has no reason to trust an unknown therapist. Trust must be earned. To become trustworthy, you must be consistent and reliable. You must meet your commitments, follow through on promises, and remain attentive to the client's spoken and unspoken fears. Trust is a fragile commodity.

Validation

The adult survivor often has problems with credibility. He or she will usually be terrified of two things: not being believed and being seen as crazy. Think before you speak. Every statement that you make must be deliberate. One careless comment, such as "That's so hard to believe," can cause the client to drop out of therapy. If the client asks, "Do you believe me?", it is best to respond, "Everything you've said is quite believable." Sometimes an eager and unequivocal "Yes, I believe you" can precipitate a client's mistrust, particularly if the client really doubts that what he or she said was true. Similarly, if the client asks, "Am I crazy?" your best response is "I have no reason to believe you are crazy." Other questions, such as "Do you think that is child abuse?" or "Do parents ever really do that to their children?" should be answered straightforwardly.

Allowing Denial

During the beginning treatment phase, denial is allowed. As I have explained, it may alarm the client if you label certain behaviors as abusive at this point. It is better simply to listen, and repeat the client's descriptions. In the middle phase, it becomes not only appropriate but also necessary to begin to correctly label the behaviors in question as abuse or neglect. A client I once saw was very angry at her young students. She was concerned and frightened about her angry feelings. During an early history-taking session she told me nonchalantly that her mother would get angry and lock her in a closet for weeks at a time. When her mother had locked her in, she would leave the house, claiming that she "needed a break." This client, at age nine, had spent a large part of her childhood locked in a closet with loaves of bread and soda pop. At first, when we discussed this, she would immediately minimize the experience by saying, "It wasn't as bad as it sounds. I just slept and wrote a lot of stories in my mind. I was really hard to handle. I can understand how she needed to get away for a while." Initially we discussed the experience in the context of her presentation—that is, of how difficult a child had been. Later, I told her that when her mother put her in the closet and left her there alone for weeks, mother was being emotionally abusive, and neglectful. I asked her if she knew any nine-year-old children. As a teacher, she knew many. I asked her to imagine how a nine-year-old might react to being left alone in a closet for weeks. I encouraged her simply to consider the situation. She reacted with some irritation. Three months later, she finally commented that she had been angry and ambivalent about labeling her mother's behavior as abuse or neglect. After thinking about it for a while, however, she realized that locking a nine-year-old child in a closet was probably "not a good thing to do to a child that age." She had begun to empathize with the child in the third person. Later she was able to identify directly with the frightened and lonely child she had been. I told her that it was important for her to explore her thoughts and feelings about these incidents, since they probably affected how she viewed both her mother and herself. This client had moved three thousand miles away from her mother and avoided all contact with her. She had become very anxious when she found herself losing her temper with the children in her classroom. She was afraid she would lose control and hit a child.

The anger towards the child was probably displaced anger she felt at her mother. Being in an authority position with a child probably precipitated the anger.

Giving the Client Choices

Because adult survivors have trouble dealing with issues of power, control, and helplessness, it is important to encourage clients to make their own decisions regarding appointment times, pacing, and content of discussion. You might say, "I have a Wednesday and Friday appointment available, one in the morning and one in the afternoon. When would you like to come in?" You should also let your clients decide what to discuss in therapy (within limits). They may choose to follow a difficult, painful session with an easy session. For example: "Last week was a particularly painful session for you. I notice that today you took care to not bring up those emotional subjects. I respect your ability to pace yourself. Another time, I would like to continue the discussion we had last week, since it's clear there are some feelings that need to be explored." The therapist both allows the client to temporarily avoid a difficult topic, and defines the limits of avoidance by announcing that the topic will be pursued at a later time. After a particularly difficult session, it usually helps the client to talk about what it was like to keep the following appointment. Many clients find coming to therapy after a painful session very difficult, and it is worthwhile to examine how they were able to overcome their resistance.

In this beginning phase of treatment, the therapist sets the structure necessary for the creation of trust and safety. The client receives validation, reassurance and support. The therapist is sensitive to the client's fear of self-disclosure and allows the client to pace the rapidity of exposure and depth of feeling. The client's defense mechanisms are observed and remain unchallenged while the client develops familiarity with the therapist. Statements are made which set the context for future discussion of difficult or painful experiences. All of these strategies contribute to the formation of a therapeutic alliance and the beginning of client trust and safety.

8.

The Middle Phase and the Termination Phase

Once the therapeutic alliance is formed, and the client has begun to trust the therapist, it is time to advance into more difficult areas for the client. In the middle phase, the therapist challenges the client's established perceptions and beliefs, and determines how they influence current functioning. In the termination phase, the therapist prepares the client to leave therapy.

During the beginning phase, the client has focused on current problems and has been given a structure within which to think about childhood issues. In the middle phase, the therapist reintroduces issues that may have surfaced earlier.

Assess the Client's Current Functioning

The following areas are now explored in order to further define therapeutic goals which address not only the presenting problems (symptomatology) but underlying concerns as well.

Assess the Developmental Stage

The first step in the middle phase is to evaluate the client's developmental level. These clients often function as adults in many areas of their lives, but their emotional age is usually lower than their chronological age. Emotionally, they have failed to mature, because the conditions necessary for growth were not provided at the appropriate developmental stages. Specifically, they lack the ability to value themselves and negotiate on their own behalf. If you have not yet taken a detailed history, now is the time to do so. Follow the information on pages 93 to 98. Start with the more general areas; then inquire about common symptomatic behaviors. Notice the client's reactions to the assessment questions. Most clients will avoid answering certain questions but will answer other questions readily and completely. Watch for affective changes, regressive behavior, and deviations from previously established interactional patterns.

Avoid asking, "Were you abused as a child?" Ask instead for descriptions of behavior in specific areas, such as the expression of anger or of physical affection within the family. Ask also for descriptions of general relationships. If the client describes abuse, ask how old he or she was at the time the abuse occurred. Ask also how the child understood the experience or explained it to others. Abuse can persist over two or three developmental stages, so it is necessary to determine when the abuse stopped. Find out why the adult (and the child) believed the abuse began, why it continued and why it ceased.

Why is it so important to determine the client's developmental level? Imagine a six-year-old child who is afraid of the dark. The parents' response can reduce the child's fears—or increase it. Reason, for example, will not reduce the fear of a child who believes that monsters will suddenly appear when the lights are turned off. The best approach is to take the child through the room, encourage him or her to look in all the dark places, provide a night-light, and reassure the child who wakes up frightened. The fear will expire more quickly if the parents use techniques that are consistent with the child's developmental age. Conversely, the fear will be exacerbated by punitive or threatening responses. Parents can also make the fear worse by rewarding it, perhaps by allowing the child to stay up late, or sleep with them.

Similarly, reasoning can be inappropriate when working with adult survivors. At some point it will be essential to educate the client about child abuse, but it will do no good to educate the client prematurely. The most suitable initial response is to listen to the client's perceptions and fears and simply try to understand how they have developed. Once the client feels acceptable, and accepted, you can raise the issue of child abuse directly if the client has not done so. In so doing, you will confront the client's illusion that he or she was responsible for having been abused. **As the illusion of responsibility fades, the horror of facing the reality**

of helplessness begins. All of this work is accomplished during the middle phase of treatment.

The following partial transcript is taken from a therapy session with a thirty-six-year-old adult survivor. Laura is struggling with self-blame and guilt over what she perceives as her failure to protect herself:

> Laura.　*I should have run away.*
>
> Dr.G.　*Where would you have gone?*
>
> Laura.　*I don't know.*
>
> Dr.G.　*Think about it a minute. You're six, you've already told your aunt, who didn't listen. Where would you go?*
>
> Laura.　*Maybe the police.*
>
> Dr.G.　*When you were six, did you know where the police lived?*
>
> Laura.　*No.*
>
> Dr.G.　*Did you know how to use the phone?*
>
> Laura.　*No.*
>
> Dr.G.　*Did you know how to look a number up in the phone book?*
>
> Laura.　*No. But . . .*
>
> Dr.G.　*But what?*
>
> Laura.　*I should have known at least that.*
>
> Dr.G.　*How do you think kids learn about things like that?*
>
> Laura.　*Well, I guess . . . somebody, probably parents, teach them.*
>
> Dr.G.　*These days education is more available.*
>
> Laura.　*I just don't know.*
>
> Dr.G.　*What don't you know?*
>
> Laura.　*I keep thinking there was something I should have done.*
>
> Dr.G.　*And if you had . . . ?*
>
> Laura.　*I could have stopped him.*
>
> Dr.G.　*But you know, Laura, you did do something.*
>
> Laura.　*What?*
>
> Dr.G.　*You told your aunt.*
>
> Laura.　*Yeah, a lot of good that did.*

Dr.G.   *That's just the point. You did what you could. It wasn't your fault your aunt dismissed the information. That was her problem.*

Laura.   *Yeah, I guess so.*

Dr.G.   *Could she have done something?*

Laura.   *Oh God, yes. She used to work for a lawyer.*

Dr.G.   *So if she had listened to you, and believed you, she might have taken some action to protect you.*

Laura.   *I guess so.*

Dr.G.   *At least she would have been better equipped to handle such a big problem. She was the adult. You were the child.*

Laura.   *Why is this so hard?*

Dr.G.   *I think it's because most abused children feel they are responsible in some way. As you concentrate on how you could have stopped your dad from being sexual with you, you forget that he was the adult, and the one responsible for stopping.*

Laura.   *Except he was drunk all the time.*

Dr.G.   *Being drunk was also his responsibility.*

Laura.   *Yeah, but after Mom died . . . he was so upset.*

Dr.G.   *Lots of men are upset when their wives die. It's hard to be left alone with small children to care for. But widowers don't become sexual with their children to cope with their grief. That was wrong.*

Laura.   *I really loved him.*

Dr.G.   *I know you did. He was your father. In many other ways, he took good care of you. When he was sexual with you, he was wrong to do that.*

Laura.   *What could have caused him to do it?*

Dr.G.   *Hard to say. What do you think?*

Laura.   *He was really lonely.*

Dr.G.   *It's OK to try to understand his motives, but there is no excuse or "good reason" for being sexual with a child. The important thing for you is to be as understanding and forgiving with yourself as you are with him.*

Laura.   *How?*

Dr.G.   *When you are ready to accept that the abuse was 100 percent your father's fault, you will stop blaming yourself. This is difficult to do. It takes time. For now, you are far more*

*forgiving of your father than you are of yourself. The reality is
that you were a child, did what you could, and you had limited
options.*

This example illustrates how, during the middle phase, the
therapist challenges the client's perceptions, and offers information regarding the issue of responsibility. The sense of responsibility developed when the child was six. When the therapist talks
to the client, the statements must be clear, short and to the point.
During the above discussion, the client is functioning at a younger
emotional age than her thirty six years would dictate. The therapist also encourages the client not to judge herself as an adult,
and reminds her that as a young child, she had limited options.

Self-Image

Adults abused as children have negative or undefined self-images.
Some clients believe that they deserved what happened to them;
that they caused it to happen by something they said or did. Other
clients feel inherently inadequate, unacceptable, unlovable, or
worthless. Still other clients may be unable to pinpoint what they
perceive as being wrong with them, but they deeply believe that
something is wrong. This sense of being "bad" has been incorporated into the client's self image. Life events serve to confirm it,
that is, if an intimate relationship does not work out, if the client
loses a job, or fails a class in school, this is seen as further proof
that he or she is worthless.

Some clients do not see themselves as "bad," but they have an
undefined self-image. These clients are unaware of their own
strengths, weaknesses, or even preferences. These clients never
received positive attention from others, and they never validate
or comfort themselves. Therefore, these clients have never
learned to address their own needs, desires, or interests. This lack
of definition can be devitalizing.

Guilt

A heinous legacy of abuse is the guilt the victim can feel at having
participated. In particular, victims of sexual abuse can feel com-
promised by their own physical reactions, such as arousal or
orgasm. Some clients have described feeling betrayed by their
bodies, which responded in spite of the client's efforts to block
the response. Later, these clients may engage in compulsive

repetition of inappropriate sexual behavior. At the very least, they usually feel guilty. These guilt feelings are difficult to assuage. Often they conflict with the client's cognitive understanding of his or her sexual responses.

You must give your clients permission to express all their thoughts and feelings about being abused. They must be able to express their guilt and shame before they can learn to accept themselves. As your clients begin to express these hidden thoughts and feelings, they may expect you to respond punitively. Afraid of incurring your disapproval or rejection, they may cancel appointments, arrive late, discuss trivial issues, or try to annoy you with provocative behavior. You must make it absolutely clear that you accept the client. At the same time, you must state explicitly what you observe. "My sense is that you're concerned how I might be reacting to what you told me last week. My guess is that you might imagine I'm angry or disgusted by what you shared. I'd like to talk about your worries or fears." This acceptance on your part help your clients to accept themselves.

Once your clients have expressed their thoughts, perceptions, and feelings, you can provide them with information. Information regarding sexuality can be both reassuring and therapeutic. Clients can begin to understand that their bodies normally react when stimulated, and that this does not mean that they participated. These new perceptions about sexuality can help to diminish the client's self-loathing. Your goal is to enable your client to reclaim his or her own body and his or her own sexuality. Body therapy with a sensitive body therapist may help to give clients a sense of body safety and appropriate touch. Maltz and Holman (1984) offer a comprehensive, step-by-step approach to repairing sexuality in victims of childhood incest.

Guilt may also be a reaction to physical abuse. Children who are hit or hurt learn that people who love them hurt them. When the only physical contact between parent and child is abusive, the abuse may be unconsciously viewed as nurturing behavior. These children may feel comforted by the pain that an important or trusted person inflicts on them. They prefer it to the pain of being ignored. Negative attention is viewed as preferable to no attention at all.

The physically abused child, then, may sometimes provoke an abusive episode. This may be done to seek comfort or attention. It may also be done in order to control the timing of an abusive incident. For example, a child who senses tension may break something to precipitate the release of tension from a parent. In either case, the provocative child may take responsibility not only for his or her own behavior, but for the abuser's behavior as well. This is never justified. The person who hits or hurts the child is always 100 percent responsible. These children must understand that their ability to provoke abuse is an inappropriate and undesirable skill and that they must stop doing it.

Guilty clients who continue to feel responsible for having caused others to abuse them may have an urge to punish themselves. They may do so by engaging in self-mutilation. This subject is discussed further in chapter 13.

Labeling Abusive Behavior

The therapist, who in the beginning phase of treatment did not challenge the client's minimizations and denial of abusive behavior, must do so now. Behavior that was abusive must be labeled abusive. In order for your clients to begin to accept the reality of their abuse, you must challenge their tendency to blame themselves or to protect the abuser. For example, one of my clients minimized her abuse to the point where she even wondered whether she needed therapy. Shrugging her shoulders, she described how her mother would put a pillow over her face and sit on it: "Well, it wasn't that often, and she never really hurt me." When I asked, "How did you react when she did this?" she said, "Oh I was scared to death. I tried to grasp for air, and a couple of times, I passed out." At the beginning of therapy I accepted the client's description and simply repeated it back to her. Once the therapeutic relationship was established, I said "I'd like to talk about what used to happen between you and your mom when she sat on your face with a pillow. It seems it's hard for you to admit this to yourself or to me, but when she did that, she was being abusive to you, and she was placing your life at risk. I'm not sure why she did that, but no matter what her reason, explanation, or excuse, she did hurt you by scaring you and putting you at risk like that, and that is considered child abuse."

Clients will respond in different ways to your statement that they were abused. They may feel relieved; they may cry; or they may argue the point. No matter how the client responds, it is critical to make definitive statements which confront denial. It provides your clients with the reality they need to lower their defenses, acknowledge the pain, and accept the past. At the same time, I cannot emphasize too strongly that confrontation of this type must be preceded by the formation of a solid therapeutic alliance. Never challenge the client before the client trusts you because they can feel victimized and flee from therapy.

Feeling Helpless

Once clients begin to accept that they were indeed abused, they usually feel the shame and confusion that are often associated with abuse. They may quickly shift from feeling loyal and protective of the abuser to feeling helpless. This is difficult for most clients. They must face their heretofore unacknowledged thoughts, feelings, and perceptions about their abusers and themselves. As people remember being helpless as children they may feel helpless now. **The truth is that they are helpless to change the past. But they are far from helpless to mobilize their resources, take controlled risks, and mold their present lives**.

Confront your client's perception of themselves as helpless by pinpointing areas where they can exercise control. Challenge them to find alternatives, options, and opportunities. Your goal is to prevent these clients from acting on their present helpless feelings while at the same time encouraging them to experience the pain of accepting their childhood helplessness.

As these previously unacknowledged feelings surface, clients may experience overwhelming sadness, anger, and pain. In the past, these clients have coped with pain by avoiding reality or re-enacting abusive situations in which they are victimized. Now they will frequently attempt to cope by avoiding, forgetting, distracting, or denying. You must help these clients to develop strategies for the gradual and safe expression of their new, deep, and frightening feelings.

Assess the Risk of Suicide and Homicide

During this stage of treatment, it is imperative to assess the risk that your client may commit suicide or homicide. Clients who are unfamiliar with their own emotions can be overwhelmed by the pain they feel when they realize that they were abused. At the same time, they can be enraged by the helplessness they feel. Clients who would find aggressive acting out against others unacceptable may turn the rage inward. They may engage in self-destructive behaviors, or highly ritualistic self-mutilations.

They may also experience severe depression. Clients usually conceal these behaviors and rarely volunteer information about them. Some adult survivors may be veteran self-mutilators, who cut or burn themselves repeatedly on areas of their body that are hidden by their clothes. Don't assume that if you don't see any scars, there are no scars. Ask directly about self-mutilation.

Likewise, feelings of intense despair may be kept hidden. You must make suicide and homicide topics of discussion, carefully evaluating the presence of clear plans to hurt self or others, impulsivity, use of drugs, and other high risk indicators.

Self-Isolation; Feeling Unaceptable

When they recognize and acknowledge that they were indeed abused, your clients may suddenly begin to feel unacceptable. Many survivors describe themselves as freaks; they feel that they underwent strange and unique experiences—experiences that brand them forever as defective. As a result, they may avoid contact with others, and may limit their social interactions to formal situations such as school or work. They may even attempt to terminate therapy when admitting that they were abused becomes too painful. These clients may blame you for causing the pain. Clients who insist on terminating individual therapy, should be referred to a self-help group. These groups can have the potential of challenging the sense of being unique or feelings of unacceptability by allowing contact with others who have survived similar experiences. Self-help groups are discussed in chapter 17.

Visibility

Up until 1964 or so, few people talked openly about child abuse. If your clients are over thirty-five, chances are it is only recently that they began hearing about child abuse and considering whether or not they themselves may have experienced it. Many adult survivors have spent their whole lives protecting themselves from the reality of childhood abuse. Recently, this has become more difficult to do, because the subject is now receiving considerable publicity. Adult survivors may have enveloped themselves in a kind of protective invisibility, maintaining their private thoughts in their private worlds. When they hear the truth spoken aloud, they become suddenly visible. This can be extremely frightening. Being visible means risking the contempt or disapproval of others. Clients who are feeling visible need to know that they can set their own limits: they can decide whom to tell, how much to tell, and when to tell. They can choose to be invisible to some people and not to others. The choices are theirs to make, and while they cannot take back secrets they have told the therapist or others, they can certainly discuss which secrets were most painful, embarrassing, or difficult to reveal.

Tolerating Pain

You must help your clients to develop the skills they need to tolerate emotional pain. These clients, who are so familiar with physical suffering, may be completely unfamiliar with emotional suffering. This is another reason why your clients may mutilate themselves—because the pain helps to distract them from the emotional pain.

The emotional pain experienced by adult survivors is very complex. Not only do they seem to experience the pain of viewing their childhood from the adult perspective, but they also seem to tap old forgotten feelings left over from that childhood—feelings that remained hidden and unexpressed. In some ways, this pain is akin to the grieving process, since the adult has to give up the image of an idealized childhood. When they accept reality, these clients experience the pain of loss. The therapist must teach the client ways of dealing with pain without feeling overwhelmed, childish, or inadequate. They need to know how to allow themselves to feel pain, how to comfort themselves, and how to seek help when the pain seems unbearable.

Dependency

The adult survivor who undergoes treatment is asked to be available in two different ways: as an adult and as a young child. The survivor is asked to recount and relive consciously what he or she may have been experienced only unconsciously. This is painful and extremely difficult. As your clients relive their early childhood, they will rely on you for support, guidance and reassurance as they develop a sense of self-acceptance.

The therapeutic relationship is inherently personal. This personal factor is crucial to the ongoing development of the abused child within the adult client. The client proceeds from one developmental stage to the next and the therapist provides a safe environment in which the client discusses fear, concerns and accomplishments.

A certain amount of dependency is likely to occur as the client relies on the therapist's guidance until self-reliance and self-direction are established.

If the therapist over-functions by giving too many directives, being over-protective or discouraging autonomy, the client can become too dependent and may fear or avoid independent activity.

During the middle phase of treatment the client's dependency and need for the positive elements of the therapeutic relationship are made explicit and the client is encouraged to make efforts to develop similar positive aspects in relationships with friends or available family members. For example, if the client values being heard, attempts are made to identify others who may also be receptive to listening to the client. The normal feelings of dependency are now slowly redirected to more appropriate resources, including friends, mates, or extended family members.

Trauma Resolution Work

Does everyone who was abused as a child have to explore the childhood abuse? Don't some people need to repress the experience in order to prevent deterioration? These are the questions that I hear most often from my colleagues.

In fact, some clients cannot accept the extent and severity of their abuse. To do so may cause severe regression and deterioration. The therapist must be cautious with clients who have a history of severe mental disorders, who have recently left an inpatient psychiatric program, or who have experienced especially severe or bizarre abuse. It may be best to direct these clients away from childhood memories, simply acknowledging the past and offering an explanation of how early abuse may impact current functioning. This explanation then serves as a bridge to current problems. If the discussion of childhood trauma causes loosening of associations, incoherence, psychotic thoughts, catatonic states, or severe dysfunction, this type of work is counterindicated on an outpatient basis.

Many other clients, however, will benefit from trauma resolution work. Trauma resolution work is the process of guiding the client to remember an abusive episode or episodes in detail. (See chapter 12 for illustrations of this process.) This process is also known as implosive therapy or abreaction.

Trauma resolution work is not always necessary. It is indicated when the client has a negative trauma resolution that results in the constant unconscious re-enactment of childhood abuse, which, in turn, disturbs adult functioning. It is also frequently indicated when a client presents with symptoms of post-traumatic stress disorder (see chapter 11).

A trauma is comprised of three elements: (1) unexpected onset; (2) induced feelings of helplessness; and (3) heightened emotional and physical arousal. Most physically or sexually abused children have experienced trauma. Chronically abused children generally use defensive strategies to cope with the experience of repeated trauma. As we have seen, a typical defensive strategy is the use of dissociation.

Positive Resolution

Trauma must always be resolved in order to be put in proper perspective. Resolution may be positive, negative or functional. A positive resolution occurs when the adult is able to process the trauma in a realistic way, experiencing whatever levels of pain, anger, or loss are elicited by a clear memory of the event. The person perceives the event accurately, and does not feel irrationally responsible for having caused it. The person is able to understand that the experience occurred in the past, and no longer feels devastated by the memory of the event, as if it were a clear and recurring danger in the present. Above all, the person does not feel compelled to repeat the event, either consciously or unconsciously. Adults who have experienced a positive resolution generally feel that they are in control. They do not suffer from chronic intrusive thoughts or images, nightmares, or intense emotionality.

Negative Resolution

In direct contrast, a negative resolution is both destructive and constrictive. The adult avoids, or attempts to avoid, thinking or speaking about the trauma, out of fear or an inability to tolerate feelings that surface when he or she does so. The person feels controlled or trapped by sudden memories, which intrude into consciousness accompanied by a flooding, or surge of distressing or disorienting emotion.

Adults who have experienced a negative resolution often find themselves repeating the familiar, abusive dynamics in their relationships. Over and over again, they find themselves being criticized, taken advantage of, humiliated, or abused. They do not want to be in these relationships, but they feel unable to escape, or to find less abusive ones. Their belief systems give them negative messages. "You asked for it." "You're getting what you deserve." "What do you expect? It's always going to be this way." These adults approach life with a distorted view of themselves and others, and this affects all aspects of their lives—their jobs, their relationships, their health, and so forth.

The most insidious aspect of negative trauma resolution is that the adult feels permanently victimized and helpless. He or she engages in destructive and dysfunctional interactional patterns—choosing abusive mates, tolerating abusive patterns, in general doing everything to reinforce the message that "It's always going to be this way." Adult survivors who recreate an abusive adult environment will remain emotionally underdeveloped, will continue to be victimized, and will expect some outside force to rescue them.

The following clinical example illustrates a client with negative trauma resolution.

Sherry is thirty-nine years old. She has been married five times. She married three men who were physically abusive and two who were verbally abusive. All five marriages were stormy and brief. (In this she resembles her father, who was married six times.) Sherry describes her relationships with men by saying matter-of-factly, "I guess I'm just not cut out to be a wife."

Sherry has been single for the last two years. She drinks every night; she feels lonely and very unacceptable. She has considered killing herself and is despondent much of the time. She has no close friends. She goes to bars every other night, frequently picking up men, or being picked up. One out of three times she winds up getting beaten. Sherry constantly asks herself, "Are all guys assholes?" She answers, "Yes."

When asked to describe her childhood, Sherry smiles and looks away. She says she was sexually abused from the time she was about eight until she was fourteen. She says her mother would get drunk every night and fall asleep on the couch. Her father slept every night with her, he would get up before her mother did. Her father began having sexual intercourse with her when she was eight. Before that, she says, he "just fooled around" with her.

Sherry believes that all men want sex first, and if you're good enough at it, they may stick around. She believes that she is highly skilled at sex, but she also feels that she must perform. "Personally," she says, "I don't know what all the fuss is about. Most of the time I have to force myself to 'be there' when I'm with someone."

She adds, "The sexual stuff wasn't as bad as everything else. When he wasn't in my bed, he was beating up on me. He used to whip me good. No reason I can remember. He was just moody, I guess." When I asked her to tell me how she viewed what was happening to her at eight, she says, "I figured I was my dad's wife, now that my mom couldn't be. He always acted like he owned me. I guess he did." She cannot describe any contact with her mother. She doesn't remember her being around that much. "When she was, she was sleeping or listening to the radio."

This is Sherry's first time in therapy. She talks readily about her childhood sexual abuse; it is as if she were talking about someone else. She has very little affect associated with the abuse and seems uncertain what to think of it.

Sherry is seeking therapy for her depression. She is beginning to think that she will never remarry or have children, and she does not like feeling alone and lonely. She has gained eighty pounds in the last two years; she finds this devastating.

Initial therapeutic responses include a suicide assessment. I also attempt to stabilize Sherry's depression, and I refer her for a medical workup and ask that she be evaluated for the possibility of being prescribed antidepressants. Sherry responds readily to directives about exercise, diet, and social activities. She had been prescribed anti-depressants but decided against taking them. Once her depression is mediated and she seems reengaged with friends and activities, I begin to help her to understand the impact that childhood sexual abuse and living in an alcoholic family have had on her. My goals are to help her to enhance her self-esteem, to help her to learn to recognize dangerous situations where she will be revictimized, and to help her to explore her view of her own sexuality. Obviously, Sherry needs to resolve her own feelings about her father in order to stop generalizing those feelings onto all the men she meets. Also, she needs to acknowledge her father's negative traits and behaviors, so she does not continue to be compelled towards men who are like him.

Sherry has not achieved a positive trauma resolution. She does not accurately perceive the experience of childhood abuse and her feelings about it are unresolved. Like others who achieve a negative resolution, Sherry is reenacting the dynamics of abuse in her current life, perhaps in an attempt to master the situation, or as a self-fulfilling prophecy based on her negative self-concept. As a result, she continues to feel victimized and powerless. It is important to do trauma resolution work with Sherry in order to gain access to the abused child's perceptions. It is often beneficial to enter the child's world in order to understand these early views. Once you understand them, you can challenge them and eventually replace them with a realistic view of the experience. For example, a young child may believe he was beaten because he was a bad baby who cried too much. New information can be provided about the natural tendencies of babies to cry, with concurrent information that some parents are underprepared to respond to normal babies. Once the child's view of the abuse is understood, a statement of fact can be made.

The following partial transcript of a session with Sherry illustrates how trauma resolution work is done:

Sherry.

Dr.G. (<u>Looking at pictures of the client as a child</u>) *How old would you say you were in this picture?*

Sherry. *Oh God . . . maybe three or four. I don't know.*

Dr.G. *Who took these pictures?*

Sherry. *Mostly my grandmother.* (<u>She has not mentioned her grandmother before</u>.)

Dr.G. *Did she live with you?*

Sherry. *Yeah, until I was about eight. I think she died when I was eight.*

Dr.G. *Had she been sick, or did she die suddenly?*

Sherry. *I don't know. I think she was sick, but I don't remember.*

Dr.G. *What do you remember about yourself at this age?*

Sherry. *Almost nothing.*

Dr.G. *How do you react when you look at this picture of you?*

Sherry. *It's hard to believe it's me.*

Dr.G.   *What do you think?*

Sherry.   *She looks so peaceful.*

Dr.G.   *Yes, she does.*

Sherry.   *She's kind of cute.*

Dr.G.   *I agree.*

Sherry.   *She looks like a doll . . . you know, not real.*

Dr.G.   *So you don't think she looks real, eh?*

Sherry.   *Not really.*

Dr.G.   *How do you feel looking at her?*

Sherry.   *OK. Nothing really. I like this picture better.*

Dr.G.   *It seems you're a little older.*

Sherry.   *This is the only class picture I could find.*

Dr.G.   *What grade?*

Sherry.   *Third, I think.*

Dr.G.   *So about what - eight?*

Sherry.   *I guess.*

Dr.G.   *What do you like about this picture?*

Sherry.   *Well, she looks strong somehow.*

Dr.G.   *How?*

Sherry.   *In her eyes. She looks gutsy or something.*

Dr.G.   *Do you think that's how she felt?*

Sherry.   *Oh God, I don't have any idea. I don't remember anything about this age.*

Dr.G.   *What do you think as you look at this picture?*

Sherry.   *Just what I said. She looks strong.*

Dr.G.   *Do you like what you see?*

Sherry.   *Oh, I don't know.*

Dr.G.   *Well, think about it a minute. (*Long pause*) Any reactions?*

Sherry.   *This seems like another lifetime.*

Dr.G.   *What was that lifetime like?*

Sherry.   *I can't remember.*

Dr.G.   *I think it's hard to remember a lot about being young sometimes.*

Sherry.   *Yeah.*

Dr.G.   *You know, Sherry, I'd like you to sit back and get comfortable.*

Sherry.   *Oh, oh.*

Dr.G.   *Oh, oh, what?*

Sherry.   *Well, it's just not going to help. It's a blank.*

Dr.G.   *I know you don't remember a lot. I just want to see if we can talk a little about what it was like when you were this age.*

Sherry.   *You're the doctor.*

Dr.G.   *OK. Now, you can either close your eyes or not. But I'd like you to see if you can remember where you used to live when you were that age.*

Sherry.   *Oh, God. Who knows?*

Dr.G.   *Did you move around a lot when you were a kid?*

Sherry.   *No.*

Dr.G.   *How many houses did you live in?*

Sherry.   *Just one.*

Dr.G.   *OK. Let's pretend for a minute that you are going to that house, and you're getting close to it, and you spot it. Describe it to me.*

Sherry.   *What, you mean (Laughing) what kind of paint and stuff?*

Dr.G.   *Try to picture it in your mind, and tell me what you see.*

Sherry.   *It's a big house. Really big. It has two floors, upstairs and downstairs.*

Dr.G.   *Good; you're doing well.*

Sherry.   *It's got a big tree in front. I don't know what kind. I don't know much about trees . . . but it's the kind that looks like a Christmas tree, and it's real tall.*

Dr.G.   *Did you ever climb that tree?*

Sherry.   *Did I ever climb that tree?*

Dr.G.   *Yeah.*

Sherry.   *Ummm. You know once I think I tried to. There was a squirrel climbing up it, and I really wanted to catch it.*

Dr.G.   *How old were you?*

Sherry.   *Well . . . I would guess about the size of the kid in the picture.*

Dr.G.   *Did you spend a lot of time outside?*

Sherry.   *No.*

Dr.G.   *What did you think about squirrels?*

Sherry.   *I used to make up stories that I woke up and was a squirrel, and then I went running to other people's trees, and I was free. I liked that story.*

Dr.G.   *Did you make up a lot of stories?*

Sherry.   *I'm not sure. But I remember the squirrel thing.*

Dr.G.   *OK, so there was a big tree in front of your house, and squirrels climbed up the tree, and once you tried to climb the tree yourself, correct?*

Sherry.   *Yeah . . . Then there was . . . no . . . there used to be a seat my grandma sat in on the porch. Then it was cut down when she died.*

Dr.G.   *Can you picture your grandma sitting on the seat?*

Sherry.   *Ummm . . .*

Dr.G.   *Take your time. Try to see yourself outside, at about eight years, and your grandma is sitting on the seat.*

Sherry.   *Oh God, I haven't thought about her in years.*

Dr.G.   *What are you thinking right now?*

Sherry.   *How she was nice to me.*

Dr.G.   *So your grandmother was nice to you.*

Sherry.   *Yeah . . . she used to hold me in her lap and we would rock in that seat.*

Dr.G.   *What did your grandma look like?*

Sherry.   *She was really wrinkled. She was really fat, too. Soft . . . I do remember sitting on her lap, and when it was really hot, her skin would stick to mine, and I hoped that it would stick so hard that she would never be able to move away from me.*

Dr.G.   *How are you feeling right now?*

Sherry.   *Oh, you know.*

Dr.G.   *No, I don't.*

Sherry.   *Well, it sort of makes me feel sad.*

Dr.G.   *Thinking about her makes you feel sad. Tell me more.*

Sherry.   *A little funny . . . let me see . . . no, I can't explain it.*

Dr.G.   *Sometimes feelings are hard to explain.*

Sherry.   *Yeah, I know.*

Dr.G.   *Do you remember what your grandma wore?*

Sherry. *Always the same rubber shoes. I used to polish them for her.*

Dr.G. *What color were they?*

Sherry. *White.*

Dr.G. *And how would you polish them?*

Sherry. *With a cream that was sticky.*

Dr.G. *What did the cream smell like?*

Sherry. *Oh, something awful. I've never smelled anything like that since. It was really strong.*

Dr.G. *What did Grandma smell like?*

Sherry. *She smelled like Noxzema. She used to love Noxzema. She used to put it on every night and every morning. I liked that smell.*

Dr.G. *Did you talk when you and your grandma sat on the front porch?*

Sherry. *Nope. Not that I remember.*

Dr.G. *It sounds like you might have really liked sitting there with her.*

Sherry. *Yeah, I did.*

Dr.G. *Were there other things you liked then?*

Sherry. *Sometimes we'd cook together . . .*

Sherry continued to describe these pleasant scenes with her grandmother. Unfortunately, her grandmother had died shortly after she turned eight. She remembers being very sad, but she couldn't think too much about it because she was busy now all the time. She had to cook, wash, clean the house, and take care of her mother who seemed to drink more after the grandmother died.

Sherry was eventually able to give a very crisp description of the house. I asked her to draw a floor plan, and she brought one to the next session. It was very sketchy. As we talked, she filled in the details. She was able to "walk through" the house, pointing out the location of various rooms. She was able to describe the furniture and the wallpaper in detail. She identified favorite possessions. She remembered the furniture particularly well because she had had to dust it every other day, or her father would beat her. She described her walk to school, approximately twelve blocks. She talked about her school and some of her friends. She felt alternately proud and depressed as she remembered what seemed to be a very deficient and abusive childhood, with little joy or warmth after her grandmother died.

She was able to describe her bedroom as messy and cluttered. She did not have to clean this room, since her father only came in at night, after the lights were out and her mother never asked her to do so.

As I helped Sherry to fill in the gaps in her memory, she began to reenter the world she had inhabited as a child. Although she had been able to talk about her father's sexual abuse, she had done so up until now in an impersonal way. I wanted to gain access to the child who had experienced the abuse-to hear that child's opinions, thoughts, questions, and feelings. At this point, I began to ask some more specific questions:

> Dr.G.   *When was the first time your father became sexual with you?*
>
> Sherry.   *The first time?*
>
> Dr.G.   *Yes.*
>
> Sherry.   *I was sleeping . . .*
>
> Dr.G.   *Were you in your room?*
>
> Sherry.   *Yeah.*
>
> Dr.G.   *OK*
>
> Sherry.   *I was sleeping, and the next thing I knew, my dad was sitting on the side of the bed.*
>
> Dr.G.   *When you opened your eyes, what did you see?*
>
> Sherry.   *My dad.*
>
> Dr.G.   *How did he look?*
>
> Sherry.   *I don't know . . . sleepy I guess. He didn't look mad. I remember asking why he was there . . .*
>
> Dr.G.   *What did you say?*
>
> Sherry.   *I said, "What's going on?"*
>
> Dr.G.   *What did he say?*
>
> Sherry.   *He didn't say much . . . He pushed the hair from my eyes. I used to have long bangs . . . like in the picture you saw.*
>
> Dr.G.   *I remember.*
>
> Sherry.   (<u>pause</u>) Do you want to know more?
>
> Dr.G.   *Yes. So far you've told me you woke up, he was sitting at your side, he pushed your hair away, you asked what was going on. Did he respond?*

Sherry. *He said, "Oh, nothing . . . "*

Dr.G. *What happened next?*

Sherry. *Let me think . . . He would always . . . no . . . that was later.*

Dr.G. *Let's stay with this first time. He pushes your hair back.*

Sherry. *Then he just looked at me . . . and he put his hand on me . . . He was kind of rubbing me . . . first on the shoulders . . . Then . . . I remember this part real well . . . his hand went down my front, and he kept going down . . . He was getting near my crotch . . .*

Dr.G. *What was your reaction?*

Sherry. *I thought something was wrong.*

Dr.G. *How did you feel?*

Sherry. *I guess scared . . .*

Dr.G. *What was your body doing?*

Sherry. *What do you mean?*

Dr.G. *As your dad rubbed his hand down your front, what did your body look like?*

Sherry. *I was just lying there . . . kind of pushing my bottom on the bed.*

Dr.G. *Could you move?*

Sherry. *No.*

Dr.G. *How were you breathing?*

Sherry. *How was I breathing? . . .* (She closes her eyes and pauses, obviously trying to picture herself in this situation) *You know, I think I just held my breath.*

Dr.G. *Uh-huh . . . a lot of kids do that when they're scared.*

Sherry. *Then he held my crotch.*

Dr.G. *Were you still looking at him?*

Sherry. *No . . . I looked away. I wasn't enjoying this.*

Dr.G. *That's understandable. You're six years old. Your dad, who hardly ever speaks to you, or beats you, or spends time away from you, is in your room, has woken you up, and is holding your crotch.*

Sherry. *I remember his hand was curled inside my legs, and he kind of pushed one finger down . . . I kind of flinched.*

Dr.G. *What happened then?*

Sherry. *He just left.*

Dr.G.   *So you're lying there, after your dad has left the room; what do you think to yourself?*

Sherry.   *Think? Let's see . . . I think I said to myself, "What was that?"*

Dr.G.   *And then what happened?*

Sherry.   *I went back to sleep.*

Dr.G.   *Before you went to sleep, what did your body do?*

Sherry.   *I curled up . . . I covered myself up . . . Then I went out.*

Dr.G.   *What do you mean by "I went out"?*

Sherry.   *I went to sleep.*

Dr.G.   *Any feelings you remember?*

Sherry.   *Nope.*

Dr.G.   *How about now, as you've described this first time, any reactions?*

Sherry.   *I really remembered his hand curled up around my crotch. His hand must have been huge.*

Dr.G.   *And your vagina was small, because you were a little girl.*

Sherry.   *Yeah, I guess that's true too.*

Dr.G.   *And when you remember that, how do you react?*

Sherry.   *I don't know . . . Is this the fun part?*

Dr.G.   *What do you mean?*

Sherry.   *Oh, it's just a joke . . . I'm sorry.*

Dr.G.   *I can see this is hard for you to talk about. Sometimes jokes are a way to keep from feeling bad.*

Sherry.   *It didn't used to be hard for me to talk about . . .*

Dr.G.   *This is a good sign Sherry, believe it or not.*

Sherry.   *That's easy for you to say.*

Dr.G.   *You're right. But I think you're doing a good job. All these old feelings have to come out, so your life can get better today and tomorrow.*

Sherry.   *I know, I know, that's what you keep saying.*

Dr.G.   *And you're really trusting me on this. I appreciate that.*

Sherry.   *I'd like to stop talking about this now . . . for today . . . .Is that OK?*

Dr.G.   *Of course. You did a lot of good work.*

Sherry is now bringing up memories that do not devastate her, but they do upset her considerably. During this period, I make myself more available between sessions. I help Sherry to structure her time so that she is always able to contact at least one friend. We discuss what to do with random feelings, memories, and dreams, and she agrees to write them in her journal and bring the journal into therapy. Three sessions later, she is able to describe how she dissociated when her father abused her. She sees how dissociating kept her from feeling anything while her father was having sexual intercourse with her. As she pictures these experiences in her mind, she begins to feel angry and disgusted with her father, and as she does so, she begins to stop blaming and belittling herself. Now she is able to express indignation.

Next, Sherry explores her feelings about her mother and her grandmother. This work involves grieving. It also involves acknowledging the dependency, longing, and loneliness she had felt. She leaves therapy for a few weeks, overwhelmed by her feelings, and needing a respite. We are in phone contact once a week. She claims she wants to go back to ignorance, which is "really bliss." But she is not as depressed as she was when she entered therapy, and she has confidence in her ability to deal with her depression.

Sherry remained in therapy for another six months. She terminated her therapy when she

- could assess her strengths and weaknesses realistically;

- felt motivated to achieve specific goals (for example, to enter a weight loss program);

- could be alone without becoming severely depressed;

- could deal with depression (that is, she knew what to do when she was depressed in order to keep from becoming dysfunctional);

- could choose where and when to socialize;

- could socialize without depending on alcohol;

- had established a friendship with another woman and had begun to enjoy being outdoors;

- could recognize that she had not caused her father to abuse her;

- could recognize that her father had ben abusive to her, and had confronted him about this;

- could recognize her own various feelings about the abuse, her father, her mother, and her grandmother;

- had chosen not to confront her mother for the time being but thought that she might confront her in the future;

- could say no to sex and could choose when she wanted to have sexual contact (although she had not yet learned to enjoy it completely); and finally

- had joined a group on sexuality and sexual dysfunctions. She found this helpful, although hearing about normal sexuality made her realize how she had been damaged by her father's abuse, and this made her even angrier at her father.

Sherry left therapy with the understanding that she could come in again whenever she needed to. She had been in treatment for a total of two years. She did not begin to discuss childhood abuse, beyond the initial reference in the first session, until the sixth month of therapy.

This was a very successful case. Not all cases of childhood abuse resolve this well.

Functional Resolution

The final type of resolution, is functional. In functional resolution, the adult negotiates the trauma by avoiding distressing stimuli in an idiosyncratic way. People who use this technique protect themselves by controlling their exposure to the feared stimuli. Functional resolution can be effective for a limited time, but it ceases to be effective if the person's circumstances change.

Deanna is twenty-nine years old. Her father beat her from the time she was four until she ran away from home at fifteen. Her functional resolution was to avoid any intimate contact with males, and she structured her environment accordingly. She created a safe, functional life for herself, one in which she never had to confront her negative feelings about men.

One of Deanna's sisters had a baby boy. When the child was seven or eight and began occasionally to act aggressive, Deanna found herself unable to maintain contact with the child she had previously loved and nurtured. Her unresolved feelings towards males were no longer controllable. At this point, Deanna sought therapy in an attempt to resolve her feelings towards her nephew in particular and men in general.

In order to discuss her previously unacknowledged and re-pressed feelings, I had to help Deanna to gain access to her childhood memories. Some of the techniques I used are described in chapter 4. This client was motivated to seek resolution of her feelings, and she progressed rapidly. She learned to differentiate between her father and other males, and she eventually returned to a warm, affectionate relationship with her nephew. Her moti-vation to seek out male friends was neither high, nor avoidant. She had actually started going to coffee with a male work acquaint-ance from time to time and found the contact pleasant.

The middle phase of therapy is where most of the in-depth work is done. The beginning phase sets the stage, by creating a safe environment and establishing a therapeutic alliance. Sensitive exploration and assessment follows, defining the impact of abuse on the client, and determining the individual's developmental stage. If it seems necessary to recreate the traumatic event through trauma resolution work, attempts are made to help the client remember and experience the feelings associated with the memory. While this process occurs, the client's perceptions of the abuse are challenged and new information is provided. If the client cannot tolerate memories and shows signs of decompensa-tion, this work is stopped. The client is encouraged to stay focused on current problems or concerns. When the client experiences the pain associated with ahuse, suicide and homicide assessments are undertaken. During this phase of treatment some dependency is likely to occur before the client develops self-reliance and self-direction. The therapist must be available for increased contact as needed. As the therapeutic relationship becomes valued by the client, he or she is directed to duplicate those positive elements of the interaction with others.

The Termination Phase

In the termination phase of treatment clients are prepared to leave therapy and they are self-motivated to act in their own behalf. The therapist's first goal, then, will be to determine whether the client is ready to leave the middle phase.

Is the Client Ready?

The best way to assess your client's readiness to shift from the middle phase to the termination phase is to evaluate the following factors:

Self-Concept

Does your client have a realistic self-image? Can he (or she) evaluate his (or her) own strengths and weaknesses? Is he more reasonable about his own physical appearance and his own personality traits than previously? Clients who have a more realistic self-image are free to explore opportunities that may render greater returns, such as rewarding relationships, jobs, recreational and educational endeavors.

Self-Esteem

Does your client like himself? Does he believe that he is worthwhile, that he has something to offer, that he deserves good things? The client who has learned to accept, value, and love him or herself will likely attract others who are respectful and caring. Likewise, interactions that are negative or abusive will not be tolerated or sought.

Trauma Resolution

Can your client tolerate his (or her) own reactions to his (or her) memories of childhood abuse without feeling emotionally paralyzed, victimized or enraged? It is critical that all of these reactions be explored, expressed, and resolved so that they do not interfere with adult functioning or impart renewed feelings of helplessness or despair. The client who has positive trauma resolution understands the impact of the trauma, but is not compelled to make unconscious reenactments of the event in order to attempt to master the situation. This client places the trauma in the past, and has the freedom to be in the present unencumbered by past events that cannot be changed or relived.

Grief

Has your client grieved for the loss of the idealized parents in his childhood? Is the past now in perspective so that it no longer impedes the client's functioning? The client who gives up the illusion of a happy or nonabusive childhood faces reality and the pain stored up by the hurt or angry child within the adult. Being free from the illusion allows an energy release which can be used to create a rewarding present and future.

Pain Tolerance

Can your client tolerate, express, and resolve pain? Does he know how to deal with it so that it doesn't overwhelm him, or leave him feeling victimized? Many abused children learned ways to defend against pain. We have seen some of the coping mechanisms that are employed so pain does not overwhelm. When the pain is not felt as it occurred, it can become stored, just as water in a reservoir. Once the reservoir is tapped, large amounts of water can surge forward. Thus, the adult survivor may be reticent to feel pain, out of fear of being overwhelmed or engulfed in feelings that are dark and hopeless. Clients need to learn how to experience pain in tolerable amounts, nurture themselves once pain has been felt, and seek assistance and comfort internally and externally. Eventually, the pain becomes more tolerable and the client has developed competence in the knowledge that he or she will not die from feeling pain. As a matter of fact, acknowledging and experiencing pain can result in self-acceptance and resolution.

Depression Management

Your client may continue to suffer from periodic depression. Have you helped him establish the tools he will need to manage it successfully? The client who can manage depression successfully will not be panicked by the onset of depressed feelings. He will recognize that more optimistic feelings will surface, and will be able to manage periods of depression.

Visibility Tolerance

Can your client tolerate being seen, heard, and valued by others? Initially, this will be difficult for adult survivors. But they must build a tolerance for being visible, experiencing these interactions as non-threatening and potentially rewarding.

Entitlement

Does your client know his (or her) personal rights, and can he (or she) assert those rights when it is appropriate to do so. Formerly abused children have usually not been taught that they have a right to be seen, heard, respected, valued, cared for, and to be treated in safe ways with dignity. Clients must develop a healthy sense of entitlement. Once the entitlement is felt and believed, clients are likely to stay away from situations in which their basic rights are violated or minimized.

Dependency

Can your client acknowledge his own dependency needs without seeing dependency as a weakness? Is he exhibiting the ability to depend on others when necessary? At the same time, can he also function independently when autonomy is called for? This ability is important for anyone, and critical for adult survivors. They have not had their needs met in the past, and consequently may have learned to ignore or avoid them. They must first pinpoint their needs, accept them, and discover how to get them met. In the process they may discover that there are times when they must rely on others. The ability to rely or depend on others must be seen as a strength.

Meeting Needs

Can your client act as an agent on his own behalf? Can he recognize and meet his own needs in a safe and constructive way? Some of these needs may be for human contact, and yet seeking others out may be threatening. Clients must know that they can reach out and try to get their needs met from others, and at the same time, that they can become a resource to themselves. For example, if they have a need for companionship and friends are not available, they should be able to do something alone that gives them a sense of well-being.

Expression

Can your client express a range of thoughts and feelings? For example can he or she talk about anger, joy, sadness, fear. If you find that the survivors choose to express a prevalence of one feeling, you need to direct them to explore other feelings as well. Clients need to learn that there are numerous forms of expression that are not limited to verbal expression. Often, the creative arts provide a way of releasing feelings in a very powerful way.

If your client shows moderate improvement in all of these areas, he or she has probably entered the final or termination phase of treatment.

The Termination Phase

New Challenges, New Anxieties

At this point, clients have worked through most of the acute pain and grief. Now they are starting to experiment with new ideas, new feelings, new behaviors. This experimentation, in turn, raises new doubts and new anxieties. Clients still lack self-confidence, which is understandable. If their efforts do not produce immediate results, they may stop trying. Also, the new experiences themselves are frightening. Clients may be torn between exhilaration and despair. New memories may surface, and the client may experience a setback. All of these issues must be dealt with in the termination phase.

In a developmental context, most clients at this point are passing from adolescence to young adulthood. Some identity issues are still prominent, but overall the client is learning to function as an adult. This takes time and much experimentation. In this final phase of therapy, you must identify your client's problem areas and encourage him or her to take risks. Applaud successes, but also failures. The outcome is less important than the attempt. Clients should be encouraged to take controlled risks in the following areas:

Establishing Control

Clients must be encouraged to seize every opportunity to behave in ways that let them feel in control. The feeling of being in control is one of the greatest deterrents to feeling victimized.

Exercising Options

Emotional paralysis occurs when clients feel trapped, when they believe that they have no options. Clients who keep exercising more options-and acknowledge that they have options- will rarely feel paralyzed.

Seeking Help

Everyone needs to know how to seek help. It is not a show of strength to stand alone, feeling scared or hurt. It takes skill and courage to ask others for help. Clients need to be taught how to reach out. Clients may be able to ask for help in therapy; now they must learn to use this skill in other areas of their lives. Clients are usually adept at helping others. Now you must teach them to reciprocate by asking for assistance when they need it.

Developing Problem-solving Skills

Clients will continue to have problems. This is perfectly normal; what matters is how they resolve their problems. Clients need to know how to define the problem, generate options, attempt solutions, and continue to keep this up until the problem is solved.

Seeking Rewarding Exchanges

In order to recover, clients must be able to seek out rewarding exchanges and avoid situations they know to be dangerous or repetitive of abusive interactions. The clients must seek out these exchanges freely, believing that they are desirable and rewarding. In order to do this, the client must first have developed some self-esteem. That is, he or she must feel worthy of positive interactions, rather than deserving of negative ones.

Seeking Affiliation

Clients should now be strongly encouraged to seek affiliation with others. This is a good time to refer the client to support groups, community activities, and other environments that facilitate contact.

Transferring Skills and Terminating Therapy

In this final phase, your clients will transfer the knowledge and skills they have acquired in therapy to other areas of their lives. For the first time, perhaps, they have been recognized, valued, supported, encouraged, and challenged. The client has been able to experience these new and perhaps anxiety-provoking experiences in a safe relationship which provided clear guidelines.

It is often painful for clients to terminate therapy. They may have ambivalence about facing the world alone. You must recognize what a big step this is for your clients and be sensitive to their needs when you plan for termination. Feelings of abandonment, grief, or anger must be discussed openly. These are natural responses for many. Others may express an eagerness to leave, and yet it is still important to discuss a range of feelings about termination. Do not terminate therapy abruptly. I recommend a six month period in which sessions are gradually reduced to bimonthly to monthly to quarterly. At the final session I make a follow-up appointment in six months, which clients are free to keep or cancel. Your clients should know that you will be available to them in the future in cases of emergency. At the same time, other resources can be discussed and your confidence in your client's ability to cope with difficulty must be conveyed.

This section has provided guidelines for treatment phasing. The therapist sets a structure for the client, anticipating the client's fears, and making efforts to create a safe environment and become trustworthy. The therapist initially provides more directives and guidance, allowing the client to rely on them, until self-reliance and self-direction are developed. As self-reliance develops, feelings of confidence and competence grow.

The therapist later encourages risk-taking, conflict resolution, autonomy, and affiliation. Previous perceptions and explanations of abusive childhoods are made explicit, then challenged.

The overall goals of heightened self-esteem, feelings of repair and motivation to act on behalf of the self are accomplished. The client recognizes options and feels empowered, entitled, and free to make choices about the present and the future. Healing and recovery is well underway, although new changes bring new anxieties and these must be recognized and addressed.

Part 4

Therapeutic Issues and Techniques

9.

Dissociation

In the next three chapters, I shall discuss various disorders that are relevant in the treatment of individuals with a history of childhood abuse. The first of these disorders is dissociation.

The Diagnostic and Statistical Manual of Mental Disorders (DSM-III-R,1987), defines dissociation as "a disturbance or alteration in the normally integrative functions of identity, memory or consciousness"(1987). There are three types of dissociative disorders. Multiple Personality Disorder exists when the disturbance occurs primarily in identity. That is, the person's customary identity is temporarily forgotten, and a new identity may be assumed or imposed. Depersonalization disorder exists when the customary feeling of one's own reality is replaced by a feeling of unreality. Psychogenic amnesia and psychogenic fugue exist when the disturbance occurs primarily in memory, and important events or specific time periods cannot be recalled. I will present some basic general information on the dissociative process in this chapter, particularly how dissociation is an effective initial defense against abuse, which becomes counterproductive later in life. The following chapter will highlight multiple personality disorder since recent research has pointed to a high correlation between this disorder and early, severe childhood abuse.

The Relationship of Dissociation with Child Abuse

Dissociation is an innovative defense against trauma. Childhood abuse is a psychic trauma as we saw in Chapter 8. However, not all victims of childhood abuse dissociate as a response to trauma. Kluft (1986) states:

> Highly traumatic events promote the use of dissociation as a psychological/behavioral defense in persons with an inborn biopsychological capacity to dissociate. If the dissociative individual's psychosocial environment is chronically and inconsistently permeated with traumatic events, then the individual instinctively resorts to dissociation as a defense because the trauma is simultaneously perceived as <u>unpredictable and overwhelming</u>. Such persons are likely to develop MPD especially if inconsistency of love and abuse is present and repeated. If the individual's psychosocial environment has a low potential for psychological trauma, then this person is likely to use dissociation as a defense and typically is a normal, highly hypnotizable individual. However, in individuals with little or no dissociative capacity, the occurrence of chronic but unpredictable traumatic events is likely to stimulate denial as the primary psychological defense. (8).

In my clinical experience, three types of victims are especially vulnerable to dissociation. These are victims of chronic physical and sexual abuse, victims of more than one abuser, and victims of ritualistic or bizarre abuse.1 If the abuse is chronic and inconsistent, then dissociation becomes the preferred form of defense because it minimizes the perception of trauma. When a client presents with any of these histories, an assessment of dissociative phenomena is warranted.

Assessment & Treatment of Dissociation

Why is it important to identify dissociative phenomena? And once identified, what is an effective therapeutic response?

Dissociative phenomena tends to block access to cognitive, sensory, motoric, or affective memory. The client can therefore develop amnesia to certain times or events. In addition, dissociation can interfere with the client's ability to cope effectively with reality.

When dissociation is a prominent defensive strategy, it is best to begin by determining the type and extent of that dissociation. Learning how and when the client uses the dissociative process allows the therapist to interrupt learned responses and assist the client to generate alternatives, thereby experiencing a choice to stay in reality. In the following example, the client discusses those feelings which trigger a dissociative response, explains how she is able to dissociate, and reviews her options. Learning about this client's dissociation was critical in that one of her symptoms was self-mutilation, and that self-destructive behavior put her life at risk. Once I helped her stop mutilating, I asked her to tell me if she dissociated under other circumstances.

Justine was a twenty-seven-year-old client who came to therapy with feelings of despair and lack of direction. Self-mutilation was uncovered during the initial assessment, although it was not her presenting problem. At first, Justine grossly minimized the extent of her self-mutilation; she refused to talk about it, and it did not come up in therapy until I had been working with her for four months and had achieved moderate success in reversing her depression. When I asked <u>specifically</u> how many times a day she hurt herself, or thought of hurting herself, the self-mutilation became a focus in therapy. Justine explained that she often remembered picking up a razor, and as she put it, "the next thing I knew, I was bleeding." It was evident that she was dissociating, and to stop the self-mutilation, dissociation had to be discussed. In chapter 13 I will describe the techniques I used.

After Justine had decreased her self-mutilating behaviors, we went on to discuss other times when she dissociated.

In the following transcript, Justine describes how she dissociates:

<u>Justine.</u>

    Dr.G. *I'm glad that you're feeling more in charge, Justine. I think you've done some important work, so even if you do <u>want</u> to cut yourself in the future, you have some tools for controlling the urge.*

Justine. *Yeah. I do think about it sometimes.*

Dr.G. *What times are those?*

Justine. *Same as before . . . when I feel bad, or bored, or aimless.*

Dr.G. *Like there's nothing to live for.*

Justine. *Yeah. Like, 'What's the use?'*

Dr.G. *I think everyone gets down sometimes. The important thing is to know what to do with the feelings.*

Justine. *And for me, I gotta stay away from sharp things.*

Dr.G. *That's right.*

Justine. *If I can.*

Dr.G. *Well, you're doing well so far. Even if you do have a relapse, you'll learn something from that too.*

Justine. *I hope so.*

Dr.G. *Speaking of learning something, one of the things that I found out about you is that you're able to split. Remember, we talked about that?* <u>(Justine nods positively)</u> *You're able to split from time to time, like when you cut yourself, and I was wondering if there are other times when you've found yourself doing that?*

Justine. (<u>Pauses</u>) *. . . I guess when I have sex.*

Dr.G. *When you have sex alone or with someone else?*

Justine. *Only with someone else . . . .*(<u>Giggles</u>) *. . . When I'm alone I don't, you know, worry.*

Dr.G. *And when you're with someone else you worry?*

Justine. *I guess that's the best way to put it. I don't feel relaxed.*

Dr.G. *I'd like to hear a little about the split that happens when you have sex with someone else.*

Justine. *Well, like what?*

Dr. G. *Give me an example of a time this happened.*

Justine. *Well . . . last time I was with Rachel.*

Dr.G. *Uh-huh. That was about six months ago, right?*

Justine. *Yeah.*

Dr.G. *Tell me about it.*

Justine. *Well, I don't know what you want to know really. I don't like talking about this stuff.*

Dr.G. *I know it's difficult for you to talk about sex. What I want to know is when you first remember splitting.*

Justine.   *Well, let me think . . . .I guess at first, you know.*

Dr.G.   *I'm not sure what you mean by "at first."*

Justine.   *When we first start doing it.*

Dr.G.   *When you first start having sex?*

Justine.   *No, way before that.*

Dr.G.   *OK, let's just try to figure this out. Did it happen this last time, when Rachel walked in the door.*

Justine.   *Oh, I get it.-No, no. Not at all.*

Dr.G.   *Tell me what happened.*

Justine.   *We had a good time. We had dinner. Rachel helped me set the table. We ate and then listened to music.*

Dr.G.   *What kind of music?*

Justine.   *Van Morrison.*

Dr.G.   *Just curious.*

Justine.   *Then we were watching an old movie on TV. We were laying on the floor, and we were still eating off and on . . . munching, you know.*

Dr.G.   *OK*

Justine.   *And then it got weird.*

Dr.G.   *What do you mean, "weird"?*

Justine.   *Rachel leaned over and kissed my neck.*

Dr.G.   *What did you do?*

Justine.   *I got tense.*

Dr.G.   *Did you say anything?*

Justine.   *No.*

Dr.G.   *Then what happened?*

Justine.   *I just kind of went numb.*

Dr.G.   *Any particular place, or all over?*

Justine.   *Just all over.*

Dr.G.   *Did you move parts of your body, like touch Rachel, or push Rachel away, or try to get up, or anything?*

Justine.   *Nope.*

Dr.G.   *What's it like to talk about this now?*

Justine.   *It makes me feel weird.*

Dr.G.   *Describe "weird."*

Justine.   *Kind of nervous.*

Dr.G.   *How do you know you're nervous?*

Justine.   *It's hard to talk . . . .My throat is dry.*

Dr.G.   *What else?*

Justine.   *I don't know.*

Dr.G.   *How does your body feel?*

Justine.   *Heavy in the chair.*

Dr.G.   *Do you feel numb now?*

Justine.   *Not really.*

Dr.G.   *Stand up, stretch, and take some deep breaths. Good.* (Rachel sits down again). *Let's talk some more about when Rachel reached over and touched you.*

Justine.   (Interrupting) *KISSED me.*

Dr.G.   *Sorry, kissed you, and then you went sort of numb.*

Justine.   *Yeah.*

Dr.G.   *What happened next?*

Justine.   *Well, then things just, you know, took their course.*

Dr.G.   *What does that mean, "took their course"?*

Justine.   *They got worse.*

Dr.G.   *I'm not sure what you mean.*

Justine.   *OK, Rachel took my shirt off and started sucking my tits.*

Dr.G.   *And when Rachel did that, could you feel your breasts?*

Justine.   *No, I just wasn't there anymore.*

Dr.G.   *So, sometime between when Rachel first kissed you and then unbuttoned your shirt and kissed your breasts, you left.*

Justine.   *I guess so.*

Dr.G.   *See if you can describe to me what specifically happened. Wait . . . let me get the dolls.*

Justine.   *Oh no, not that again.*

In a previous session, this client had great difficulty visualizing the self-mutilation and found it hard to provide the specific details I needed in order to understand what she was doing. I brought out the anatomically correct dolls and asked her to recreate the situation. Although she was initially reluctant to use the dolls, they had enabled her to illustrate behavior that she found difficult to describe. I found that the dolls also encouraged her to remember details, because they provided a concrete image for her to observe. For many individuals who dissociate, the process of observing from afar is a familiar process.

Dr.G.   *Well, it helped us the last time.*

Justine.   *OK, OK.*

Dr.G.   *This time I brought two dolls. This one is you, from before. This one is Rachel.*

Justine.   *OK. Looks just like Rachel.* (Laughs and moves the dolls' bodies into position) *My legs were crossed like this.*

Dr.G.   *And how about Rachel?*

Justine.   *Like this.*

Dr.G.   *OK, then show me what happened.*

Justine.   (Manipulating the dolls) *Rachel came across like this, and kissed me here.*

Dr.G.   *Now take a minute and try to remember what this was like. Look at the dolls, and now close your eyes and think about this scene.*

Justine.   (Opening her eyes) *. . . OK, I see it. Rachel leaned across me and kissed me, and I went cold.*

Dr.G.   *Now look at the doll's body. You. What does your body do?*

Justine.   *My arms just dropped, like this. My legs stayed the same. My head turned away.*

Dr.G.   *Were your eyes open or closed?*

Justine.   *Open.*

Dr.G.   *Where did you look?*

Justine.   *Where did I look?*

Dr.G.   *Yes. What were you looking at?*

Justine.   *I guess the wall.*

Dr.G.   *Any specific part of the wall?*

Justine.   *A painting.*

Dr.G.   *A painting of what?*

Justine.   *I don't know . . . let me think.*

Dr.G.   *Take your time.*

Justine.   *I guess . . . well . . . I'm not sure.*

Dr.G.   *Just pretend you're looking at it. What do you see?*

Justine.   *A mountain top.*

Dr.G.   *A mountain top?*

Justine.   *Yeah. It's some kind of outdoorsy picture. I always look at the mountain peak.*

Dr.G.   *OK, so you turned and looked at the mountain peak.*

Justine.   *Yeah.*

Dr.G.   *And then what?*

Justine.   *Then . . . I don't know . . . I don't remember.*

Dr.G.   *Look at the dolls.* (I review what we have discussed so far) *What happens next?*

Justine.   *I guess I'm gone right away.*

Dr.G.   *When do you come back?*

Justine.   *Huh?*

Dr.G.   *What do you remember next?*

Justine.   *I'm putting on my pants and getting up to get more food.*

Dr.G.   *What happens after that?*

Justine.   *We stayed up to watch David Letterman.*

Dr.G.   *So it sounds like you left your body until the sex was over?*

Justine.   *Yeah, that's what I usually do.*

Dr.G.   *Well, people sometimes do that when they feel in some kind of trouble.*

Justine.   *What do you mean, "trouble"?*

Dr.G.   *When something's happening that you don't like, or scares you, or confuses you, or something.*

Justine.   *I like Rachel. I don't know why I do that.*

Dr.G.   *You can like Rachel and not like what Rachel does sexually.*

Justine.   *I guess that's it.*

Dr.G.   *I think that there are some better ways of dealing with your feelings, whatever they are, when you feel in trouble, other than splitting off.*

Justine.   *Seems to work.*

Dr.G.   *Oh, it works . . . for the moment. But how do you feel about what happens when you're split off?*

Justine.   *What do you mean?*

Dr.G.   *I mean, when you look at this scene,* (pointing to the dolls) *what's you're reaction?*

Justine.   *I don't know . . . .I don't like it.*

Dr.G.   *What's the "it"?*

Justine.   *What Rachel is doing.*

Dr.G.   *And do you think Rachel knows that?*

Justine.   *Knows what?*

Dr.G.   *That you don't like being touched sexually?*

Justine.   *I never thought about it. I don't know.*

Dr.G.   *I don't know either. Do you think you're taking care of the problem by splitting off?*

Justine.   *Only at the moment?*

Dr.G.   *That's my guess. The rest of the time you continue to feel "weird," as you call it, about sex, and you have a difficult time talking about it.*

Justine.   *Yeah . . . .*

Dr.G.   *And, Justine, you seem to like Rachel.*

Justine.   *Yeah, I do. More than anyone before.*

Dr.G.   *What do you like about Rachel?*

Justine.   *Rachel is sweet and honest. She makes me laugh. I feel comfortable.*

Dr.G.   *I've never asked you this before. Would you describe your feelings towards Rachel as love?*

Justine.   *If I had to.*

Dr.G.   *No one's forcing you to label what you feel. I'm just interested in how you would describe your feelings.*

Justine.   *I guess I do love her.*

Dr.G.   *You know, sometimes when people love each other, they show it in many ways, including in a physical, sexual way.*

Justine.   *I know.*

Dr.G.   *Have you ever considered showing Rachel your love in a physical way?*

Justine.   *You know how I hate that stuff.*

Dr.G.   *I know that sexual contact makes you afraid and tense.*

Justine.   *I don't know if I'll ever feel differently.*

Dr.G.   *I don't know either. But I'm wondering if you think you would even want to feel differently?*

Justine.   *What do you mean, "want to feel differently"?*

Dr.G.   *Would you like to be able to show your feelings in a physical way, maybe to Rachel, maybe to someone else you meet later?*

Justine.   *I'm just not sure. I . . . (<u>long pause</u>)*

Dr.G.   *Well, I'd like you to think about that for now. We can talk about it some more later.*

Justine.   *I guess my vote in this doesn't count.*

Dr.G.   *Sure it does. What's your vote?*

Justine.   *I say, ignore the stuff.*

Dr.G.   *I have registered your vote. Think about what we talked about today, OK?*

Justine.   *Yeah, yeah.*

Over the next eight months of therapy, Justine learned to describe exactly how she dissociated. As she put it, "First, I tend to feel weird in some way. I get scared or upset, or I feel strong feelings of some kind that I don't know what to do with. Then, I usually pick something out and I focus on it. I let my body go limp . . . .I get heavy . . . .I say to myself, Think about spring, think about spring. I like spring. And then before I know it, whatever it is is over."

The sequence that Justine described consisted of (1) a specific trigger (distress); 2) flight response; (3) visual focus on an inanimate object; (4) body limpness; and (5) a cognitive (trance-inducing) statement, over and over. This client's specific way of dissociating was clarified for both of us. In order to interrupt the process, attention was paid to all these aspects. For example, to block body limpness, the client was instructed to move physically at the moment she felt distressed. This client took up running and when she experienced boredom or anxiety she ran outside or up and down her apartment stairs. We spent considerable time discussing her flight response and what would happen if she felt her feelings instead.

Slowly Justine began to want to "stay with" whatever feeling she was experiencing. She was motivated to change her flight response primarily because Rachel had threatened to leave her unless Justine was willing to participate in a full, loving relationship, including sexual reciprocity. Justine's first reaction was to forget about Rachel, but she found that her feelings for Rachel were deeper than she had supposed, and she felt empty and lost without her. If Rachel had not imposed this external threat, it is difficult to say whether Justine would ever have been motivated enough to understand and change her flight response, which had enabled her to endure eight years of childhood sexual and physical abuse.

I gave Justine a number of behavioral tasks designed to give her control over her responses. One of the main characteristics of dissociation is the client's sense of being out of control. Dissociation is often described as something that happens spontaneously. Clients often say, "The next thing I knew . . . " to describe the reawakening of conscious awareness. In order to help these clients to regain control, I have them experiment with deliberately trying to dissociate. This makes the unconscious processes conscious, thus bringing the process under conscious control.

Justine was asked to pretend that something had happened that left her feeling "weird"— her term for one of the feelings that triggered her dissociative response. She was then asked to dissociate (or pretend to do so) both in and out of the therapist's presence. Some clients will be too frightened of dissociating in someone else's presence. Ask these clients to dissociate at home, either alone or in the company of someone they trust, and to do so for a set period of time. In order to stop dissociating, the client must use a stimulus that effectively interrupts the dissociative state. Some clients may need to set a timer or ask a friend to telephone at a specific time. In a therapy session, you can call out to the client, touch the client lightly, or turn brighter lights on, depending on what the client finds most helpful.

Another technique for mastering dissociation involves instructing the client to increase or decrease the intensity of the dissociative state. I use a rating system in which zero represents no dissociation and ten represents extreme dissociation. Once the client can deliberately dissociate at, say four, ask him or her to try to increase the intensity to five or six or decrease it to three or two. As the client learns to do this, he or she is learning to exercise control over the dissociative process. Clients do not usually resist this technique as they might if you simply asked them to try to "stop" dissociating. Resistance might be elicited by asking the client to "stop" dissociating.

The most successful interventions are made at the beginning of the flight response, right after the trigger feeling is registered. Once the client registers the trigger feeling, the therapist suggests alternative responses (other than flight through dissociation). Help the client to explore these alternative responses, which may include withdrawing physically from the situation; describing the discomfort to self or others; trying to identify the source of the discomfort ("Why do I feel threatened right now, and is it a realistic fear?"); and looking for healthier ways to respond ("What can I do instead of spacing out?") You should also encourage the client to keep the past and the present separate. For example, say someone yells at your client, and they feel an immediate sense of fear. The client can say to him or herself, "This is probably a safe situation. Just because someone raises their voice does not mean that I am going to be hit. People yelled and hit me when I was a child. I am an adult. I will not let anyone hurt me. I am safe. I can protect myself. I will ask this person to lower his voice." This client may also give him or herself other directives such as, "Breathe in," "Move your legs," and "Speak out."

Before I began to focus on dissociation, Justine had known that there was something terribly wrong with her childhood, but she had avoided remembering, saying that there were big gaps in her memory. Over a period of months, as we worked on dissociation, she retrieved partial memory. Justine had suffered abuse at the hands of both parents. Her mother had been sexually abusive, and her father had beaten her and her mother regularly. To seek refuge from her father, she would run to her mother's bed, and her mother would orally copulate with her. Justine did not see this as painful or harmful in any way, and had great difficulty in accepting this as sexual abuse. "If it had been my dad, I could see it as abuse. My mom was just lonely." At the same time, she felt that being sexually abused by her mother set her apart from any other survivor, and deep inside she felt ashamed and confused about her mother's sexual abuse.

Her denial about the impact of sexual abuse by her mother continued for months. I gave her a book to read about mother-daughter incest (Evert 1987) and the book penetrated her denial. She suffered greatly as she admitted her mother had been wrong. She had felt her mother was all she could hang onto as a semblance of caring and nurturing. I referred her to a group for women sexually abused by mothers and she found the group very valuable. She was eventually able to separate the appropriate from the inappropriate attention she had received from her mother and she chose to forgive her and not dwell on this aspect of her relationship to her mother. Mostly, she continued to feel a great deal of empathy for her mother, and persisted in maintaining the caretaking role with her.

During the time that the treatment focused on her mother's sexual abuse, Justine became severely depressed and she was hospitalized briefly. She stayed in therapy for an additional year. There was a great deal of transference. She viewed me as the nurturing parent whom, for a time, she relied on for guidance and direction. As could be expected, she also saw me as punitive, sexualized, and withholding. She had strong and deep feelings to express, and I encouraged her to express them.

At the same time, I remained consistent and predictable in my responses. I set limits; I reassured; I was appropriate and safe. My limits were clear: I would not hit her, I would not be sexual with her. This client, more than any other, asked for repeated reassurances on these two points. She separated from Rachel many times, but eventually made a long-term commitment. They attended couples therapy for a while and they moved to Washington, D.C. Justine stays in touch and told me that she and Rachel are very content and stable. She was in therapy with me a total of two years and three months.

Dissociation was a functional, creative way for Justine to deal with early childhood abuse. She had simply split off from an unbearable reality. In so doing, she perfected a process which was later a reflex reaction which she experienced as out of her control. The treatment helped her to control her dissociative process, and a number of feelings were then experienced and expressed.

Dissociation is a common occurrence among adult survivors. The ability to dissociate is a life-saving, pain-sparing survival strategy. However, useful as dissociation is during trauma, it can later interfere with conscious participation in reality. Dissociation is also a frequent precursor to amnesia, which can be disturbing to adult survivors and keep them confused about current reactions or life situations which might be more easily understood if more information about early experiences is available.

10.

Multiple Personality Disorder

The Diagnostic and Statistical Manual of Mental Disorders defines multiple personality disorder (MPD) as follows:

> The essential feature of this disorder is the existence within the person of two or more distinct personalities or personality states. Personality is here defined as a relatively enduring pattern of perceiving, relating to, and thinking about the environment and one's self that is exhibited in a wide range of important social and personal contexts. (1987).

The DSM-III-R goes on to describe people suffering from multiple personality disorder as having "unique memories, behavior patterns and social relationships". The numbers of personalities may vary from two to one hundred or more, and the transition from one personality to another tends to be sudden. These are the diagnostic criteria established in the DSM-III-R:

A. The existence within the person of two or more distinct personalities, or personality states (each with its own relatively enduring pattern of perceiving, relating to, and thinking about the environment and self).

B. At least two of these personalities or personality states recurrently take full control of the person's behavior.

Putnam (1985) has identified several types of personalities, or alters, that may coexist within a person who has MPD. Child personalities serve to hold or buffer traumatic experiences. Persecutor personalities inflict pain and punishment on the host or central personality (often through suicide attempts or self-mutilation). Helper personalities offer advice or perform functions that the host is unable to accomplish. <u>Recorder</u> or <u>memory personalities</u> maintain continuous awareness in spite of the amnesias experienced by other personalities. In working with MPD, it is imperative to contain and restrict the activities of the persecutors, while engaging the helpers actively on behalf of the host.

The Problem of Credibility

Perhaps no other mental health disorder encounters the degree of skepticism that is inspired by multiple personality disorder. As Goodwin (1985) observes: "Most present day psychiatrists were confidently taught, and tried to believe just as confidently, that multiple personality did not occur, but might be mentioned at times by female patients who were malingering or attention-getting, or who had been persuaded that this was their diagnosis by clumsy or cunning hypnotists; and that intrafamilial childhood sexual abuse (incest) did not actually occur, but might be mentioned at times by female patients who mistook their oedipal longings and fantasies for realities" (2).

Popular media depictions of multiple personality disorder, such as <u>Three Faces of Eve</u> and <u>Sybil</u>, as well as media reports linking mass murderers to multiple personalities, may have convinced the professional and lay communities that MPD is a dramatic, not to say sinister, condition. The fact is multiplicity is a creative response to a sinister and dramatic environment.

Prevalence

Putnam (1985) affirms that "the incidence and prevalence of this disorder is unknown" (70). In graduate schools across the country, students of mental health have been consistently taught that MPD is extremely rare and there has been sparse training on the detection and treatment of the disorder. Consequently, many mental health professionals do not assess for the existence of this condition and would be unlikely to report high prevalence within their caseloads. The accurate prevalence of this problem is therefore currently an impossibility, although there seems to be a current surge of interest in MPD. Putnam states that "in the last few years, a number of case collections have been published, allowing the further characterization of multiple personality disorder"(71).

Correlation with Childhood Abuse

The reason I am discussing MPD in this book is that there is a strong correlation between the development of MPD and a history of childhood abuse. Indeed, Wilbur (1985) believes that "without abuse, we would have few cases of multiple personality disorder"(26). A number of studies have provided evidence that sexual abuse, particularly incest, is involved in the majority of reported (and studied) cases of MPD (Boor 1982; Greaves 1980; Bliss 1980; Putnam 1983; Wilbur 1984; Saltman and Solomon 1982; Stern 1984). Convincing evidence is offered by Putnam (1983) and Schultz (1985). Putnam found that 97 out of 100 patients with multiple personality disorder had histories of childhood abuse. Schultz found that 97.4 percent of 309 MPD patients were abused or neglected.

In their forthcoming book, Sachs, Goodwin, and Braun discuss why some abused children develop MPD and some do not. In 1985, Sachs found that "the major difference between child abuse victims who do and do not develop MPD is based on the degree to which the ability to dissociate is available in their biological repertoire of responses" (47). She found that the development of MPD depended partly on the nature of the abuse. "The abuse must be frequent, unpredictable, and inconsistent . . . .Chronic abuse stimulates repeated dissociations which, when chained together by a shared affective state, develop into a personality with a unique identity and behavioral repertoire." Finally, Sachs found that "multiple personality child abuse victims . . . are usually subject to sadistic and bizarre abuse in addition to, or without, reactive aggression".

Assessment and Treatment of MPD

When adult survivors present with a history of severe, chronic, bizarre, or ritualistic abuse, or evidence of dissociative states (current or past), the therapist must assess for the presence of Multiple Personality Disorder.

Once MPD is identified, a therapist unfamiliar with its treatment is advised to read extensively and if possible, to receive training in the treatment of this disorder. Most experts in the treatment of MPD are optimistic about the outcome of treatment. This is especially true in the case of children who are diagnosed and treated early.

Kluft (1986) identifies thirteen issues which can be identified as basic considerations in the psychotherapy of MPD. These are "1) developing trust, 2) making and sharing the diagnosis, 3) communicating with each personality state, 4) contracting, 5) gathering history, 6) working with each personality state's problems, 7) undertaking special procedures, 8) developing interpersonality communication, 9) achieving resolution/integration, 10) developing new behaviors and coping skills, 11) networking and using social support systems, 12) solidifying gains, and 13) following up." (9).

Kluft states that fusion is an important goal and occurs when there are three stable months of continuity of contemporary memory; absence of overt behavioral signs of multiplicity; subjective sense of unity; absence of alters on hypnotic re-exploration or other intensive probe; modification of transference consistent with coalescence of alters; and clinical evidence that the unified patient's self-representations include acknowledgements of attitudes or awareness previously segregated into alters. When fusion has persisted for two years, it is considered to be "stable fusion." (Some of my clients prefer to think of fusion as cohabitation in which alters function in greater harmony.)

A Caution

In my work with clients with MPD, I have found that it is critical to identify the presence of persecutor personalities. It is advisable to gain access to the persecutor in an assertive manner. I ask my clients to invite (or challenge) this alter into treatment. If the persecutor refuses to participate in therapy, messages to it are communicated through other alters. Dangerous or harmful alters (like offenders of any other kind) can be firmly confronted. In dealing with them, you must set firm and consistent limits; if they test these limits, tell them that their behavior is unacceptable and will be stopped. External controls might need to be set. At the same time, these alters can be given an opportunity to explain why they want to hurt the client, and give them tools to express their hostility harmlessly. In addition, you must convene the helper personalities and encourage them to form a protective coalition. Most clients find strength in numbers, and it is useful to conduct group therapy sessions with the helpers to develop clear strategies for self-protection.

Because adult survivors are vulnerable to revictimization, lack self-esteem, and may find self-disclosure difficult, it is important to keep asking the helpers (and the client) if the client is safe. It is also important to keep talking to the persecutor about its current thoughts, feelings, and behaviors.

The development of multiplicity is a highly creative response to extremely abusive situations. Without the ability to dissociate children might develop long-term psychiatric illnesses and impaired functioning.

Multiplicity can create numerous problems for the adult survivors, particularly if the client views the disorder as a sign of mental illness, or if alters place the client's life at risk. Also, MPD clients can be misdiagnosed and treated with medications or hospitalizations which do not adequately treat the disorder.

Multiples are capable of understanding MPD and its function. They can learn to work with their alters, eliminating the threat of persecutors, while engaging helpful or nurturing alters to provide general assistance or companionship.

Multiples can benefit from trauma resolution work designed to explore the childhood trauma towards healing and recovery.

Kluft (1986) offers strategies for treatment of MPD. Those strategies in combination with strategies for survivors of abuse offer the fundamental elements of therapy for survivors of abuse with multiplicity There is a great deal of research data available and efforts to diagnose and treat this disorder are impressive. I encourage you to read <u>Chilhood Antecedents of Multiple Person-</u>

ality by Dr. Kluft, and <u>Treatment of Multiple Personality</u> edited by Dr. Braun.

11.

Post-Traumatic Stress Disorder

The Diagnostic and Statistical Manual of Mental Disorders defines Post-traumatic stress disorder (PTSD) as the development of characteristic symptoms following a psychologically distressing event that is outside the range of usual human experience (i.e., outside the range of such common experiences as simple bereavement, chronic illness, business losses, and marital conflict). The stressor producing this syndrome would be markedly distressing to almost anyone, and is usually experienced with intense fear, terror, and helplessness. The characteristic symptoms involve re-experiencing the traumatic event, avoidance of stimuli associated with the event or numbing of general responsiveness, and increased arousal. (1987).

The DSM-III-R notes that the most common traumata involve a threat to the subject's life; that the trauma may be experienced while the subject is alone or in the company of others; that stressors include natural disasters, accidents, and that they can be reexperienced in a variety of ways, including recurrent or intrusive memories, distressing dreams, or the "reliving" of the traumatic event. There can be intense psychological distress when the subject experiences an event that resembles or symbolizes the traumatic event. There may also be persistent avoidance of associated stimuli.

The DSM-III-R proposes the following diagnostic criteria for Post-traumatic stress disorder:

A. The person has experienced an event that is outside the range of usual human experience and that would be markedly distressing to almost anyone, e.g., serious threat to one's life or physical integrity; serious threat or harm to one's children, spouse, or other close relatives and friends; sudden destruction of one's home or community; or seeing another person who has recently been, or is being, seriously injured or killed as the result of an accident or physical violence.

B. The traumatic event is persistently reexperienced in at least one of the following ways:

(1) recurrent and intrusive distressing recollections of the event (in young children, repetitive play in which themes or aspects of the trauma are expressed)

(2) recurrent distressing dreams of the event

(3) sudden acting or feeling as if the traumatic event were recurring (includes a sense of reliving the experience, illusions, hallucinations, and dissociative [flashback] episodes, even those that occur upon awakening or when intoxicated)

(4) intense psychological distress at exposure to events that symbolize or resemble an aspect of the traumatic event, including anniversaries of the trauma.

C. Persistent avoidance of stimuli associated with the trauma or numbing of general responsiveness (not present before the trauma), as indicated by at least three of the following:

(1) efforts to avoid thoughts or feelings associated with the trauma

(2) efforts to avoid activities or situations that arouse recollections of the trauma

(3) inability to recall an important aspect of the trauma (psychogenic amnesia)

(4) markedly diminished interest in significant activities (in young children, loss of recently acquired developmental skills such as toilet training or language skills)

(5) feeling of detachment or estrangement from others

(6) restricted range of affect, e.g., unable to have loving feelings

(7) sense of a foreshortened future, e.g., does not expect to have a career, marriage, children, or a long life

D.   Persistent symptoms of increased arousal (not present before the trauma), as indicated by at least two of the following:

(1) difficulty falling or staying asleep

(2) irritability or outbursts of anger

(3) difficulty concentrating

(4) hypervigilance

(5) exaggerated startle response

(6) physiologic reactivity upon exposure to events that symbolize or resemble an aspect of the traumatic event (e.g., a woman who was raped in an elevator breaks out in a sweat when entering any elevator)

E.   Duration of the disturbance (symptoms in B, C and D) of at least one month

Prevalence

It is virtually impossible to give a specific figure to indicate the prevalence of post-traumatic stress disorder. PTSD is associated with military combat, and particularly with the problems manifested by veterans of the Vietnam War (Janoff-Bulman 1985). Trimble (1985) cites literature that refers to "long term psychological sequelae of survivors from Nazi persecution, or more simply to survival of other extreme situations, such as hijack or hostage . . . even variants of the 'Rape Trauma Syndrome'"(12). Janoff-Bulman adds that PTSD also "aptly describes the reactions of individuals who have experienced other traumatic events such as serious crimes (e.g. rape, kidnapping), accidents (e.g., car accidents with serious physical injury, airplane crashes), and disasters (e.g. floods, large fires)". She argues that "even though there is a tendency to try to understand psychological responses within each category rather than across victimization, many emotional reactions cross a wide range of victimizations." (16) These reactions include shock, confusion, helplessness, anxiety, fear, and depression.

Correlation with Childhood Abuse

Most clinicians can cite anecdotal evidence of adult survivors with symptoms of post-traumatic stress disorder. However there are very few studies that document this problem. Donaldson and Gardner (1985) specifically reviewed a sample of twenty-six clinically diagnosed PTSD clients, and studied them to determine how many had experienced childhood abuse. In the cited study, <u>all but one of the 26 clients who was diagnosed with PTSD had a history of incest.</u>

Several studies have recently been done on psychic trauma and response during childhood (Ayalon 1983; Black 1982; Newman 1976); the application of PTSD for children as previously validated for adults (Green 1983); on kidnapped children (Senior, Gladstone, and Nurcombe 1982; Terr 1979, 1981, 1983); and on child witnesses to parental homicide (Eth and Pynoos 1985). These studies have provided information about children's responses to trauma which include later symptoms of PTSD. This is relevant data since many adult survivors present with symptoms of PTSD, specifically the sense of overwhelm and threat as they remember early trauma, intrusive flashbacks, physical sensations (throbbing, stinging, internal pain), or emotionality. Many adult survivors seek therapy to relieve their symptoms of PTSD. The symptoms are disruptive and distressing and interfere with the client's functioning and sense of emotional well-being. The flashbacks may be particularly disconcerting because they direct the client's attention to previously unconscious material. Many clients come to therapy to try to remember what might have occurred to them as children.

Some clients develop these symptoms of PTSD during therapy. It appears that normal questioning about childhood history can precipitate memory and subsequent stress if childhood abuse is present.

Assessment and Treatment of PTSD

Therapists who work with adult survivors have a lot to learn from the established strategies for treating individuals who suffer from PTSD—strategies that were originally designed to treat war veterans. These strategies involve a direct confrontation of disturbing memories and associated feelings in order to stabilize the client's current functioning by establishing a safe, structured way to remember and tolerate feelings which were generated while experiencing a traumatic event.

What we ask PTSD clients to do is to remember a trauma integrating cognitive, affective, physiologic responses, thereby creating full memory and an ability to process previously repressed material. Since what is remembered elicits fear, anxiety and pain, this process must be carefully designed considering the client's ego strength, never asking the client to go too fast or too soon. If the client shows signs of decompensation, regression, or psychosis, the work must stop and a careful decision made as to when and if to continue.

Scurfield (1985) insists the client with PTSD symtoms must be "guided through tolerable doses of awareness," preventing the extremes of denial on the one hand and intrusive-repetitiousness on the other" (245). Horowitz, (1974) and Horowitz and Solomon, (1975) state that in a psychodynamic treatment approach, potentially overwhelming affective responses require active interventions to allow interpretations and clarification of specific fantasies, remembrances and impulse configurations and to reduce feelings of powerlessness. Methods to reduce, desensitize, or extinguish unwanted or aversive symptoms are encouraged. Behavioral techniques such as imaginal flooding and implosive therapy (Black and Keane 1982; Fairbank and Keane 1982; Keane and Kaloupek 1982; and Miniszek 1984), systematic desensitization (Cellucci and Lawrence 1978), thought-stopping, cognitive restructuring, behavioral bibliotherapy (Marafiote 1980; Parson 1984) and hierarchical routes of behavior (Horowitz and Solomon 1975), are useful techniques in working with PTSD. In addition, Donaldson and Gardner (1985) describe a treatment approach called "Reconceptualization of stress responses," which has been shown effective in the treatment of PTSD.

Scurfield (1985) lists five key principles in the treatment of post-traumatic stress disorders. These are (1) the establishment of a trusting therapeutic relationship; (2) education regarding the stress recovery process; (3) education regarding stress management techniques; (4) a reexperiencing of the trauma; and (5) integration of the trauma experience. In addition, Scurfield recommends a combination of individual and group therapy.

This treatment model is congruent with the treatment model described in this book.

This point cannot be emphasized enough: The therapeutic decision to facilitate recollection or reexperiencing of a traumatic event must be carefully and deliberately made. The therapist must guide the client at his or her own pace.

PTSD as a Diagnostic Label for Adult Survivors

There has been recent discussion of the applicability of this diagnostic label when treating adult survivors. Clearly not all adult survivors develop symptoms of PTSD and PTSD does not include all the symptoms of early childhood abuse. Finkelhor (1987) finds the label overused and ineffectual since it describes only a limited number of symptoms typically associated with sex abuse survivors, and offers no theoretical framework to explain the development of PTSD. I concur that the diagnostic criteria for PTSD frequently appear in adult survivors, but survivors also have a variety of symptoms and issues not addressed by this diagnostic category. Finkelhor offers his "Traumagenic Dynamics in the Impact of Sexual Abuse", as a more comprehensive theoretical framework which gives specific dynamics associated with the impact areas of Traumatic Sexualization, Stigmatization, Betrayal, and Powerlessness. This framework was developed to discuss the impact of childhood sexual abuse. However, some of the elements are applicable to victims of other forms of child abuse including physical abuse, neglect, or emotional abuse.

I have reviewed the disgnostic category of PTSD because many adult survivors present with symptoms of this disorder. In addition, I refer you to the body of work established to treat other victims of trauma, especially war veterans, who later suffer PTSD. The literature on treatment of PTSD clients is pertinent to the treatment of adult survivors of childhood abuse, particularly those who have negative trauma resolution, seek therapy for PTSD symptoms, or develop PTSD symptoms as a result of therapy for other presenting problems.

12.

Trauma Resolution Work Using Anatomically Correct Dolls

In the next three chapters, I shall discuss various therapeutic tools and techniques and their application to specific problems. The first of these techniques is the use of anatomically correct dolls.

Anatomically correct dolls are dolls that have genitals. They are usually rag dolls, and they come in a set of four: two adult dolls, male and female, and two child dolls, male and female.

Anatomically correct dolls are used primarily for interviewing children. The child manipulates the dolls to demonstrate what happened. This is often more effective than asking the younger children to describe what happened, which can result in unclear statements by embarrassed or nonverbal children. In cases of child sexual abuse, the body parts that may have been touched, fondled, penetrated, or hurt are visible and tangible on the dolls.

To date, these dolls have been used primarily in police and legal investigations. However, they are also used in therapy. With them, the therapist gives the child an opportunity to use the dolls to reenact the trauma through play. Terr (1983) describes that abused children frequently engage in post-traumatic play for long periods of time.

I will limit my comments in this chapter to the therapeutic use of anatomically correct dolls in adult therapy. I have found the dolls helpful in working with clients who cannot recall the details describe the abuse at first from the standpoint of an observer-participant.

In all of these contexts, the dolls are a useful therapeutic tool. They represent both adults and children, and illustrate in concrete terms some differences between them (the child is smaller, has less strength; looks more vulnerable). The clients can show what happens "between the dolls" from the safety of an observer participant role. If the child victim did dissociate during physical or sexual abuse or neglect, he or she is familiar with the observer role, and this familiarity may facilitate the process of remembering. The dolls allow clients to recreate the abuse scenario, and in so doing, to awaken and explore their thoughts, reactions, and perceptions to that scenario. During the recreated scenario, the adult survivor can empathize with the child doll. This third-person empathy is a first step towards self-acceptance.

This type of evocative technique is suggested only after the therapeutic relationship is strong and the client feels as safe as possible.

Procedure for Using the Anatomically Correct Dolls in Therapy

I first ask the client to choose a specific incident to remember or try to remember. This may be a vague, partial or clear memory. I then help the client recreate the event by asking relevant information which might help the client remember details. (See example on page 147). The goal is to access the perceptions and reactions which were developed during the abusive incident. The client may be unaware for example, that the abuse incident was where the negative attitude or false belief about him or herself was first formulated. If this is the case, that attitude or belief is discussed while the client is remembering the event itself. The therapist helps the client challenge and reorganize negative or false perceptions.

Once the client has chosen the incident to be discussed, I recommend that the therapist ask about responses to the event in the following sequence:

1. Instruct the client to describe what happened in the order in which it happened, and in specific detail (You sat on the chair; she put her hand on your knee; what happened next?)

2. Repeat the sequence.

3. Obtain descriptions of physiologic reactions at each point (You sat on the chair; describe what your body did, how it felt)

4 Obtain descriptions of the behaviors associated with the physiologic reactions (You went limp, tensed up, frowned, held your breath, clenched your fists, clenched your jaws)

5. Ask for cognitions - that is, ask the client how he or she interpreted what was going on (You sat on the chair; your legs got heavy and sweaty; what did you say to yourself?)

6. Review behaviors, physiologic reactions and cognitions.

7. Finally, ask the client to describe what, if anything, he or she remembers feeling.

One of the obvious goals of this kind of work is to offer the client the opportunity for emotional discharge.

My experience is that most clients find it hardest to describe feelings. If your clients cannot describe their actual feelings at the time, ask them to imagine how they might have felt, given the situation and ask them how they feel now about discussing what happened then.

It is sometimes effective to have the client go through the whole sequence from beginning to end, and then go back over it again, exploring whatever new information the client brings up each time. Clients who find it easier to describe the abusive incident may be able to provide all this information the first time around.

The therapist must guide the exploration carefully. Review the abused child's behavior, cognitions, physiologic reactions, and emotional responses. Review the coping strategies that he or she employed. Proceed slowly. Do not go beyond the client's ability to tolerate the pain or confusion that the retrieval of these memories may evoke. The client who continues to discuss the abusive incidents in an analytical way, detached from affective responses, needs assistance in acknowledging feelings attached to the memories. This client is still well-defended and will need help to process the experience so changes in the current symptomatic behavior can be made. Note any specific resistance that you encounter. Some clients, for example, can tell you a great deal about what they were thinking during the event but virtually nothing about what they were feeling.

As mentioned earlier, the primary purpose of this procedure and the use of the anatomical dolls to facilitate the process, is to examine the client's interpretations of, and reactions to, the abuse. This may shed insight on the client's defense mechanisms and on his or her feelings of responsibility. More often than not, the child unable to provide an accurate explanation, accepts the blame and responsibility for having been abused. Once you have determined that this is the case, you can intrude into the client's old belief system, and substitute more accurate information. It is important to communicate at first as if you were communicating with a child. Later, you can restate the information in adult terms. Both the child and the adult need to hear and understand what you are saying. Both the child and the adult need to acknowledge and experience their feelings.

In the following partial transcript, the sequence of behavior has been established, and I am seeking to determine the client's physical reactions. John is twenty-eight years old. He has a history of physical abuse:

John.

> Dr.G. *John, in the work we were doing last week, you selected a memory that had haunted you for quite a while, because it was the most emotionally painful beating for you.*
>
> John. *Well, it did bug me a lot because of what I told you.*
>
> Dr.G. *You mean that your dad had broken a confidence.*
>
> John. *Yeah, he used it against me.*
>
> Dr.G. *You had trusted him with your feelings about something important, and he brought it up when he was angry at you.*
>
> John. *He really got to me that night.*
>
> Dr.G. *What I'd like to do today is to talk a little about what you used to do with your body while you were getting a beating.*
>
> John. *What do you mean?*
>
> Dr.G. *I'm interested to know how your body reacted to being hit.*
>
> John. *Well, it didn't hurt, if that's what you mean.*

Dr.G.   *That's part of what I mean.   Let me set up the situation we talked about last week, and I'll explain it more as we go along.*

John.   *OK*

Dr.G.   *You were in your room, usually lying on the bed, listening to some music. Next thing that happened, your dad would drive into the driveway.*

John.   *Yeah, revving the engine like crazy, which he used to complain I did.*

Dr.G.   *When you heard the car drive up, what did your body do?*

John.   *I don't get it.*

Dr.G.   *You were lying here (<u>Demonstrating with the doll</u>) with your arms under your head; your legs crossed, like this; the music on; and you would hear your dad's car. What did your body do?*

John.   *Well, I usually sat up right away, turned the music down, and sat back on the bed.*

Dr.G.   *So here you are relaxed, you hear the car, and you turn down the music. Then you sit up in your bed, like this? (<u>Demonstrating with doll</u>)*

John.   *Yeah, like that. Except I would grab something to read and wait to hear what was going on.*

Dr.G.   *What were you listening for?*

John.   *I wanted to hear if he was in a good mood or not.*

Dr.G.   *How could you tell?*

John.   *If he started yelling or not.*

Dr.G.   *So here you are, pretending to read something, listening for what was going on downstairs. Can you remember, looking at this guy here, (<u>Pointing to the doll</u>) what your body was doing?*

John.   *I remember my knees were held together.*

Dr.G.   *Anything else? Think about your body. Your heartbeat, your breathing, tension, your stomach, your buttocks, your feet, your fists . . . anything happening?*

John.   *I remember my heart beating fast.*

Dr.G.   *How do you imagine you were feeling right at this moment?*

John.   *Probably scared some . . . You never knew if you were gonna get in his way or not.*

Dr.G.   *Then on that particular night, he was in a bad mood, yelled at your mother, found out about the fight at school, and came busting through your door.*

John.   *That's right.*

Dr.G.   *How'd your body react when he came through the door?*

John.   *I stood up.*

Dr.G.   *How was your heartbeat then, as you stood up?*

John.   *Pounding away.*

Dr.G.   *What else is your body doing?*

John.   *I used to clench my fists.   I used to pretend I was going to hit him back.*

Dr.G.   *OK, so your fists are clenched.*

John.   *Yeah . . . and my teeth are pressing hard.*

Dr.G.   *You mean you've got your jaw shut down hard?*

John.   *Yeah.*

Dr.G.   *What about your stomach?*

John.   *I would tighten it up.   That's where he usually punched me first.*

Dr.G.   *How about your legs?*

John.   *That I really don't know.*

Dr.G.   *Then he would yell for a while.   What did you do then?*

John.   *It's kind of like a dream . . . .Everything goes fast, it's like I'm not me, but someone else watching what's going on . . . .*

Dr.G.   *And what do you do?*

John.   *I just wait.   I let him scream and yell, and I look at him.*

Dr.G.   *What does your face look like?*

John.   *I don't know.*

Dr.G.   *What do you imagine it might have looked like?   Try to do that face now.*

John.   (Smiling a little) . . . *I don't know that I can.   Let's see . . . I guess sort of like this.*

Dr.G.   *Looks sort of blank to me.*

John.   *Yeah, I guess so. I didn't want to look like anything. Sometimes he'd say I looked "sassy," other times "wimpy"; no matter what I did, it didn't help.*

Dr.G.   *When he hit you, what did your body do?*

John.   *That's easy. I'd just tighten up and let him beat on me and he was pounding on pure muscle and it didn't hurt me at all.*

Dr.G.   *So you learned to tense up all your muscles, and when you did that he could beat on you all he wanted.*

John.   *That's right.*

Dr.G.   *That sounds like a good thing to have learned to do.*

John.   *I guess so.*

Dr.G.   *Do you ever have to get that way now?*

John.   *Well, you know . . .*

Dr.G.   *What?*

John.   *That sometimes at work, when my boss asks me to do something that I think is unreasonable, I get all tense.*

Dr.G.   *And your body muscles all tense up.*

John.   *Yeah. But the problem is that it doesn't go away. That's when I get those really bad pains in my gut.*

Dr.G.   *So it sounds like one of the ways you responded to tension when you were a kid, scared and about to get beat up, was that you tensed up all your muscles. Now when you get tense at work, because your boss expects too much from you, the same thing happens.*

John.   *Yeah, except he doesn't hit me or anything.*

Dr.G.   *He doesn't hit you, but he does make you nervous and tense, and your body goes into automatic.*

This client's defense mechanism, valuable in his youth, is no longer an advantage but a disadvantage. His physiologic reactions to fear, high expectations, or tension occur immediately and reflexively, causing his body undue stress, which has resulted in a bleeding ulcer. It is important to help John to understand the connection between his current problem and this learned behavior, so that he is motivated to develop new methods of responding. Eventually, John was able to say to himself, "This is not my dad; this is my boss. My boss is not going to hurt me. I can relax." In addition, he learned to make eye contact, to sit down so that his legs would not shake and make him feel unstable, and to hold something in his hands that he could manipulate. He also learned to ask his employer to sit down and talk with him. All these methods were successful in helping him break old habits and gain some confidence, but they could not have been undertaken without a clear understanding of his original responses.

Although it can be tedious, it is well worthwhile to explore each level of response to the abuse. To do so can provide you with data that you may not be able to obtain in any other way. In my opinion, we cannot alter the client's negative self-concepts without knowing the cognitive distortions that exist in his or her perception of the abuse. Children usually cannot conceptualize abuse accurately. Their loyalty to, and dependence on, the abusive person leads them to blame themselves for the abuse, as I have explained. If left unchallenged, these distorted views reinforce a negative self-image.

Consider the following example. Mary, a forty-one-year-old sales clerk, discusses her rejecting mother:

Mary.

> Mary. *When my mom would push me off her lap and send me to my room, I would go curl up under my covers and suck my thumb.*
>
> Dr.G. *What did you say to yourself as you lay there curled up with your thumb in your mouth?*
>
> Mary. *I'd tell myself I was dumb.*
>
> Dr.G. *How did you phrase it?*
>
> Mary. *I'd say, "You are dumb."*

I have already used the dolls to help this client to explain the physical abuse and the neglect that she suffered in her childhood. Now I reintroduce them:

> Dr.G. *Let's take the Mary doll for a few minutes. Show me how you used to lie down under the covers.*
>
> Mary. (Arranges the doll into a fetal position, with thumb in mouth and eyes shut)
>
> Dr.G. *I'd like you, Mary, to say the words to this little doll that you used to say to yourself.*
>
> Mary. (In a soft little voice) *You did it again, Mary. You are so stupid. Mommy was loving you, and you were stupid and made her get mad and throw you away. She was*

*being so good to you, and you screwed it up again. You always
ruin everything. You are so dumb.*

Dr.G.   *What did Mary do that was so dumb?*

Mary.   *She made Mommy mad.*

Dr.G.   *What did she do that made Mommy mad?*

Mary.   *I don't know.*

Dr.G.   *Try to remember. What you've told me so far is that
Mommy was drinking her bottle, holding little Mary in her
lap.   Then Mommy pushed Mary away and sent her to her
room, saying, "Get away from me, you dumb little shit."-What
do you think Mary did to make Mom angry?*

Mary.   *I really don't know.*

Dr.G.   *Let's see if we can figure it out together.   What could
have made Mommy mad?*

Mary.   *Well, she got mad if her TV shows didn't come on.*

Dr.G.   *OK, so that's something that didn't have to do with
you that could have made her mad.   What else?*

Mary.   *Maybe I was too heavy.*

Dr.G.   *How old were you Mary, five or six?   Do you think
you would have been too heavy?*

Mary.   *Well, Samantha weighs a lot more than I did then
and she's not heavy.*

Dr.G.   *Why else could your Mom have gotten mad?*

Mary.   *If she ran out of stuff to drink?*

Dr.G.   *That's another really good reason she could have
gotten mad that didn't have to do with you.*

Mary.   *God, I wish I had known what to do so she would
have never gotten mad at me and thrown me off her the way
she used to do.*

Dr.G.   *And I wish you could see now that it was not you
who were stupid or dumb.   You were just a little girl who liked
to sleep in her Mommy's lap.   You didn't do anything to make
her mad.   Sometimes she just got mad because of other things.
Can you see that?*

Mary.   *I guess so . . . ."*

Dr.G.   *But it's hard for you, because there's a little part of
you that wants to think it was your fault.*

Mary.   *Why would I want to do that?*

Dr.G.   *What do you think?*

Mary. (Wipes away a few tears and blows her nose.)
I guess if I'm to blame, then she isn't mean or a drunk.

Dr.G. *I think that's probably true. But Mary, your mom
is not alive anymore and you are; and it would sure be nice if
you could stop thinking of yourself as a bad little girl, who is
dumb and who nobody would want. You are a very smart and
pretty woman, who has a lot to offer.*

Mary. *I just hate saying she's a drunk. I once hit a kid in
the face who laughed at her and called her a drunk.*

Dr.G. *It's very hard when others call your parents names
and laugh at them. The truth is Mary, that your mother was
an alcoholic and had a serious disease. She was not able to
get help with that problem. Because she drank she was not the
best mother in the world. She was very hard on you.*

Mary. *I hate hearing you say that.*

Dr.G. *I know you do. But Mary, it's time to face the truth,
and allow yourself to move on. You don't have to protect her
anymore. You have to protect, and nurture, yourself.*

Mary. *I wish I knew how. I can't seem to do anything
right.*

Dr.G. *It takes work to see yourself differently than how
you've grown up thinking of yourself. You are improving all
the time as far as I can see. Wasn't it just last month that you
stood up to that verbally abusive salesperson?*

Mary. (Smiling) *Yeah. But that person was really off
base.*

Dr.G. *Yes. And you were able to recognize that you were
entitled to be treated with respect.*

Mary. *I guess so.*

Dr.G. *You are not stupid. You are learning quickly about
your strengths.*

This client's self-esteem had been severely affected by an emotionally abusive, alcoholic mother. Mary's mother gave her spo-
radic physical attention, which the child came to crave. When the
mother's mood changed, she would abruptly push the child away
or hit her and the child came to believe that this was her fault. If
only she were smarter, nicer, prettier, Mommy would not push
her away or hurt her. Mary felt totally responsible for the abuse

and neglect she had suffered at her mother's hands. Her need to maintain an idealized image of her mother was extremely strong.

Once you have uncovered the client's cognitive distortions, you must help the client to replace them with statements that are realistic and non-punitive. This is done by offering the client new input, and by helping the client to identify his or her own strengths. Mary, for example, was an excellent mother, and she had no doubts about her parenting and nurturing abilities. It was necessary for her to accept that she was not responsible for her mother's rejection; that her mother was in fact an alcoholic. Accepting her mother's alcoholism was extremely difficult for Mary.

She preferred to think of her mother as a sad and lonely person whose reasonable requests she could not meet. In other words, she had chosen to remain loyal to an idealized memory of her mother. When Mary finally did acknowledge her mother's alcoholism, she discovered a great deal about herself and about the relationship she had maintained with her mother. She joined a group for Adult Children of Alcoholics (ACA), and she gained strength through affiliation with other abused children. As her self-esteem flourished, her fear of being abused by employers, which had originally brought her to therapy, diminished.

As I have explained, most adult survivors find it difficult to recognize or express their feelings. The child within the adult must be encouraged and praised for doing this. Very few abused children live in an environment that values or elicits introspection. Children may create an internal world in which their thoughts and feelings remain largely unexplored. Many abused children, for example, when asked how they feel, will answer "Hot" or "Cold." Sometimes abused children learn to keep their feelings to themselves. These children become proficient at not showing what's going on inside. Some children attempt to ignore their feelings, or avoid having any, because they find them too distressing.

Adult clients may or may not experience any feelings while they are exploring painful memories. If they do experience any feelings, they may not acknowledge them. It is helpful to stop from time to time and ask clients how they are feeling at the moment. If the client can identify how he or she is feeling, you should immediately acknowledge this insight and support it. You should also attempt to weave together the present and the past by making statements such as these. "So at age five, lying there alone, you felt you were bad. Looking at that little five-year-old now, what are your thoughts?" Or, "So at ten you couldn't tell anyone what was going on. At twenty-eight, who could you talk with if something hurt your or confused you?" The therapist must constantly emphasize the fact that there is a difference between <u>what was</u>, <u>what is</u>, and <u>what will be</u>. The adults need encouragement to feel empowered and capable of change.

Introducing the Dolls

Not all clients require dolls as props. Many clients are able to provide a lucid verbal description of their abuse. At the beginning of this chapter, I described the types of clients who benefit, in my experience, from the use of the dolls. Introduce the dolls to these clients by saying simply, "These are special dolls. I've brought them in to help you talk about what happened to you when you were a child."

Clients react to the dolls in a variety of ways. Usually they smile and make some comment about the dolls, "They sure have a funny look on their faces." (Actually, most of the dolls do, so it's a very appropriate remark.) I ask clients what they find funny about the dolls' faces. Some clients say the dolls look scared; others say they look angry, others say they look startled. I tell clients that these dolls are special for two reasons. First, the dolls will help them to show me what happened to them, how they felt about it then and how they feel about it now. Second, the dolls have all the parts of their bodies, which will make it easier for them to show me what happened to them as children.

Men frequently object to working with the dolls. They may specifically resist, saying, "Guys don't play with dolls"; "I'm not into this kind of thing"; "I can't take this seriously." However, men can benefit from working with the dolls if their resistance can be overcome. On occasion I have shown men a videotape of another man using the dolls to reenact his abuse. (The other man had given permission for the tape to be used in this way) The tape desensitizes the issue; after viewing it, the first man usually decides that the technique is effective after all.

If a client refuses to work with the dolls, or feels offended or patronized at being asked to do so, I do not insist. It is important not to engage in power struggles over any specific aspect of therapy. If you do this, you are fighting a losing battle, and you may end up recreating the dynamics of abuse (such as power imbalance, lack of choice, and helplessness). If the client is willing to work with the dolls, however, I next ask him or her to choose an incident to work on.

Note that when you are working with dolls, you should introduce them early in the session. I recommend scheduling longer sessions when the dolls are going to be used. This work can go slowly or quickly, but clients who rush through it are probably trying to avoid recognizing or experiencing their own feelings. In such cases, it is best to take your time. It is important to give the client explicit permission to stop the work if he or she finds it overwhelming. There may also be times when you yourself decide, for a variety of reasons, that it is not in the client's best interest to proceed. I worked with one client who became obsessed with recreating each and every abusive episode that she had experienced. I concluded that she was being self-abusive by forcing herself to reexperience the pain without altering any of her current views or behaviors. I limited her to one episode per month, and eventually advised her that she had done enough work recreating abusive incidents. She was angry at being limited in this way and I acknowledged that fact, using it as a bridge to working on current issues in her life. I asked "What's it like for you to be angry with me?" I encouraged her to express her anger using poetry, art, movement, physical exercise and eventually, verbal statements. She was alternately immobilized and energized by directing her anger at me. She was able to tolerate having two feelings towards me at the same time. She valued me as her therapist, and she was also able to be angry at me. This brought the client back to the present and important work that eventually helped her to forgive her abusive parent, while accepting the love she also felt. This combination of forgiveness and acknowledgement of love worked for this client.

Using the Dolls

The following clinical example illustrates the use of anatomically correct dolls in trauma resolution work. Paula is a forty-year-old mother of five, whose daughter was recently sexually abused by a cousin. Her daughter's abuse brought up a series of memories about her own abuse and concurrent feelings of guilt about her failure to protect her daughter. A few months into therapy focused on helping her child, Paula wanted to discuss her own abuse and yet had trouble remembering exactly what had happened. Because she was not able to remember through more traditional methods, I brought out the dolls to give her a visual stimulus.

<u>Paula.</u>

Dr.G.   *Have you chosen one of the vague memories you wish to work on?*

Paula   *Yes, I have one in mind.*

Dr.G.   *OK. I would first like you to pick out which one of these dolls is you.*

Paula   *This is me.*

Dr.G.   *How old are you?*

Paula   *About eight.*

Dr.G.   *What grade are you in?*

Paula   *Third grade.*

Dr.G.   *Where were you living at that time?*

Paula   *Arkansas.*

Dr.G.   *Who did you live with?*

Paula   *My two brothers, Mom, Dad and a great-uncle.*

Dr.G.   *How old were your two brothers?*

Paula   *Thirteen and fifteen.*

Dr.G.   *OK. Can you tell me, Paula, who else is in the memory you've chosen to work on today?*

Paula   *My brothers.*

Dr.G.   *Can you choose which of the dolls they will be?*

Paula.   *This one . . . and I guess this one, although he was bigger.*

Dr.G.   *OK. Now tell me who's who.*

Paula.   *This one is Chuck, my thirteen-year-old brother, and this one is Kevin, my fifteen-year-old brother.*

Dr.G.   *OK. This is you, Chuck, and Kevin.*

Paula.   *Uh-huh. I can't believe how nervous I feel.*

Dr.G.   *Say some more.*

Paula.   *My heart is beating fast. My stomach is so tight, and my hands are sweating.*

Dr.G.   *Tell me what you think is making you most nervous.*

Paula.   *Just the idea of talking about this to someone else.*

Dr.G.   *Have you ever told anyone what happened?*

Paula.   *No, I've always been too embarrassed. Wait . . . I take that back. There was a girl friend in high school I told.*

Dr.G.   *Did you tell her everything you wanted to tell her?*

Paula.   *Oh, no. I just got halfway there and then I stopped.*

Dr.G.   *What caused you to stop?*

Paula.   *Her reaction.*

Dr.G.   *How did she react?*

Paula.   *She laughed and told me to stop making up stories . . . that I was a pervert.*

Dr.G.   *What was your reaction to what she said?*

Paula.   *Well you know, I kind of believed her, because that's what I thought anyway.*

Dr.G.   *You knew what pervert meant when you were eight?*

Paula.   *Oh, no. This was when I got to high school.*

Dr.G.   *Oh, I see. So it was a few years before you told anyone, and then when you did, you got a negative reaction, and then you shut down.*

Paula.   *That's right.*

Dr.G.   *What kind of reaction do you expect from me?*

Paula.   *You know, it's funny. I know you hear this kind of stuff all the time . . . .*

Dr.G.   *And how do you expect I'll react?*

Paula.   *I think you're going to think I'm really bad.*

Dr.G.   *And how will it affect you to have me think you're really bad?*

Paula.   *I'll just feel like you're right. I really am bad.*

Dr.G.   *Have other people told you you're bad?*

Paula.   *All my life. My brothers used to tease me about how I was the reason they couldn't control themselves. I was the bad one, not them.*

Dr.G.   *How do you feel about that now?*

Paula.   *You mean now?*

Dr.G.   *Yes. As a forty-year-old adult woman, how do you feel about what they said to you about being bad and causing them to lose control?*

Paula.   *Part of me says "bullshit."*

Dr.G.   *And the child part?*

Paula. *The other part, maybe it's the kid . . . I don't know. The other part says, "Yeah, I'm really bad."*

Dr.G. *And so your fear is that I will agree with them, and others, and think of you as bad?*

Paula. *Yeah.*

Dr.G. *And what will I do if I think you're bad?*

Paula. *Well, I know you won't do anything.*

Dr.G. *Yeah, but the part of you that's afraid . . . what's the worst thing I could do to you?*

Paula. *Well, this is probably very stupid, but I imagine that you could tell me you don't want to see me anymore and that it's my fault Sara was abused.*

Dr.G. *So you would be so bad, I wouldn't want to work with you anymore, and I would think it was your fault Sara was abused.*

Paula. *You know even as you say that, I can feel myself getting really scared. Pretty stupid, huh?*

Dr.G. *Well, I don't think you're stupid. I think that you have thought all these years that your abuse was your fault, and that you were to blame.*

Paula. <u>(Paula struggles to keep from crying, wiping her tears away)</u> *Yeah, I guess so.*

Dr.G. *I want to assure you I have never fired anyone from therapy. (Pause) I also want to assure you that the only person to blame for Sara's abuse, is the abuser.* (<u>Pause</u>) *How are you feeling right now?*

Paula. *Well, a little less nervous . . . .I also feel reassured.*

Dr.G. *I'm glad. Let's talk some more about where this memory takes place. Where are you and who is with you?*

Paula. *Well, I'm in the attic at my house.*

Dr.G. *OK. Show me what you're doing.*

Paula. *Well, I'm sitting down here.*

Dr.G. *Are you doing anything?*

Paula. *I'm reading a book. I used to like to go upstairs and read and play cutout dolls.*

Dr.G. *Remember what you're reading?*

Paula. *No...Something by Judy Blume I think . . . or somebody like her.*

Dr.G. *What happens next?*

Paula.   *Well . . . it's after school, and my Mom is making dinner.*

Dr.G.   *OK, which one of these is your Mom?*

Paula.   *This one.*

Dr.G.   *Let's put her where the kitchen would be.*

Paula.   *It was pretty far.* (She places the doll on the other couch)

Dr.G.   *Anyone else home?*

Paula.   *No.*

Dr.G.   *OK. So you're reading, and what happens next?*

Paula.   *Well, my brothers come upstairs.*

Dr.G.   *Did they used to come up there a lot when you were alone?*

Paula.   *Well, I picked the first time. So this time I remember being surprised they came there.*

Dr.G.   *What did you say when you saw them?*

Paula.   *I just said "Hi, what are you guys doing up here?"*

Dr.G.   *What did they say or do? Show me with the dolls.*

Paula.   *Well, Kevin said, "We wanted to come see what you were doing, and we have a new game to show you."*

Dr.G.   *What did you say or do?*

Paula.   *I just said, "OK".*

Dr.G.   *Keep going.*

Paula.   *Kevin came over to me, and Chuck was behind him.* (She walks the two boy dolls over to the girl doll) *This is where I get fuzzy . . .*

Dr.G.   *OK. Take a deep breath. Now look at the dolls and just let yourself picture the scene and see what happens next.*

Paula.   *Oh, I know . . . Kevin told me to lie down, and he kneeled down next to me.*

Dr.G.   *Alright. Just stay with the picture and see what happens next.*

Paula.   *Then he pulled my dress up.* (She reenacts this motion with the doll) *He pulled my panties down like this.*

Dr.G.   *What is the little girl thinking?*

Paula.   *She goes blank.*

Dr.G.   *How is her body reacting?*

Paula.   *Her heart is beating fast.*

Dr.G.   *What else?*

Paula.   *She curls her knees up.*

Dr.G.   *How do you think she's feeling?*

Paula.   *I think she's scared.*

Dr.G.   *Go on.*

Paula.   *Chuck comes up here (<u>She indicates the top of the girl doll's head</u>) and holds my arms down. Kevin straightens out my legs. Oh, this is hard to remember.*

Dr.G.   *Of course it is. You are this little girl. Your brothers are hurting you. How do you feel now?*

Paula.   *I feel scared . . . my heart is racing . . . my stomach is in knots . . . I, I, I can't believe they were so mean. I'm so little.*

Dr.G.   *Yes, you were little. How do you think you felt when you were this little"?*

Paula.   *Oh, just like I do now . . . .(<u>Terrified. She tries to move her legs and arms and can't.</u>)*

Dr.G.   *Paula, is this a "bad little girl" right now?*

Paula.   *(<u>Tears come down her cheeks</u>) No. Not now. It's not her fault.*

Dr.G.   *Who's bad?*

Paula.   *The boys. Chuck and Kevin.*

Dr.G.   *Why are they bad?*

Paula.   *Because they're forcing her . . . . Because she doesn't know anything about sex or what they want.*

Dr.G.   *Why else is what they're doing bad?*

Paula.   *I don't know . . . (<u>looking embarrassed about crying</u>)*

Dr.G.   *They're bad because they're big, you're little, and they are making you do something that feels scary. They were wrong to do that. (<u>Pause</u>) Paula, look at yourself and your brothers. What do you see?*

Paula.   *How little she is . . . .How she can't move . . . .*

Dr.G.   *How does that make you feel now?*

Paula.   *Sad.*

Dr.G.   *Anything else?*

Paula.   *No . . . .Just sad.*

Dr.G.   *Talk about feeling sad.*

Paula.   *Just thinking about this whole thing. It makes me wonder what was going on with them that they did this to me.*

Dr.G. *I can understand your feeling sad and confused.* (She waits as Paula cries)

Paula. *I also keep thinking of Sara and what she's been through. It makes me sick to think about her being held down.*

Dr.G. *It's hard to understand why anyone would hurt a child, whether it was you, or Sara. But one thing is clear . . . .It was not your fault you got abused, and it is not Sara's fault.*

Paula. *Somehow looking at these dolls has helped me see that. I had forgotten how small I was. I just really don't know how I feel.*

Dr.G. *Well, it looks like its painful to remember.*

Paula. *It's amazing how little I had thought about this first time. I always remembered the other times, when I kind of liked what they were doing, and I didn't even try to stop them.*

Dr.G. *And you had forgotten how it all began, and how it might have felt for the little girl to be forced and scared?*

Paula. *Yeah.*

Dr.G. *Sometimes people who go through these experiences give themselves a hard time by seeing themselves as the cause of what happened.*

Paula. *I really had always felt it was me . . . something evil in me . . . because I did like it when they touched me sometimes . . . and I never could find the voice to yell or say something . . .*

Dr.G. *You know, Paula, when girls or women are touched in certain places on their bodies, their bodies react. . . . It feels good. It's not bad that your body reacted this way.*

Paula. *I know that in my head. But deep inside I think I was somehow dirty to enjoy being treated this way.* (Talks very quickly) *I just wish I'd done more . . . you know . . . to object . . .*

Dr.G. *Well, you have to remember how little you were, and look at the size difference. There's not much you could have done.*

Paula. *Maybe if I can really feel that way, I'll quit being so mad at Sara for not telling me right away.*

Dr.G. *Maybe. Sara told you as soon as she could.*

Paula. *I can sort of see she might not have felt she had much of a choice* (Pointing to the dolls) *Chuck held my arms down, and Kevin pulled my pants down and spread my legs . . . like* *this . . . . Then . . . he opened my vagina and stuck his tongue in there.*

Dr.G.   *What was your reaction?*

Paula.   *I tried to close my legs, but he held them apart. I yelled, "Don't do that!"*

Dr.G.   *Oh, I thought you had never objected?*

Paula.   *Well, I did at first. I told them to stop.*

Dr.G.   *Did he?*

Paula.   *He told me to be quiet. He said this was a game that was going to feel good, just to relax.*

Dr.G.   *Did it feel good to you?*

Paula.   *Not then. I thought it was gross, and I didn't like it.*

Dr.G.   *What did your body do?*

Paula.   *I just got real tight in my stomach. I felt nauseous . . .*

Dr.G.   *How about your face?*

Paula.   *I closed my eyes tight and looked away.*

Dr.G.   *How about your heartbeat?*

Paula.   *It was going real strong.*

Dr.G.   *Anything else?*

Paula.   *Not that I can remember.*

Dr.G.   *Were you breathing?*

Paula.   (Looking at the dolls) *You know, I think I was holding my breath.*

Dr.G.   *What happened next?*

Paula.   *Kevin put his head up and looked at Chuck. He said, "This tastes kind of sour."*

Dr.G.   *What did Chuck say?*

Paula.   *He said, "Hurry up. It's my turn."*

Dr.G.   *What did you say?*

Paula.   *I said, "Chuck, no . . . I'll tell Mom." Chuck said, "You tell Mom and you're dead." Kevin put his fist in my face and said, "I'll beat the shit out of you if you tell anyone, you hear? Anyone!"*

Dr.G.   *How did you feel then?*

Paula.   *Scared. I just knew they weren't kidding, and I also knew I was stuck and couldn't fight them off. Then Chuck had oral sex with me for a long, long time, and Kevin kept*

*trying to get him to stop. He finally had to let go of my hands
and get him off me . . . Then they ran down the stairs.*

Dr.G.   *So the boys run off. What do you do?*

Paula.   *She just lays there.*

Dr.G.   *What are you thinking?*

Paula.   *She's just blank. And her vagina hurts. And the
muscles here* (Pointing to the doll's legs) *hurt. I remember
shaking.*

Dr.G.   *So she's blank . . . lying there, hurting and shaking.
What does she do?*

Paula.   *She gets up, pulls her pants up, and goes to her
room.* (She pulls the doll's pants up and walks her away)

Dr.G.   *What do you do next?*

Paula.   *I took a shower and a bath, and I remember
throwing my underwear away. Then I went downstairs for
dinner.*

Dr.G.   *What was that like?*

Paula.   *I didn't say anything. Chuck and Kevin kept
looking at me and smiling. I didn't know what to do.*

Dr.G.   *Anything you said to yourself?*

Paula.   *Just that I hoped they wouldn't make me do that
again.*

Dr.G.   *And did they?*

Paula.   *Over and over again. Probably for about four
months.*

Dr.G.   *That's a very long time.*

Paula.   *Yeah, and they kept trying more and more things
with me.* (Looks away)

Dr.G.   *We'll talk about what happened later on. I think
this has been a good beginning. What's your reaction to
talking with me?*

Paula.   *I just don't know. It feels kind of good to get it out.
It also feels kind of funny.*

Dr.G.   *Funny how?*

Paula.   *I don't know. I feel kind of empty.*

Dr.G.   *Well you know, you've carried this secret around for
a long time. Once you get it out, it leaves a kind of emptiness
where the secret used to be.*

Paula.   *Yeah, that makes sense.*

Dr.G.   *Any other thoughts or reactions?*

Paula.   *No . . . just how funny it is that I hadn't remembered that much about how weird this whole thing really was. I only remembered much later, when it had turned to something else . . . and I felt more responsible in a way for what was going on.*

Dr.G.   *Sometimes that happens. But it's real important to keep the facts straight. You weren't bad. You didn't ask for sexual contact from your brothers. You were forced. That is child abuse.*

Paula.   *Yeah, I can see that now.*

Dr.G.   *It's time to stop for today. Any questions or comments?*

Paula.   *Do you see other people who had brothers do this to them?*

Dr.G.   *Yes I do.*

Paula.   *Do you think it's as bad as if it's a parent or someone much older?*

Dr.G.   *Yes, it can be.*

Paula.   *I always kidded myself . . . saying it was just my brothers . . . it wasn't that bad.*

Dr.G.   *Yeah. Sometimes people do that—minimize what's happened to them for all kinds of reasons. But abuse is abuse, and as you showed me what happened it's clear you were forced, scared, and abused. That can leave you feeling like you were bad, as it obviously has; and we will keep talking about that some more.*

Paula.   *OK. There's one more thing. (*<u>Looks embarrassed</u>*) I don't know if you work a lot with adults and marital stuff, but I've realized today that what they did to me might explain why I sometimes don't like to have sex with my husband . . . . By that, I mean, certain kinds of sex.*

Dr.G.   *My guess would be that since you had oral sex forced on you at an early age, that maybe you don't particularly enjoy that type of sex. Is that correct?*

Paula.   *Oh, I'm so relieved I can talk to you about it. Exactly. And the problem is Mark likes that the best, so sometimes I let him do it, but then I feel pretty bad afterwards.*

Dr.G. *I think it's great you brought this up. Next time, let's talk about it some more, and figure out what will help you feel better, OK?*

Paula. *OK. Thanks a lot.* (<u>Hands me the little girl doll and leaves the boy dolls on the floor</u>.)

In conclusion, I want to mention that I have used anatomically correct dolls in one other way. That is with clients who have no specific memory of abuse, but who come to therapy wanting to remember what happened. As one of the techniques to help them remember, I ask these clients to identify each doll as a specific family member. Then I give them the dolls to take home. I ask them simply to put the dolls out somewhere, where the client can see them, in different settings, at different times of day and night, and doing different things. This frequently triggers specific memories of family interactions, activities, relationships, and so forth. Later, when the client uses the dolls in specific memory work, he or she is well identified with them, and it is that much easier to do the exercise, since some of the ice-breaking work has already been accomplished. (Other specific techniques for helping clients to remember their past are discussed in chapter 14.)

In summary, then, the anatomically correct dolls can be an effective tool in working with adult survivors. They provide a visual stimulant that can help generate detailed memory. After events are recreated, the dolls can also be used to have the client verbalize or do the things he or she would have liked to do to the abuser. Dolls can be an effective tool in assisting clients to visualize the discrepancy in size between abused and abusers, and the differential control issues between someone who is being coerced, forced, tricked, or emotionally bribed, and the person in control.

The dolls allow clients to awaken and explore their thoughts, reactions, and perceptions of what occurred. During the recreated scenario, the adult survivor can empathize with the child doll. This third-person empathy is a first step towards self-empathy and acceptance.

13.

Self-Mutilation

Self-mutilation occurs when the client causes physical damage to his or her body. The damage may be inflicted by scratching, biting, cutting or piercing, or by other means. Clients who mutilate themselves may do it chronically, ritualistically, or sporadically. Most of them hide the evidence, but a few of them flaunt it. Likewise, some clients employ very dramatic methods of self-mutilation, while others may, for example, simply scratch too much.

Clients who mutilate themselves do so for a variety of reasons. Children who dissociate may develop a bizarre reliance on pain as evidence of being alive. When the mind splits from the body, and the child becomes the observer, the body can seem unreal and robotlike. These dissociated children may cut themselves simply to prove that they are really flesh-and-blood human beings.

Physically abused children often associate pain with love. Some children in foster care have a deep longing for their abusive parents, missing them and worrying about them constantly. These abused children may induce pain in an effort to feel close to the absent parent. Self-mutilation can also be a form of self-punishment. Abused children sometimes believe they are bad inside and out; they want to destroy their bodies and their souls. Carried to the final extreme, this self-punitive tendency leads to suicide.

Finally, some abused children are in dire need of attention and have learned that they will get it if they hurt themselves. Being taken to the doctor, receiving medication, and being interviewed by social workers or counselors all prove to these children that someone cares about them. Often it is the only proof they have.

It is important for the therapist to know what purpose the client's self-mutilation serves. You can find out about motives by asking about a sequence of events such as what was happening (externally and internally) before and after the mutilation. It is possible the client feels punished, comforted, reassured, inadequate or calm, before or after mutilation and this points to a possible motivator. Then you can discuss what you observe, describing alternative ways of reaching the desired outcome.

As opposed to those who seek attention, most self-mutilators tend to hide their problem. During the initial assessment, you should ask questions that will encourage the client to reveal any self-mutilating behavior. Ask about pain, including self-inflicted pain. Even if the client chooses not to disclose the behavior now, these questions can set the stage for future disclosure and communicate your familiarity with the problem and willingness to have an open discussion.

Once the client has acknowledged the self-mutilation, you can address the issue directly. In order to address self-mutilation in therapy, you must obtain the answers to the following questions:

What type of self-mutilation does the client practice?

Does the client require hospitalization?

What instruments does he or she use?

What time of the day does he or she do it?

What is the most extensive form of self-mutilation that the client has engaged in?

Is the self-mutilation accompanied by any rituals or ceremonies?

What problems does the self-mutilation cause for the client?

Has the client attempted to stop the self-mutilation? How?

Who knows (or knew in the past) about the self-mutilation?

Is there anyone special the client would like to tell about it?

Is there anyone special the client would be afraid to tell about it?

What does the client think about the self-mutilation?

What does the client believe that others think about it?

When did the self-mutilation begin?

How many times a day, a week, a month, does the client do it? Does the client medicate or treat the scars?

Is there anything special that the client does, or avoids doing after engaging in self-mutilation?

Is there something that the client hopes will happen after he or she has engaged in self-mutilation. (For example, is the client harboring rescue fantasies?)

What does the client like about engaging in self-mutilation?

What does the client dislike about it?

Does the client wish to stop doing it, or to continue? In either case, why?

What does the client perceive as the therapist's reaction to self-mutilation?

Does the client engage in self-mutilation alone, or in the presence of others, including pets?

Does the client mutilate others, or domestic pets?

Does the client seek others to mutilate him or her?

The best way to obtain answers to these questions is to ask directly, in a matter-of-fact way. Once you have this information compiled, you can obtain more specific information during the session. The following clinical example illustrates this process.

Justine, whose case I described in chapter 9, has been mutilating herself since she was thirteen. She entered therapy for feeling despair and lack of direction, but now, after four months, the therapy is focused on the self-mutilation which was revealed nonchalantly during the initial assessment:

> Dr.G. *How did you do this week with your self-mutilating?*
> Justine. *Not bad.*
> Dr.G. *How many times during the week did you cut yourself?*
> Justine. *Just once.*
> Dr.G. *What's your reaction to that?*

Justine.   *I feel OK about it.*

Dr.G.   *Once a week is a definite change. Last week you cut yourself five times.*

Justine.   *Yeah.*

Dr.G.   *Tell me about the time you did it. I remember you mentioned earlier that it was right before going to sleep. Where were you?*

Justine.   *In the bathroom.*

Dr.G.   *What were you doing?*

Justine.   *Going to sleep.*

Dr.G.   *No, I mean, what were you doing in the bathroom?*

Justine.   *Oh. I took a shower, and I was just drying off.*

Dr.G.   *OK, so you stepped out of the shower. What happens next?*

Justine.   *I wrapped one towel around my body, and one towel around my hair.*

Dr.G.   *And then what happened?*

Justine.   *I was taking off my makeup with cream.*

Dr.G.   *So you were looking in the mirror.*

Justine.   *Yeah.*

Dr.G.   *What did you see?*

Justine.   *Mostly I was looking at my eyes, but then I spotted some of the scars on my chest.*

Dr.G.   *And when you saw your scars, what did you think?*

Justine.   *I don't know that I thought anything . . . but I know I felt weird right away.*

Dr.G.   *Describe "weird."*

Justine.   *Just funny.*

Dr.G.   *Did you say anything to yourself?*

Justine.   *Not really.*

Dr.G.   *What happened then?*

Justine.   *I don't know. The next thing I knew, I had cut myself and I was bleeding.*

Dr.G.   *Where did you cut yourself?*

Justine.   *Same place.*

Dr.G.   *How deep?*

Justine.   *No more than usual.*

Dr.G.   *Well, on a scale of zero to ten.*

Justine.   *About a two.*

Dr.G. *OK. So two means that you must have caught yourself pretty early.*

Justine. *I think when I saw the blood.*

Dr.G. *That's much better than waiting until the blood drops. I think this is progress. What do you think?*

Justine. *I'm just impatient. I want this to be over.*

Dr.G. *I understand that, and I think you're doing a really good job trying to figure out how this happens so you can stop.*

Justine. *Yeah.*

Justine was abused by both her parents, as we saw in chapter 9. She refused at first to discuss her self-mutilation, as I have explained. After approximately four months in therapy, she changed her mind, largely because she had a new lover and was embarrassed to let her see the scars. At this point the self-mutilation became the primary therapeutic issue.

I asked Justine to do a number of things, and she cooperated. She filled out a daily chart showing the location and severity (on a scale of zero to ten) of each injury. The chart also showed the times of day and what she was doing before and after she mutilated herself. Justine filled out the chart religiously and during the first month, the self-mutilations decreased by half. Not only did the incidence decrease, but the severity of the injuries decreased as well. During the second month, however, she suffered a relapse.

This made Justine impatient. She grew tired of making the effort to stop the mutilation. She refused to show her lover, or anyone else, her scars. In order to ascertain the extent of her injuries, I asked her to show me where they were, using a drawing of a nude female (Groth 1986). The mutilation was confined to the chest, neck, and arms. I asked her to count the scars. There were 135 of them, and Justine was surprised and embarrassed; she had thought there were thousands and felt as if she had been misrepresenting herself to me. I assured her that 135 cuts was a very serious problem. I told her to stay away from the risk environment—in her case, the bathroom. I instructed her to buy a small cosmetic mirror to look in when she removed her makeup. Apparently Justine's self-mutilating behavior was triggered by seeing her old scars in the mirror and subsequent feelings of being bad and needing to be punished.

Justine did as I told her. She stopped self-mutilating and felt proud of her accomplishment. Eventually, she gained insight into her behavior, which was an expression of her feelings about her breasts. It turned out that her breasts had been fetishized during sexual abuse, and she had grown up with an unconscious disregard for her breasts, which she believed had caused the abuse to happen.

When working with self-mutilators, it is best to take a very matter-of-fact approach. Once these clients acknowledge their behavior, you should review it from different angles, to try to determine how the client does it, and why. Next, you should provide clear directives designed to break up the rituals that trigger the abuse. Once you have identified the times and places where self-mutilation usually occurs, you can label them high-risk areas. At first it is best not to tell the client to avoid these situations, unless of course, there is a risk that the client may kill him or herself or cause serious bodily harm. Rather, you should provide an alternative. For example, I did not tell Justine to avoid looking in the mirror. I told her to buy and use a smaller mirror. Being told prematurely to stop doing something is likely to make the client rebel. If the self-mutilation threatens the client's life, you should treat it as a suicide attempt. In my experience, chronic self-mutilators have learned to inflict pain in as safe a way as possible, that is, they consciously or unconsciously make efforts to stay away from life-threatening injury. I am not however, minimizing any type of self-mutilation and work very hard to stop the behavior.

The underlying goal of therapy is to make the self-mutilating behavior open and ego dystonic. This will help the client develop internal motivations rather than relying on external motivators, such as the therapist's directives. Like any habitual behavior, change is problematic but not impossible. In summary, adult survivors mutilate themselves for many reasons—to punish themselves; to prove that they are alive; to feel closer to a loved, abusive person; or to elicit nurturing attention. Most self-mutilators hide their problem; let them know that this behavior is not uncommon, and can be changed. Once the client has acknowledged the self-mutilation, it must become the focus of therapy. Ignoring or minimizing self-mutilation may elicit escalation of the behavior on the part of the client. Explore with the client the circumstances under which the self-mutilation occurs. Identify risk factors and provide a behavioral program that offers clear alternatives. Try to determine the purpose of the self-mutilation, but remember that behavioral management comes first. I reiterate that the goal of therapy is to make self-mutilation a conscious process; this will enable the client to control it. Not allowing it to be a hidden process is also helpful to the client. Eventually, the client must build internal motivators to stop the behavior because it becomes ego dystonic to him or her.

14.

Memory Work

Clients can seek therapy remembering little or nothing about their childhood. This may trouble them for many reasons. Some clients suspect that they endured some kind of childhood abuse, and that they are repressing painful memories. These clients tend to expect to feel better once they remember. Before commencing memory work, it is wise to evaluate the client's expectations. "Tell me a little about what you hope to remember" or "Tell me a little about what you're afraid you might remember."

Once you have identified the client's hopes and fears, find out what the client's expectations are. What does he or she expect will change once the lost memories are retrieved? Some clients' expectations are moderately or completely unrealistic (I expect I'll be able to get pregnant, to find someone to fall in love with, to get a raise). Other clients' expectations are more reasonable (I'm afraid of physical contact, and I'd like to find out why). Whatever the expectation, you should emphasize that it may not be realized, and that to avoid disappointment, it is best to begin memory work with this fact in mind.

The next step is to determine where the gaps in memory are. The gap may cover a specific period; it may cover two or three years; or it may cover most of the client's childhood. I have worked with clients who have selective memory deficits—that is, they cannot, for example, recall any contact with one parent, but they can clearly remember contact with the other parent. There are three concepts that I find very useful in helping clients remember. First, the therapist is attempting to gain access to memories of events that were perceived and stored by a young person. To do so requires understanding of the child's ability and method of receiving and categorizing information. Second, visual cues can stimulate the retrieval of information. (Visual cues through recognition tasks will be discussed in chapter 14.) And third, when a traumatic event has occurred, the memory has been stored during an experience that produced arousal and helplessness in the victim. Allowing the client to experience anxiety or fear during the session, the therapist may be able to help the client retrieve memory. This may be a challenge with some clients who approach the task of remembering in an analytical way, as if they were discussing someone else's life, not their own. With these clients it will be important to help them achieve congruency of affect and content. These clients may react to watching a videotape of a victim or offender to generate arousal states or empathy states.

Perry (1987) best summarizes the relevant issues of perception and memory:

As long as children pay attention to an event, they can perceive it accurately.

Young children have some difficulty ordering and interpreting events. However, lack of ability in sequencing events should not suggest that other elements of a child's testimony necessarily are erroneous.

Children can remember material directly relevant to their daily lives. When they are asked about peripheral events however, their memories may fail . . . questions should focus primarily on events about which the child has established knowledge base.

The immaturity of the child's brain, particularly before age five, limits the ways in which perceptions are registered and communicated. The young child may well be able to register a mental "snapshot" of an incident, but likely will focus only on more salient, global details unless specifically instructed to explore the mental image in detail. Using questions that tap into all five senses may help the child to explore the image further.

Even if the child can explore a remembered event in detail, communication of what is remembered may be limited or misleading. It is best, therefore, to have the child report simple details of the remembered event, and to avoid asking for interpretations or judgments about the incident.

It is important to use simple sentences phrased in active voice. Words that unnecessarily complicate the sentence, such as adjectives, adverbs, and double negatives, should be avoided.

Simple, direct (nonleading) questions or use of recognition tasks appear to be viable means of eliciting factual information. In addition, reconstruction tasks that involve the use of props may be helpful. (518-522)

While Perry is concerned primarily with the memory of children called upon to testify in court, I find that these principles are helpful as we assist adult survivors to recover childhood memories.

Recognition Tasks

Recognition tasks are tasks which provide visual cues to the client. These cues can facilitate memory.

The client's first recognition task is to find photographs of himself or herself at as many ages as possible. Some clients have to write to their family to obtain these photos. Most people have some photos, but I have worked with clients who could not come up with any. (This situation is discussed below.)

Next, have the client arrange the photos in chronological order and paste them into a notebook one to a page. The process of reviewing and ordering the pictures may stir latent memories. Now ask the client to bring in one photo and discuss it with you. Document the client's observations and reactions. Ask the client the following questions:

Who are the important people in the child's life?

How does the child spend his or her time?"

Where did the child live?

Who is the child closest to?

What is the child's favorite activity?

Have the client bring in a new photo or set of photos each week and discuss any memories that the photos trigger. If the client is unable to obtain photos, (or after the work with the photos has been done), he or she can write to one or more relatives and ask them what they remember about the client as a child. Most clients have at least one relative whom they are willing to contact. The relative may be able to provide some clear descriptions of events or interactions which can trigger off the client's memories. I have had some clients receive these letters from relatives and find one or two incidents helpful in triggering recall. If the client has no relatives, proceed to the second recognition task. Ask the clients to remember a house in which he or she lived. Clients who cannot remember a specific period of their lives should be asked to try to remember the house they lived in during that period. If they cannot, encourage them to choose any house they can remember. Ask them to draw the outside of the house. Then ask them to draw a floor plan of the inside of the house. Make it clear that you are not asking for artwork, only for a simple sketch. If they cannot attempt even a simple sketch, help them by making a sketch based on their description. This procedure was illustrated in the clinical example of Sherry on page 115. Once you have a floor plan, ask the client to imagine that you are a visitor, and that you would like the client to show you around the house.

The first trip through the house is usually quick. Note any changes in the client's affect (gasping, swallowing, hyperventilating, holding the breath) or physical responses (twitches, rapid eye movements, clutching, pain). Note any spontaneous statements or reactions ("I feel nauseous"; "I can't breathe"; "I hated this room"). You may wish to explore these reactions with the client. Ask the client to take the sketch home and try to remember the colors, furniture, pictures, and so forth in each room. Ask the client to try to remember specific smells, textures, lighting, and other sensory information. The goal of this exercise is to help the adult to remember by discussing sensory cues that were probably relevant to the child. Sensory cues often trigger spontaneous recall. Maltz and Holman (1987) studied thirty-five adult survivors of incest. They found that memories of the incest were triggered, in their subjects, by smells, sounds, tactile sensations, as well as by a number of nonsensory stimuli.

Familiarity Tasks

A recognition task provides a visual cue that can help the client remember. A familiarity task provides the client with familiar people, events, situations in the hopes that discussion will trigger memories. Most children's lives include memories of school, friends, pets, hobbies and people in their families. While these topics may have been superficially discussed during intake, these topics are now discussed in greater detail.

Keeping in mind the client's developmental age during the period in question, ask him or her to think about schools attended (favorite subjects, report cards, school activities, awards, teachers, walking to school); about friends of both sexes (their names or nicknames, how they laughed, what they looked like, where they lived, what their parents were like, what they did together, music they listened to); and pets (dogs, birds, cats, rodents, and their names or nicknames.) Ask clients for specific details concerning the nature and extent of their relationships with parents or parent substitutes. Ask if they can remember specific family activities, eating or sleeping rituals, chores they had to do, types of punishment, arguing at home, vacations, parents' friends and so forth. This focused attention usually liberates some memories. It may also elicit flashbacks or other symptoms of post-traumatic stress disorder, in which case the symptoms are discussed and treated. It is beneficial to prepare the client for a variety of responses such as flashbacks, emotionality, or nightmares so they are not frightened by them. I ask clients to record all responses so they can be discussed in session.

Uncertain Memories

Even after they have done all this work, defensive mechanisms may prevent clients from remembering clearly. Memories may remain vague, dreamlike, and tentative. Not everyone obtains picture memories to work on. Reassure the client that he or she has done as much recalling as seems appropriate at this juncture. Later, the client may remember more specific details. However, the client is advised not to make a heavy investment in retrieval of detailed memories. In my experience, trying too hard to remember can be counterproductive. Resistance to remembering mounts, and the client grows more and more frustrated. If I conclude that too much self-pressure is being applied, I will ask the client about other topics for a while.

I have on occasion directed clients to focus on the present and future and leave the past untouched. I believe that memory work is counterindicated in cases where they provoke a severe depression, disorganization, or deterioration. This is most common when the abuse is chronic, bizarre, severe, or occurred during the preverbal stages. Remembering can cause an extreme regression and distressing levels of helplessness and despair.

On other occasions I have referred the client to hypnotherapy to obtain more detailed memory. This has been very effective with many of the survivors I treated, and I recommend the referrals be made to hypnotherapists who are familiar with the issues of childhood abuse.

If the client is unable to remember or retains vague memories, I usually discuss what they believe the memories might signify and how they will accept the fact that the memories may continue vague. Sometimes, clients have surmised that something traumatic did happen and they have come to believe it was child abuse. I then ask them to imagine that it was abuse or was not abuse, and explore their reactions to each possibility. In other words, what meaning does it have for them to believe they were abused as children? Does the abuse help explain some current problem? Does the insight help them change their attitudes and behaviors?

It is difficult for clients to leave therapy if they have not been able to remember or somehow validate the possibility of childhood abuse. Yet some kind of resolution is important so that the client does not see him or herself as disturbed, dramatic, hysterical or crazy, and more importantly, so the client can focus on today and tomorrow, not yesterday. The vague memories are accepted as such, without judgmental messages about failure to remember. The meaning of the possible abuse is explored, connections are drawn to current problems, and attempts are made to change the problematic behavior.

To summarize, many clients seek therapy to remember details and fill in the gaps in memory. These clients may fear that the gaps in memory represent the presence of a traumatic event. It can be helpful to these clients to make concentrated efforts to help them gain memories, using recognition and familiarity tasks.

Hypnotherapy can also be used to help clients access repressed memories. Asking about sensory information frequently helps.

Some clients retrieve partial or full memories while others cannot. Picture memories may never materialize. Those who have vague memories should be helped to accept this fact without feeling like they have failed. Trying to remember may elicit resistance and in some cases clients who do not focus on the material they want to retrieve, can have spontaneous recall through unexpected external stimuli at a later time.

15.

Group Therapy

Group therapy can be of immeasurable value to adults abused as children (Gordy 1983; Steward et al 1986; Sgroi and Bunk 1988). The group experience provides an opportunity to interact with others, to get positive feedback, to experiment with issues of safety and trust, and most importantly, to meet and affiliate with others of similar background. Adult survivors frequently feel freakish about their experience. Associating with others of similar background helps them to feel more normal—to feel less responsible for having been chosen as a victim.

Group therapy should be preceded by a period of individual therapy, during which these clients have had a chance to discuss their childhood abuse and have learned to tolerate their own feelings without being devastated. Some clients who enter group without prior individual therapy may be overwhelmed by the topic of abuse; indeed, they may be so frightened or overwhelmed that they will drop out.

Some Initial Decisions

Before you can organize a group, you must make several key decisions. Some of these decisions are discussed below.

The Target Population

There are a great many groups for adult survivors of sexual abuse. There are very few services in general, and groups in particular, for adult survivors of physical and emotional abuse, or for adults who were neglected or abandoned as children.[1] There are also very few groups or services for men.[2] While it is true that, in general, women tend to seek counseling more than men do, men abused as children will respond to services that are specifically designed for them. Child abuse in all its forms can have devastating long-term consequences. In choosing your target population, bear in mind the need to serve these neglected groups.

First, then, decide whom the group is to be for. Next, decide whether you want to run a mixed group. Some clinicians provide groups exclusively for victims of child sexual abuse. Others include in the same group victims of physical, emotional and sexual abuse. This works well as long as there are an approximately equal number of victims of each type of abuse. The only mixed group that is difficult to conduct is one in which most of the clients were abused in one way, while one or two were abused in another way (for example, eight victims of incest and one victim of physical abuse). This tends to split the group. It also encourages the minority members to feel isolated, misunderstood, and undeserving of help. (The tendency of adult survivors to compare themselves unfavorably to one another is discussed later in this chapter.)

In my work, I have found that there are many more similarities than differences among adult survivors. The therapeutic issues tend to be the same, and the biggest potential problem is the victim's attempt to isolate him or herself by presenting his or her abuse as particularly rare. Clients who are allowed to maintain a posture of uniqueness miss most of the likely benefits of group interaction. If the abuse has been particularly rare, as in the case of ritualistic abuse, groups can be formed to address that specific type of abuse.

Format

The next decision is whether to offer a short-term or a long-term group. Each has its advantages. I prefer to begin with a short-term group of approximately ten to fourteen sessions and then recontract with the same clients for additional sessions. Clients usually feel nervous about joining a group that will focus on memories that they have probably suppressed for years. If the group has a foreseeable end, clients may feel more able to make the short-term commitment. Once they have experienced its benefits, they are more likely to commit for additional sessions.

Usually a core group develops over time. One or two members may drop out, which will make room in the second series of sessions for one or two new members. Often the core group becomes a long-term group. Long-term groups offer special benefits: now the work deepens as trust and motivation increase. On occasion I have interviewed clients who want the security of starting from scratch in a long-term group. These clients seem to find comfort in the fact that the group will be there for a good, long time with limited substitutions in membership.

Coleaders

I have led groups alone and with a cotherapist. Either way is effective, but I prefer to work with a cotherapist. That way there are two of you to share the enormous responsibility and challenge of this type of group, and to support each other. It is extremely painful for group members to talk about their childhood abuse, and of course the therapists will be personally affected, given the highly charged material. Two therapists can share the work of responding to the various group members and can use each other for planning meetings, setting individual and collective goals, and reviewing previous sessions. Two therapists provide the clients with two different perspectives and approaches. And they can demonstrate effective interactions, providing two positive role models rather than one.[3]

If you decide to have men and women participate in the same group, it is best to have male and female cotherapists. This will give each client the opportunity to identify with a therapist of the same sex, and it will also allow for interaction with a role model of the opposite sex. Many adults who were abused as children have learned to fear all the members of the same sex as the person who hurt them.

Finding Clients

The next step is to recruit your clients. One excellent source of referrals is your local Child Abuse Council. Child Abuse Councils are coordinating and educational bodies that keep files on community child abuse prevention and intervention services. In Southern California, the Adult Survivor Program provides a comprehensive listing of services for adults abused as children throughout the country. (Call 1-800-4-A-CHILD for information.) Many prospective clients call these resources to obtain information about local services.

You will need to prepare a flyer which can be mailed out to prospective clients and referral agencies. Many referral agencies are unaware of available services and need to know if they are to provide assistance to their callers.

The flyer or brochure should clearly specify the target group. It should give dates, times, location, and fees. It should briefly describe the goals or purpose and the theoretical orientation of the group. Most referring parties will want to know that the group leader is licensed, and that he or she is trained in the prevention or treatment of child abuse. Agencies that might refer potential clients to the group include county welfare, local Police and Probation, and county Mental Health. Look in your local telephone directories to identify related resources, such as alcohol and drug programs, parenting and childcare organizations, eating disorder programs, and other community services. In addition, local Child Abuse Councils compile listings of services specific to the prevention and treatment of child abuse. Services such as Parental Stress Hotlines, Suicide Prevention Hotlines, Parents Anonymous, and Emergency Family Caretakers are likely to receive calls from adults abused as children and are therefore a good source of referrals.

One of the best investments you can make is to engage in networking with community agencies. If you do attend meetings, exchange information, express an interest in solving problems around child abuse coordination, these agencies, in turn, will refer potential clients to you or your organization. Joining a local Child Abuse Council, or attending child abuse seminars and conferences, can be beneficial to all concerned.

Screening Clients

Screen your potential clients before you enroll them in the group. Most clients welcome the opportunity to meet with the group leaders first and get their questions answered. This kind of personal contact makes the client much more willing to attend the group. It also gives you an opportunity to screen out those clients that are not good candidates for group.

In screening, several factors must be assessed. The most important of these factors is the client's preparedness. Clients must be able to talk at least a little bit about their abuse, about their current problems and about what they hope to gain by attending a group. If the client has not been in therapy before, or cannot talk about the abuse at all, it may be more beneficial to provide individual therapy first. This will prepare the client for the exploration of abuse within a group. There are exceptions to this rule. Some clients have done enough trauma resolution work on their own that they can enter a group without previous individual therapy.

If the client seems excessively vulnerable or fragile, and has not had previous therapy, a group may not be appropriate or even safe. Clients who exhibit these characteristics may be completely overwhelmed by listening to other members describe their abuse. Such clients usually do better initially in individual therapy.

Clients who have drug and alcohol problems should not be allowed to participate in group unless they are also enrolled in an appropriate drug treatment program. A client in a drug and alcohol treatment program who comes to group drunk or high, should be asked to leave the meeting. If this occurs more than once, the client must be asked to leave the group permanently. The drug and alcohol program should be notified of the client's non-compliance with the group. You should obtain evidence of the client's participation in such programs, since adult survivors are familiar with secrecy, and many people with addictive disorders conceal their failure to follow through with treatment. You should also screen out clients who are actively suicidal or homicidal. The group may exacerbate their difficulties. These clients must be stabilized before they are allowed to join a group.

Clients who engage in highly volatile or aggressive behavior will be disruptive, frightening, and counterproductive in the group—particularly since so many adult survivors are terrified by outward signs of anger and feel unable to protect themselves. You should screen out these clients if you can. Sometimes the problem behavior does not surface during screening but only after the group has begun. If this happens, you must make every effort to contain the aggression and attend to the group's reactions. If the aggression does not respond to firm limits, you should refer the aggressive client to individual therapy and not allow the client to return to group.

Another destructive factor is manic behavior. One manic client can monopolize the group time and often fails to empathize with others. For these reasons, manic people are not suitable group members. Hypomanic people must be carefully assessed. These clients should be admitted only if they are reasonably able to control their verbal output and physical agitation, and to respond to the other members' needs.

Finally, you should screen out clients who have an actively psychotic process or disorientation. These clients cannot participate well in groups. They tend to interrupt the group process, and they usually generate a great deal of caretaking on the part of other group members. If they are heavily medicated, their ability to interact with others is limited. These clients are usually being followed by mental health practitioners in hospitals or mental health clinics and they should be referred back to those clinicians.

Laying the Foundation

During the first few sessions, you will lay a foundation for the work that will be done later within the group. This initial phase usually lasts five or six weeks. During this time, you and the group will perform the following tasks.

Group Rules

During the first meeting it is important for you to provide a safe structure by explaining the group rules. A good set of rules will ensure that:

- Members can say as much or as little as they want about their childhood abuse

- There will be opportunities for everyone to speak[4]

- No member will be hit or hurt in any way

- No one will be forced to do or say anything

- No threatening behavior or abusive language will be tolerated

- Members will keep what goes on in the group confidential

- The groups will begin on time and end on time

- Members will be expected to arrive promptly and to attend all meetings

- There is a clear understanding about collection of fees

- The limits of confidentiality are understood

Group Structure

The next step is to give members an idea of what will happen during group sessions. They were probably given this information during the screening interview, but this gives you a chance to reiterate the goals of the group and clarify any misunderstandings. If there are two therapists, they should make the introductory comments together, in order to convey a sense of joint responsibility. They might take turns saying something like this:

> **Dr.G.** *I'm Eliana, and this is my colleague, Enid. I've spoken to all of you before you came here tonight, and what I'm going to say will sound familiar. Enid and I would like to tell you a little about what we are planning for this group.*
>
> *First of all, groups are all different from each other. Each group develops a personality all its own. Once we know about this group, we'll be able to decide what to do that will best meed the needs of this group.*
>
> *This is a group for adults who were abused as children. We will be trying to understand how the abuse affected each of you, how it might be interfering with your life now, and how to help you to continue to grow and feel better about yourselves.*
>
> **Enid.** *At the beginning of this first group, we will go around the room and have each of you say what you're looking to get from being in this group, and what specific issues you want to work on.*
>
> *At the beginning of future groups, we will have a check-in time to see how everyone is doing, and if something special came up during the week that someone would like to discuss. We will either spend our time each week talking about one or two persons' problems, or else we will talk about a topic of mutual interest and concern. Next week we will get an easel in here so we can write down all the things that people might want to talk about during group.*
>
> **Dr.G.** *At the end of the group we're going to ask each of you to turn to the person on your right and say something positive to that person. We have found it very important to do this at the end of group since most of you benefit from hearing positive things.*
>
> *We sometimes give homework assignments for people to bring in the following week. No one gets grades; the assignments are set up to help you think and talk about issues that may be important for you.*
>
> *Everything that is said in group is confidential. There are only two exceptions, which I would like to mention now. We will need to take action, which may include talking to a professional outside of group, if we believe any of you are going to hurt yourselves or someone else. And we will take action if*

we suspect that the person who hurt you may now be hurting another child.

We have prepared a list of questions for you to take home and read. These questions are for you to start thinking over since these general topics and others will be discussed in group. (See Appendix)

I think that covers it. Any questions about anything Enid or I have said so far?

If anyone does ask questions, of course, you should answer them. It is my experience that there are few questions at this stage, since members are reluctant to be seen or heard too much. Once in a while, however, a client may become aggressive, hostile, and quite verbal about a specific issue. If you cannot address the client's underlying issues and regain control and focus of the group, it is best to tell that client the you or your cotherapist will speak with him or her individually later. As I have already explained, many adult survivors are hypervigilant to signs of anger. They may freeze, expecting a violent confrontation. It is important for you to demonstrate that you can protect them by defusing hostile conflict and responding to the underlying issues. It is also important to encourage adult survivors to respond verbally, rather than freeze, when they themselves are threatened.

More specific directives about the content and process of each session are provided later in this chapter.

Group Goals

The first question that you should ask each member is "What do you want to accomplish in group?" This is an opportunity to define goals and make contractual agreements with each client. You should help the clients to develop realistic, measurable goals. This process has the added advantage that it allows each new member to receive positive attention from the group. Defining goals for the whole group will take one or two sessions. The contracts are made among the member, the group, and the therapists. As goals are clarified, you can make statements that will encourage group cohesion. For example: "One of the things you would like the group to do is to check with you, Ann, when you become too quiet and isolated." This process will also remind group members of what they have in common.

It is useful to repeat this goal-setting and contractual procedure after five or six weeks, when the group is half over. With open-ended groups, goals can be reevaluated at the therapist's discretion.

The following clinical example illustrates the goal-setting procedure as I began one of my groups:

Group.

    Dr.G.   How about you, Lynn? Tell the group what brings you here at this time and what you would like to work on in the group.

    Lynn.   Well, basically I just would like to feel better about myself.

    Dr.G.   In what way?

    Lynn.   Well . . . I feel that I don't get out and meet people or make friends very well.

    Dr.G.   How do you explain that?

    Lynn.   I want to, but I don't know . . . something holds me back.

    Dr.G.   What do you think that might be?

    Lynn.   I think basically I don't think anyone is going to like me.

    Dr.G.   How come ?

    Lynn.   I don't know.

    Dr.G.   What won't they like?

    Lynn.   Well, I think I'm kind of dumb . . . and I can hardly talk to people.

    Dr.G.   What happens when you do?

    Lynn.   I get nervous. I say the wrong things.

    Dr.G.   What are the wrong things?

    Lynn.   You know . . . something dumb. I just don't feel like I have anything to say.

    Dr.G.   Well, it sounds like you do have things to say, but when you get around people, for some reason it's hard for you to talk. Does that sound right?

    Lynn.   Yeah, 'cause actually, I'm kind of opinionated.

    Dr.G.   What do you mean?

    Lynn.   I have lots of opinions about lots of things.

Dr.G. *So you really have a lot to say.*

Lynn. *That's right.*

Dr.G. *But you think if you say it, people will think you're dumb.*

Lynn. *That's right.*

Dr.G. *Is that a familiar feeling for you?*

Lynn. *What?*

Dr.G. *Feeling dumb. Like no one will want to hear what you have to say.*

Lynn. *I was told I was dumb all my life.*

Dr.G. *Who told you that?*

Lynn. *My parents . . . and my brothers.*

Dr.G. *Anyone else?*

Lynn. *Not really.*

Dr.G. *Any teachers tell you that?*

Lynn. *No. They just used to say I was too quiet.*

Dr.G. *What's it like for you to be quiet.*

Lynn. *Umm . . . (*Long pause*) I guess it's better than being told you're dumb.*

Dr.G. *So it's safe.*

Lynn. *Yeah.*

Dr.G. *Lynn, let me ask you one more thing. How else do you see yourself? Sounds like you worry about being dumb. Any other things you say to yourself about you?*

Lynn. *Well . . . just that I'm, you know, ugly and fat.*

Dr.G. *I see.*

Lynn. *Pretty stupid, huh?*

Dr.G. *No. It's not stupid. It's sad.*

Lynn. *I can't believe I can't get over this stuff. I haven't lived at home for ten years now.*

Dr.G. *So physically you've left your parents.*

Lynn. *Yeah, as soon as I could.*

Dr.G. *And emotionally, it sounds like you carry a little part of them with you.*

Lynn. *What do you mean?*

Dr.G. *Well—the little tapes that get played in your head, when you tell yourself you're dumb, ugly, fat—whose words are those?*

Lynn. *Mostly my Mom's.*

Dr.G.   *So you carry your Mom around with you.*

Lynn.   *Except they're actually much more positive about me now that I'm grown up.*

Dr.G.   *Yeah, but those words were very important back when they said them. Do you know why?*

Lynn.   *I don't know.*

Dr.G.   *Why would the things a parent says to a child be important to that child?*

Lynn.   *Because they're little. They don't know any better.*

Dr.G.   *Yeah, and kids get their sense of self from the important people in their lives, usually their parents or brothers and sisters and grandparents. They trust the adults who take care of them. They listen to them. Like you did.*

Lynn.   *It makes me mad to think they have this much importance now.*

Dr.G.   *You would like to be in charge of what you think of yourself.*

Lynn.   *Yeah, I really want to feel better about myself.*

Dr.G.   *Most people want that. You're not alone.*

Lynn.   *How do I do that?*

Dr.G.   *I think the first step is to figure out what you think of yourself now, and give yourself some credit for knowing. Also, start giving other people in your current life some credibility. So when they tell you you're pretty, smart, whatever, you can at least consider that they may be right.*

Lynn.   *Sounds hard.*

Dr.G.   *None of this is easy. We're talking seeing yourself differently than you have for thirty-six years. It took thirty-six years to get here. It will take a little while to change that perception.*

Lynn.   *If it's possible.*

Dr.G.   *I've seen it done. (*<u>Pause</u>*) So for you, Lynn you'd like to use the group to see if you can get some new information about yourself, how others see you, and start working on a new self-image.*

Lynn.   *Yeah.*

Dr.G.   *So by the end of the group, you'd like to have some other things to say to yourself besides "stupid, fat, or ugly," and you'd like to say more of what you think.*

Lynn.   *Yeah.*

Dr.G. *To do that, we'll also probably talk about when and how those tapes first got made.*

Lynn. *Uh-huh.*

Dr.G. *And it will be important for us to help you express your opinions in the group, even when you might feel afraid people will think you're dumb.*

Lynn. *Yeah.*

Dr.G. *And it sounds like it would be important for you to hear from others in the group how they see you as they get to know you better.*

Lynn. *Yeah.*

Dr.G. *OK, Lynn. Thanks for being so clear about what you want from the group. Let's move on . . . .*

The therapist can make mental notes of the key issues each member presents and the specific interactional patterns he or she employs.

Group Time

Be attentive to time restraints. It is very important in this initial phase that all group members feel that they receive equal time. Adult survivors are hypersensitive to rejection. Many of them employ a coping skill that consists of trying to become invisible when they are afraid of being ignored. Some members will get particularly quiet; their physical posture will collapse, as if the air were leaking out of a balloon; their breathing slows down, and their affect goes flat. These members can give the impression of being just fine, while experiencing an overwhelming internal despair. On the other hand, they may become totally deadened, in essence putting themselves outside the group. Cotherapists share the responsibility for observing and interrupting these responses. These members need to learn what triggers their need to become invisible, blocks their ability to express themselves, and to find other more effective ways to respond.

Group Cohesion

The first five or six sessions are, in a sense, experimental. During these sessions, the members develop a rapport. They begin to share their feelings with one another, testing the response to and outcome of, their risktaking. Some of them may seem to be taking fewer chances and joining in less than others, but they too will be reaping benefits by carefully monitoring the other members' interactions.

Anything that happens in the group offers an opportunity for discussion of relevant issues. These issues can be brought out in the open. Once explicit, they are discussed. For example, "I notice that a group of you sits over on this side of the room every week, and you seem to exchange a lot of glances and smiles during the session. What's that like for you?" Once these members have expressed their reactions, it is useful to ask the other members of the group to say how they feel. There will be many opportunities to talk about feelings of acceptability, comradery, unacceptability, rejection, and so forth.

As I said above, the group provides a familylike environment for its members. Some of their reactions within the group will mirror their reactions as children within the family. This will provide many chances to gain insight, as well as to experiment with new alternative behaviors.

Group Homework

During this initial phase, it is useful to give assignments that all group members will complete and share. For adult survivors, this is difficult, yet rewarding. Adult survivors have low self-esteem; they expect criticism; they feel devastated by criticism; they compare themselves to others and come out on the short end; they minimize their accomplishments; and they often have trouble completing tasks. In giving assignments, you address these issues.

Make your presentation of the task clear and brief to avoid increasing anxiety or causing confusion. Make sure that group members understand that they will not be evaluated, graded, accepted, or rejected as a result of what they do. If clients do not complete tasks they are asked to imagine that they did complete the task and presented it to the group. Then the client is asked how they imagined the group responded, and what the client's fears, hesitations, hopes were before and after presenting the completed task. I always give clients a second chance to complete the task prior to the following group.

Draw Yourself

Adult survivors both withdraw from and gravitate towards drawing. They can withdraw out of fear or shyness and yet they gravitate to the experience of play. Ask each member of the group to draw a picture of himself or herself. When everyone has done this, members take turns showing their drawings and introducing themselves. The person who made the drawing and the other members can make comments about it. For example: "You're frowning." "Your head is a lot bigger than your body." "You look very tense." and so forth. This allows each member to get feedback on the discrepancies between his or her own and the groups' views.

Strengths and Weaknesses

Members are asked to list their strong and weak points and discuss them. Notice how they do this. Strengths, being less familiar and less credible, will usually be described quietly, shyly, or nervously. Weaknesses, being more familiar and therefore more credible, will usually be described with conviction. Ask members each to select one strength that they feel fairly confident of possessing and state it slowly while making eye contact with their fellow members. The cotherapist might then record a group members' strengths and weaknesses on index cards.

Replacing Internalized Messages

Internalized messages are those that the client repeats to him or herself consistently. The positive internalized messages are those which encourage, support, or validate the client. The negative statements judge, criticize, or put down the client. The positive internalized messages are seen as affirmations of strengths; the negative internalized messages are seen as punitive and judgemental.

Once a client has internalized negative messages, these are very difficult to eliminate. They cannot simply be stopped. They must be replaced with positive messages. These positive messages will eventually become habitual and will encourage the client forward, rather than being a constant source of pessimism. Clients who begin to believe in the positive messages they give themselves may find their behavior affected by their enhanced self-image.

For example, Janice was a thirty-two year old single mother, who had been severely emotionally abused by two alcoholic parents. When she first came to therapy she was extremely depressed, feeling as if there was no reason to live. Her internalized messages were: "Nothing you do is good enough." "You'll never amount to anything." "No one could possibly be interested in you," and "Nothing ever works out for me."

She repeated these statements to herself so frequently that she was reinforcing her sense of doom and failure. One of the therapeutic responses was to help her challenge each of these statements, make a more realistic statement, and see what impact this would have on her intensely negative self-view. In fact, as we were able to ascertain, she had completed two years of college, therefore she was good enough to get the grades to be in school; she had been married and dated frequently, therefore men had been and were interested in her; and she had managed to hold a job for three years, raise a beautiful ten-year-old child, and find housing which was financially reasonable. Together, we put her negative messages on one piece of paper with black marker, crossed them off, and replaced these messages with positive ones underneath in yellow and orange marker. Doing this helped her some, and obviously there were many other issues to be addressed in this young woman's deprived childhood. Yet working on the replacement of negative statements with more realistic positive statements was a concrete strategy that she found helpful. She commented to me that when she would start getting down, she would take her list out and read it. As she started being less critical of herself, she seemed more motivated and once again registered in school.

Similarly, in group, each client has been asked to identify their strengths and weaknesses. They are now asked to pinpoint their internalized positive and negative messages. On individual pieces of paper their negative statements are written in black ink then scratched out, and the new positive statements are written underneath in brighter colors. Members may need the help of the group to formulate new positive statements. The group is asked to give feedback to each member regarding perceived strengths.

Childhood Pictures

Once trust has developed among group members, ask them to bring in photographs of themselves as children. Ask them to choose photos that move them or otherwise interest them. The process of seeking out these photos can be disconcerting to many clients. Some of them have avoided looking at childhood memorabilia for years. Others have never shown photos of themselves to people outside the family, or have never really acknowledged their own feelings about these early photos. And of course some have seldom or never been photographed at all, and must struggle with yet another manifestation of neglect.

With photographs in hand, ask members each to say a little about what they see in the picture, about themselves, or about what was going on when the picture was taken.

Journal

You should encourage group members to record in a journal anything they think about, remember, or experience during the group. This is useful not only because it gives them an opportunity to remember and bring up important issues, but also because it provides a structure for working outside the group.

Readings and Audiovisuals

Members can be asked to read some particular book or part of a book that is relevant to childhood abuse. Suggested books are listed in the bibliography. The book is then discussed in meetings. The group can also watch a videotape or film, and discuss their reactions to what they saw.

These activities promote group cohesion since it is a shared experience. Make sure the book is short, easy to read, and won't overwhelm the resistant client. My experience with both reviewing books or watching videotapes has been very positive. Group members have found these techniques powerful and moving.

Suggested Format

In this section, I shall suggest guidelines for a twelve-week support group for adult survivors. My intent here is to suggest the content and process of each individual session. Therefore, some of what I say in this section repeats what I said in the preceding section. This format is not rigid. Depending on the group, some tasks may take longer periods of time. As you read this, feel free to experiment with the ideas presented.

Sessions One and Two: Group Rules, Group Structure and Goals

You can assume that most of the people who are entering group are experiencing a great deal of free-floating anxiety, anticipation, and stress. Your first task is to put them at ease by providing a structure. Give everyone a name tag. Have them all write their names and put on their tags. Now make your opening statement and explain the group rules. Examples were given in the preceding section. To summarize, you should cover the following points.

Structure

The group will last twelve weeks. The group is structured so that group members can say as much or as little as they want to about their childhood abuse.

There will be a check-in time each week. This will usually be brief—no more than ten minutes per person. Each member will say how the previous week went, whether anything special has come up that needs attention, and whether he or she wants to discuss any of the specific issues that have come up before. At the end of the check-in time you and your coleader will decide whether a specific topic will be discussed for the first hour, or whether the time will be distributed among the group members. This decision will be based on the individual and collective needs of the group.

<u>Specific topics</u> will be discussed. Topics will be selected and listed in order of priority by group members. However, selected topics will take second place to individual issues.

There will be a <u>closure exercise</u> each week. In this exercise, each member will turn to another member and say something positive to him or her.

There may be <u>homework</u>. Give examples. Members may be asked to read something, write something or draw something. They may be asked to think about or try a new behavior.

The group is a <u>safe place</u>. Aggressive verbal confrontations, physical threats, and violence will not be tolerated.

It is important to state that the group is for <u>adults abused as children</u>. This gives members the message that the issue will not be skirted, and that they are permitted—indeed, encouraged—to break silence.

Many people come to group expecting to feel great immediately, or to have all their problems quickly solved. Tell group members that <u>people move at their own pace</u> for good reasons. Not only may they not feel great right away, but they may feel worse. Ask them to buy journals so that they can document their thoughts, feelings, and reactions from one session to the next.

<u>Group leaders are advised to be available</u> by phone between group sessions. Members should feel free to contact them if they wish to ask questions or need reassurance. Phone numbers for group leaders should be made available in writing. (Later in the group, members may want to make up a list of their own phone numbers so that they can be in contact with each other between sessions. They should not be required to do this, however, and it is useful to give them a chance to think of it for themselves. If they do not, you may want to bring the subject up for discussion at the third or fourth meeting.)

What is said in group is <u>confidential</u>, with two exceptions. These are, first, potential suicide or homicide, and second, current child abuse. It is critical to state that if you suspect that a child is currently at risk, you will report the matter to the authorities.

Adult survivors tend to compare themselves unfavorably with other adult survivors. That is, each person usually feels less abused, less justified in feeling abused, and less entitled to group time than anyone else. These comparisons can make people feel misunderstood or alone. <u>Everyone's abuse is important and</u>

<u>everyone</u> <u>deserves</u> <u>help</u>. Make sure that all group members understand this.

State your policy with respect to <u>fees</u>. I collect fees at the beginning of each session. Some group leaders prefer to collect at the beginning of each month, which reminds members of the ongoing nature of their commitment.

After you have discussed group structure and group rules, ask members to introduce themselves and briefly state their goals. "Let's go around the room and have everyone tell us their name and anything else they feel like saying about themselves. Then we would like people to say what brings them to the group and what they are hoping to accomplish." I find it useful to have one cotherapist take notes for each member (having first informed the group that this will be done).

Help each member to define his or her specific behavioral goals. It is not sufficient to say, "I want to feel better about myself." The member must propose specific ways of feeling better. You can help by asking, "When you leave the group, in order for you to look back and feel like you made the best possible use of the group, what changes would you have made?" You should keep each member's specific goals on file so they can be reviewed with each client. Often, group members are unable to gauge their own progress and do not acknowledge small steps they may have taken towards accomplishment of stated goals.

At the end of this first meeting, the group leaders demonstrate the closure exercise and every one has his or her turn giving someone else positive feedback. Members are told that returning to group the following week may be difficult and they should feel free to call group leaders to discuss hesitancies.

Sessions Two and Three: Prioritizing Goals

At the beginning of this session there is a check-in time. Ask each member to say what their previous week has been like, and in addition, ask them to say what things they said to themselves about attending their second group meeting. This will give them permission to discuss their hesitations, and so help to prevent them from feeling isolated.

Be sure each member stays to the allotted check-in time. Usually this early in the group most people still expect and need to have the leaders set the structure. By the fifth or sixth session, you can have one member time the other members during check-in. Meanwhile, the job of the time-keeper should be shared by both leaders. It is also best to rotate the job of primary therapist, so that both leaders share equally in this responsibility.

At this point, the discussion focuses on establishing group goals. The group is asked to begin suggesting topics for discussion in the group. I usually list a couple of topics to get the discussion going, drawing from the previous discussion of individual goals.

Certain common topics are discussed in most survivor groups. These include:

- Trust, or the lack of trust

- Fear, or the dangerous lack of appropriate fear

- Low self-esteem

- Poor self image

- Anger

- Depression

- Shyness

- Intimacy and Sexuality

Once the list is complete, ask the group to rate the topics on a scale of one to ten, with one being "fairly easy to think about or discuss" and ten being "extremely difficult to think about or discuss." (If the topic of child abuse is not on the list, be sure you add it.) The rating is done by consensus. If the group will not volunteer their opinions, ask them to vote. Most of the time they will reach a speedy consensus, which has the effect of drawing them closer. If the group cannot agree on one item, put it somewhere in the middle, say at four or five. If more than one topic receives the same rating, rank them by means of a random drawing.

When this rating process is complete, the group has charted its course. The topics rated one through five will be discussed during the first few weeks, and the topics rated six through ten will be discussed later.

Discussing the less threatening topics first gives the group a chance to feel safe before they are faced with more threatening topics. It is almost always beneficial to deal with self-esteem and self-image early on. A discussion of these topics helps people to get to know one another. It also encourages self-disclosure.

The task of setting goals and rating them should take no more than one hour. This leaves the remaining hour for issues that were raised during check-in time.

When specific topics are discussed, you can ask a number of questions to stimulate dialogue. For example, if the topic chosen is trust, you might ask:

> Whom did you trust as a child? Why did you trust that person? What qualities in you are brought out when you trust someone?
>
> How do you know you trust someone?
>
> What do you say to yourself about that person?
>
> How do you behave differently or the same with people you trust or don't trust?
>
> How do you know when other people trust you?
>
> What's your reaction to being trusted?
>
> How does not trusting someone affect you?
>
> Has anyone violated your trust?
>
> Who was that person? How did you react?

Ask one of these questions and get two or three members to respond. Then ask another question and get two or three other members to respond. Point out common responses that have been made by everyone. Point out similarities between responses made by two group members. List the range of reactions. Emphasize the benefits of trusting. Discuss specifically how people think or feel about trusting or being trusted. Talk about how distrust affects people and how it may become an obstacle to establishing or keeping relationships.

Depending on how verbose group members are or how strongly they feel about a topic, they may discuss a specific topic for one

or two sessions, or they may bring it up over and over throughout
the whole twelve weeks.

Sessions Four and Five: Self-Image

The topic of the fourth and fifth sessions might be self-image. As
I have just explained, it is wise to discuss this topic early on. Start
with a group exercise. Have each member draw his or her
self-portrait. You will find that adult survivors tend to hesitate
when a drawing task is introduced. They must be reassured that
they will not be judged on their artistic ability. To prevent anxiety
from escalating, pass out the paper and pencils quickly, and set
the tone by conveying your expectation that everyone will participate in the task. Allow enough time so that nobody has to rush.
If one or two members resist, help them with their concerns while
the rest of the group begins to draw. Have an alternative task
ready for members whose resistance makes participation too
painful, or help these members to generate their own task.

When everyone has finished, ask them all to look at their
self-portraits. Ask them to notice what their reactions are. Then
ask them, one at a time, to show their self-portraits to the group
and tell the group about their own reactions. For example,
someone might say, "I noticed that I didn't draw a mouth on
myself" or, "I had a hard time drawing hands."

Ask the other members of the group to comment on what they
notice about each person's drawing. If the group is unable to do
this, you and your cotherapist can role model appropriate comments. Groups vary a great deal in their ability to generate this
type of feedback.

Finally, ask the group members to take their drawings home,
and on the back to make a list of strengths and weaknesses—that
is, of things they think they do well and things they feel they could
do better. (Another way to structure this task is to have people
list things they like and dislike about themselves.) The following
week they will be asked to read these lists out loud, so tell them
to be sure to complete this homework and bring it back next week.

At this point the group can turn to discussion or individual
work. As always, the session ends with the closure exercise.

Sessions Five and Six

The fifth week's topic might be self-esteem. There is a difference between self-esteem and self-image. Self-image is how the individual sees him or herself. Self-esteem is how the person regards or values him or herself (usually based on the self-image).

Members have brought in last week's homework. (Members who failed to complete this homework should be asked to think about what prevented them from doing so and be prepared to talk about those reasons when it's their turn. Tell those members that their homework can be reviewed the following week.) Ask each group member to read to the group his or her list of strengths and weaknesses, making them into personal statements. For example, if someone has written down, "Good sense of humor" have them state, "I have a good sense of humor." Have them start by reading the list of weaknesses (which are usually easier to acknowledge) and finish by reading the list of strengths (which are usually difficult to say out loud or with conviction.)

As each person reads out his or her strengths, you or your cotherapist should take notes. Any statements about the adult survivor should be stated in the first person. For example, if the member says "People tell me I'm easy to get along with" the statement is recorded as "I am easy to get along with." Clients usually volunteer which statements are less credible in their own minds.

After each person has read his or her own lists, ask him or her to read the new list (which the therapist has made) of personalized, positive affirmations. This should be done aloud and with conviction. Give group members their new lists to take home. Tell them to post the list in a prominent but private place where they will see it every day. Ask them to read the list to themselves every night before they go to bed. Keep their list of weaknesses on file for future comparison. Clients are often surprised to see the changes they have made in their own self-perceptions. After this group exercise, the group can deepen the discussion of self-esteem, go on to another topic, or do individual work. The session ends with the usual ritual.

Sessions Seven and Eight

By now most of the people in the group are probably beginning to feel some kind of closeness to the other members. Capitalize on this fact by introducing the topic of intimacy. This is a good time to give members a chance to help structure the future of the group so that it meets or continues to meet their needs; and to give them a chance to voice their dissatisfactions.

After check-in, have people answer the following questions:

How is the group working for you so far?

How is the group not working for you so far?

What would you like to see remain the same? What would you like to change?

How close are you feeling to other group members? What is that like for you?

How distant are you feeling? What is that like?

If a group member selects another person in group as someone whom he or she feels close to, it is useful to emphasize the qualities in the second person that appeal to the first person. For example:

Meg.   *I really feel comfortable with Pat.*

Dr.G.   *What does Pat say or do that makes you feel that way?*

Meg.   *Pat always asks how I'm doing whenever she sees me, and always has a friendly smile. She seems sincere.*

Dr.G.   *So when Pat asks about you, and greets you warmly, you feel comfortable.*

Meg.   *Yeah*

Dr.G.   *That's really good to know about you. I'm glad that you are able to trust that someone could be interested in you and express warmth towards you.*

A potential problem would arise, of course, if one group member received no positive comments from the others. It would then be up to you to explore what it's like for that person not to have been mentioned and what it's like for the others when that happens. Then discuss how people take care of themselves when they feel hurt or ignored. In fact, however, this is not likely to happen. Group members tend to be protective and vigilant with each other, as we shall see in the next section.

Sessions Eight through Ten: Childhood Abuse

By this time it may be possible to discuss childhood abuse in an environment of trust and safety. There has probably been sufficient structure, support, and bonding so that group members feel less anxious and guarded than they did at first. There is no perfect time to introduce this subject, and some members may be more ready to discuss it than others. However, your goal from now on is to help them to break the silence.

Start by reviewing the rule <u>Say as much or as little as you want about childhood abuse.</u> Encourage everyone to say something or to think about what is preventing him or her from doing so. Make it clear that this part of the work may take some time. Explain that people will be helped to work at their own pace, and that while everyone will have a chance to speak, not everyone may want to participate immediately. Explain that those who do not want, or do not get a chance, to talk about their own abuse during each session should try to participate internally, as they listen. Encourage members to write in their journals anything that comes up during the sessions, so that they can think about it later at home. Members who are unable or unwilling to speak should be asked to think about what they fear, and what they wish would happen if they did speak.

Members have probably reviewed the questions that were given to them at the first session, so the following discussion questions will be familiar:

> Say something about your childhood. Specifically, how were you hurt or abused, and by whom?
>
> What was your reaction to the abuse?
>
> What did you say to yourself about what was going on?
>
> Did you tell anyone about the abuse?
>
> What did you tell them?

How did that person react?

How does it feel to talk about the abuse here and now?[5]

After each person speaks, ask the other members of the group to offer that person their reactions and support. They may react quite strongly to hearing about another member's abuse. This ability to empathize is usually well developed in adults abused as children. They are frequently better able to identify with another's pain than with their own. These clients need to be taught to apply the same empathy to themselves that they apply to others.

This particular group discussion is the one that most members anticipate and fear. Yet talking about abuse can be very beneficial. Years and years of hidden thoughts, secret feelings, and private interpretations are brought out into the daylight and examined. Therapists and group members will confront the client's erroneous beliefs—beliefs that were usually organized in childhood. The client's task is to expel old toxic thoughts and feelings by establishing new belief systems and new behaviors.[6]

It may take two or three sessions before each member has had a chance to speak and to listen to the responses of the other members. But in fact, the topic of childhood abuse, like the topics of self-image and self-esteem, is never really exhausted. It tends to be woven into the discussion of every other topic.

The following clinical example illustrates a group discussion of childhood abuse in one of my groups:

> Alice. (Sobbing) *He shouldn't have done that. I was so little. He was really wrong to do that.* (In a strong voice) *I hate him . . . . I hate him . . . . He shouldn't have . . . .*
>
> Dr.G. *No. He shouldn't have. He was wrong to do that to you. He was wrong to be sexual with you.*
>
> Alice. *I feel so . . . betrayed . . . so . . . pissed off . . . .*
>
> Dr.G. *You have a right to feel angry.*
>
> Alice. *I really do hate him.*
>
> Dr.G. *I can understand that. You were so little. He was very wrong to use you sexually. There was no way you could protect yourself at that age.*
>
> Barbara. *That's what keeps bothering me. I feel like I should have done something because I wasn't so little. I was a lot older . . . and I still didn't stop him.*

Dr.G. *So you were physically bigger?*

Barbara. *Yeah.*

Dr.G. *But you were still a child. What do you think you could have done?*

Alice. *I should have stopped him.*

Dr.G. *Is this a familiar statement to anyone else in here?* (They all raise their hands and mumble) *I'd like to hear your answers. What should you have done to stop the abuse?*

Alice. *Fought.*

Barbara. *Told someone.*

Meg. *I kept thinking about running away, but I never did.*

Diane. *Telling my mother.*

Ellie. *I even thought of telling a nice teacher I had at school ... but actually, once I did, and the teacher didn't do anything.*

Dr.G. *OK, so telling, fighting, running away. Anything else?*

Alice. *Kicked him in the balls.*

Group. (Laughter)

Dr.G. *OK. That's the idea of fighting back. Any other ways to stop a parent or an adult or older kid from being sexual with you, or beating you up, or ignoring you?* (Nobody says anything) *Think about a little kid now. And think of how small children look physically, compared to most adults. And now think that the person who is hurting the child is a parent. The child loves that person, trusts or used to trust that person, wants approval from that person, depends on that person— What can the child do?*

Alice. *I wish I could have kicked him. I wish I could kick him now.*

Dr.G. *Wanting to do something is different from doing it.*

Barbara. *What does that mean?*

Dr.G. *What it means is that Alice is angry. It's OK to be angry. It's not OK to hit others. So Alice has to find a way to express that anger in a way that doesn't hurt someone else.*

Alice. *That sounds unfair. I'm supposed to be rational. How come he wasn't rational?*

Dr.G. *I can't answer that. He had problems he couldn't handle in the right way. He ended up doing the wrong thing. My concern right now is for you. Many of you feel frustrated and angry, sad and depressed. When you look back at what happened and realize your pasts cannot be relived, you're still having strong feelings about what was done to you.*

Ellie. (<u>Sobbing quietly</u>)

Dr.G. *I think it's good to feel these feelings, and to realize that there wasn't anything you could have done then. There are lots of things you can do now to make yourselves feel better. Alice, you can't kick your dad, but it may help you to kick some pillows, or throw rocks into the ocean, or express your anger in words.*

Alice. *It takes so long . . . . It's so unfair . . . .*

Dr.G. *I know.* (<u>Pause</u>) *I want to check in with you Ellie and ask how you're doing. I notice you've been crying quietly for a while.*

Barbara. *Yeah, I've been hoping someone would notice.*

Dr.G. *It sounds like you've been noticing, Barbara.*

Barbara. *Yeah, I have.*

Dr.G. *How did it make you feel that Ellie was crying?*

Barbara. *It reminded me of myself when I was little. I used to cry for hours, without making a peep.*

Dr.G. *Do you know why you were so quiet?*

Barbara. *I was afraid if I was loud, no one would notice and then I'd feel really bad.*

Dr.G. *Ellie, does that sound familiar to you?*

Ellie. (<u>Sobbing and looking down</u>) *Maybe . . . I don't really know.*

Dr.G. *Can you say what's going on for you right now?*

Ellie. *I don't really think so . . . .*

Candy. *I'd like to know.*

Ellie. *I just don't think I can right now.*

Dr.G. *What would happen if you did talk right now?*

Ellie. *I think I couldn't stop crying.*

Dr.G. *So you're afraid you wouldn't be able to stop yourself?*

Ellie. *Yeah.*

Dr.G. *OK, I understand your fear. Has that ever happened to you before, that you haven't been able to stop crying?*

Ellie. *Yeah. And I get really bummed out for weeks. I can't do that now. I have to study for an exam.*

Barbara. *The exam can wait.*

> Dr.G. *Well, maybe it can't.*
>
> Ellie. *No, it can't. I've got to pass.*
>
> Dr.G. *Are you in therapy now, outside the group?*
>
> Ellie. *Yeah.*
>
> Dr.G. *Will you see your therapist before our next group meeting?*
>
> Ellie. *No. He's out of town.*
>
> Dr.G. *Would you be willing to come in and see either myself or Enid before the next group meeting?*
>
> Ellie. *I think so . . . .*
>
> Dr.G. *Maybe it would be easier for you to discuss whatever is troubling you on a one-to-one basis before you talk in the group.*
>
> Ellie. *That would be a lot easier. I think, anyway.*

I decided to offer this client a private session prior to the next group meeting because she was consistently reluctant to speak out in the group. Ellie would interact with the other members by eliciting caretaking on their part. However she would not risk talking about her abuse, and this caused a schism between herself and the other members. The contract was that the individual session would prepare Ellie to speak out in the group if possible.

The individual session was very effective. Ellie's secret was that she had been sexually abused by her mother, and she felt alienated from the other members, who had been abused either physically or sexually by their fathers. She also felt ashamed to admit that she had enjoyed oral sex, and found her past experience helpful in her current sexual functioning. She felt that both of these pieces of information would be unacceptable in the group. She was reassured by my reaction. I told her I had many clients whose abusers were women, and I also told her that some survivors viewed the sexual contact as non-traumatic and pleasurable. She decided that she would open up to the group and with my encouragement she did so. Had Ellie decided against bringing these issues up in group I would have explored that choice, and allowed her to make it. (I may have brought the issues up during general discussion, kept Ellie's experience confidential, and provided education if needed.) Forcing clients to say or do things in group reenacts the experience of abuse: someone in an authority position is forcing the client to do something he or she does not want to do.

When Ellie spoke out in group, members were quick to empathize and reflect on their own sexual ambivalence. A few members mentioned that they endured great shame because they could only become aroused when they had sexual fantasies of the abuse. (This issue comes up frequently and is a source of great pain to survivors.) In addition, two other women disclosed that they had also been abused by women, one by an aunt, and the other by a former therapist. These topics resulted in very important discussion for all members and Ellie was relieved to have shared her deep, dark secrets and find others in the group both compasionae and grateful for the chance to talk together about difficult topics.

The Last Two Sessions

The last two sessions are devoted to termination, review, and feedback.

Termination

Some group members will choose not to return for a second series. This is their choice, and they must be supported. At the same time they must be given honest and useful feedback. The feedback may include your own or the group's opinion that they would be wiser to stay on. The opportunity to agree to disagree promotes each client's autonomy and self-esteem. On occasion I strongly disagree with a client's decision to leave group and will meet with them individually to tell them why.

Other members may have chosen to contract for a second series, and yet may be upset because this first series is ending, because some members are leaving, or because new members will be coming in. This will provide an opportunity to discuss separation, loss, and endings of all kinds.

Here are some sample questions for discussion:

Was there ever an ending that hurt you or confused you? Talk about that time.

What's it like for you to say goodbye?

How do you usually say goodbye?

Was there ever an ending that you felt good about? Talk about that time.

How would you like others to say goodbye to you?

How would you like to say goodbye to others?

How do you deal with the sadness, anger, or fear that you may feel when you say goodbye?

Review

Give members a chance to review what they have achieved during this first series, and what they wish to work on during the next series. They may want to consider these questions both individually and as a group. Read the cards listing each member's individual goals and have everyone comment on the progress they observe, as well as areas for future work. This review process helps members see the steps they have taken, and the steps that are yet to be taken. Without reviewing progress, clients may feel discouraged or pessimistic about their own progress. If they feel optimistic it may encourage them to keep working.

Feedback

During the last session, have each person in turn stand in the center of the room. This visibility can be therapeutic in and of itself, although it is usually stressful. Have the other members of the group give the one who is "it" constructive criticism followed by positive feedback. Giving direct, nonpunitive, constructive criticism is a skill. You and your cotherapist should model this skill in this final session as you have done throughout.

Ask the person who is "it" to refrain from speaking. Often this person's instinct will be to minimize or contradict the positive feedback and to agree with (or become defensive about) the criticism. As much as possible, help him or her to experience the criticism as nonpunitive and nonabusive.

During the feedback, write down what is said to each person. Reword these comments as you did in the session on self-esteem. That is, if Elizabeth is told that she is cheerful, write, "I am cheerful." If she is told that she sometimes puts herself down, and the group encourages her to think about all her good qualities, write, "I sometimes put myself down. It is important that I remind myself of my good qualities." Give the list to Elizabeth, let her return to her seat, and last of all, have her read the list out loud. The list is a gift that each person takes home from the group.

Group leaders also receive feedback. Ask your clients to tell you what they found helpful or unhelpful, useful or not useful. Encourage them to make whatever comments they wish to you and your cotherapist. The same rules apply: the group leaders must not speak and must read their list when it is complete.

This session usually lasts longer than the regular sessions, so you should schedule accordingly.

The Next Series of Sessions

The next series of sessions resemble the first in that each member defines his or her specific goals and group priorities are set. By this time, members rely less on structure. They will probably welcome the opportunity to help determine how group time is spent. Suggestions from the previous series can be incorporated into this one if they are realistic and consistent with group goals.

Most groups last for three series. After that, the members may decide to become a long-term group, which will meet indefinitely on a weekly basis.

Problem Behaviors in Group

As group leader, you must be prepared to deal with certain problem behaviors. Here are some of the more important ones.

Resistance

Resistance is a form of self-protection, and group members have many reasons to want to protect themselves. They may be afraid of the group's negative reactions; they may not be certain that what they think they remember is really true. They may feel that other members' problems are more urgent than their own. They may find it difficult to tolerate attention and support.

Clients protect themselves in many ways. The classic resistances of adult survivors in group include arriving late, missing sessions, insisting that they don't understand what is wanted, and refusing or forgetting to do assignments.

It is your job as therapist to decrease these resistances. The one strategy that has limited results is to apply pressure. Instead, it is best to respond by asking questions:

> What was it like to think about doing the assignment?
>
> If you had done it, what do you think would have been the easiest or hardest part of it?
>
> You're having a difficult time responding to that question. What do you think the others will say or do if they hear your response?
>
> We notice that you arrive at least fifteen minutes after the group has begun. What's it like for you to do that? How do you imagine others react when you're late? What do you think you miss when you come in late?

I always express my hope that these clients will feel able or willing to follow through the next time, because I think it will be in their best interests to do so. If they do not follow through the next time, I discuss the issue of avoidance and offer them and opportunity to try again. Most of the time this approach is effective. Once it was not, and the solution worked out by two group members was to pick up the tardy member and drive her to group. The tardy member then experienced guilt and ambivalence about the special attention from others. She also had to tolerate the fact that everyone in the group really wanted her to be on time because they valued her and wanted her attention.

Sometimes the group participates in a collective resistance. Examples of this are mutual reinforcement for avoidance of hostility, fear, or other feelings; overadaptation to group leaders; and avoidance of specific topics or intense emotions. Clients may understand that resistance is often an unconscious reaction to making changes. Discussing their fears may motivate them to regulate its occurrence by trying out alternative responses.

Hostility

Restrict open hostility and threatening behavior. Freely expressed hostility on the part of one member can cause the other members to withdraw. Furthermore, you as group leader will lose the members' trust if they think that you cannot control the hostile member. Adult survivors need above all to feel safe. You must therefore be able to model protective responses.

On occasion, it may become necessary to ask the hostile member to leave the group. This causes turmoil and distress, as well as relief. Group members may react in a variety of ways. They may feel paradoxically both cared-for and undeserving. They may also fear that they too will be expelled. To reassure group members that they are safe, clearly describe the unacceptable behavior. You must emphasize established rules, and state your willingness to enforce those rules.

Monopolizing Group Time

Another problem is posed by the client who takes up a great deal of time and does not respond well to limits. Initially, this may be a relief to other, shyer or more reluctant members of the group but eventually, if one member is allowed to monopolize the time it will elicit underfunctioning (learned helplessness) on the part of others. Then they will feel resentful.

Members who monopolize group time do so for many reasons. They may have problems with boundaries and entitlement. That is, they may not know what is enough and what is too much; and they may have an exaggerated sense of what they are entitled to. In addition, they usually have underlying problems with control. It is helpful to ask these clients what would happen if they were not filling up the time. Some people who talk incessantly are avoiding facing their own feelings, or the discomfort of silence. Silence may precipitate intolerable anxiety in people who fear they are about to be put down, expelled, exposed, forced to do something, or abused in some way.

Other clients may have a manic quality that presents with self-absorption and physical and verbal agitation. Others again have clingy, needy behavior and appear to be starving for attention. These people soak up boundless interest as if inside them there were a bottomless pit.

Members who monopolize need to be contained. That is, they need to have limits set for them and enforced. These talkative clients may become annoyed or self-conscious about being reminded. They can be helped to tolerate these reactions by learning to observe and understand what happens when they pay insufficient attention to the rights and needs of others.

Avoiding The Spotlight

Conversely, some people are terrified of expressing their thoughts and feelings, which means asking for time for themselves. They are unaccustomed to being seen or heard. They find it painfully exacting to be the center of attention, and they make every effort to avoid the spotlight.

These people need a chance to develop a tolerance for attention. Once you have identified the problem, you can set a time limit giving this timorous member progressively longer periods of time in which to speak. These people need gentle encouragement to explore their own reactions to taking up other people's time.

Remaining Mute

No matter how much support and kindness is shown to some people, they may be unable to speak. At the same time, they may be making good use of the group experience, listening to everything that is being discussed and completing all the assignments.

Group members can be asked their reactions to having an elective mute in the group. In some cases, they may not mind; in other cases they may resent it. If the group can understand and tolerate a mute member, the member is welcome to remain. However, it is useful to have the group tell the person directly how they feel. The person's decision to remain mute is best addressed in individual therapy after the group discussion.

Eliciting Rejection

One group member may repeatedly elicit rejection from others. When this occurs, point out what is happening and, with the group's assistance, help the member to understand how he or she is asking to be rejected. Sometimes eliciting rejection is a defense mechanism. In this case, it may represent a deficit in interactional skills. People who fear and anticipate rejection sometimes try to make it happen in order to halt the anticipatory anxiety. Rather than waiting until the feared rejection occurs, these people take control by causing the rejection. Taking control diminishes anxiety in the short run, but by setting up the rejection, they confirm their own worst fears: they are unworthy, and others will always reject them.

As I've explained, a number of problem behaviors can surface during groups. Some of these problems can make group members feel threatened or intimidated. You must provide group safety by quickly responding to problem behaviors and enforcing established rules. All problem behaviors are best made explicit to group members to avoid confusion about what behavior is unacceptable. When you confront the problem behavior, do it directly. When you do this, you role model appropriate conflict resolution, and you become more trustworthy to individuals in the group.

16.

Family Work and Confrontation

Family work can be highly rewarding for the adult survivor. It can also be risky. Think carefully before you decide to engage the client in family work. Make sure that the client knows what the goals of this type of therapy will be and be sure you understand the client's motives in wanting to meet with family members.

Family work gives the client an opportunity to break silence in the context where silence was first elicited. It offers a chance to break family rules—who speaks for the family, which conflicts are exposed and which are hidden, who yields the most or least authority, who is allied to whom, and so forth. These family rules, and the self-concepts they encourage, may still be exerting control over the adult client. The rules may only become visible when the whole family is together and each member is acting out his or her assigned role. By this means, the family homeostasis is preserved. Contesting the rules, then, will almost always result in change.

The family may respond to the challenge by uniting against what they perceive as an intrusion. They may strongly resist your attempts and those of the client to challenge old patterns or put the family secrets into words. If the client can persist, however, the results may be highly beneficial. For example, another family member may be able to acknowledge that he or she too was abused. When this happens, the two siblings may establish, or reestablish, a close relationship. Another example is when the non-abusing parent is able and willing to validate the client's experience and describe the factors which contributed to failing to protect the client as a child. The client may benefit from the validation, and be able or willing to express the disappointment or anger at not being protected. Again, the end goal is for the client to feel empowered by self-disclosing within the family context, and deciding what type of relationships are now possible and desirable.

At the same time, the client must be strong and well grounded to undertake this work, since there is a real risk that the family will once again absorb all the players, and the client will be temporarily or permanently lost. Clients sometimes begin to doubt their own reality in the face of consistent denial from other family members. When this happens, they may regress to pre-therapy behavior, exhibit previous problematic behaviors, and even come to question the reality of their experience.

Assessing the Client's Readiness

Before you decide to engage the client in family work, you must evaluate his or her ego strength. Ego Strength may be defined as a coherent sense of self. Ego strength enables the individual to interact flexibly, rather than rigidly, with the environment. The lack of ego strength renders the individual vulnerable to deterioration in the face of stress. One of the essential principles of therapy with adult survivors is to help them to repair, stabilize, and strengthen their ego strength. Your client may have made great strides in this area. He or she may be enjoying a new self-confidence; may have formed safe and nurturing relationships; may have learned to be more expressive, seek out rewarding interactions, to take pleasure in his or her accomplishments; and in general, may have developed control over his or her own life.

But these changes may be fairly recent. Often these clients have not yet undergone any real test of their new-found confidence. They tend to have a sense of false strength, which is inherently delicate. Prior to facilitating family sessions in which confrontation is the goal, ask the client to do a trial run with someone else to see what reactions they have as they discuss abuse with others who may have clear questions, doubts or varying degrees of empathy. Make sure the client has a realistic view of what confrontation can bring, including the common experience of family denial or minimization. Help the client experiment with both feared and desired responses so no false expectations prevail. I take great care to prepare clients because desired outcomes are rare, and confrontations can be extremely painful. It is critical that the client confront for him or herself, not in the hopes of changing family members. The greatest benefits are derived from speaking and facing the truth. The following clinical example illustrates the process of preparing the client to confront, and demonstrates the potential benefits of confrontation. It is my belief that whether or not to confront is the client's decision alone, and should not be a forced choice. The client should always have the experience of making free and fully-informed choices. In addition, the client can choose face to face, or less direct modes of confrontation such as letter writting or role playnig

Clinical Example: Susan and Her Family

Susan was an adult survivor who had been physically and emotionally abused by her older brother for seven years. She had chosen to have no contact with him as an adult. At the same time, she felt that her unwillingness to face him gave him a certain power over her. Susan wanted to resolve her feelings towards her brother so that she wouldn't have to be afraid of bumping into him at family gatherings, or of being embarrassed when her children asked about the phantom uncle.

She was thirty-five when she entered therapy. She was in treatment for eight months, remembering the pain of her childhood and experiencing and expressing a range of feelings, not only about her brother but about her parents as well. She believed that her parents had sided with her brother and had failed to recognize that she was in serious danger at his hands. Remembering the childhood abuse triggered feelings not only about her family of origin, but also about her current family. Her two children fought constantly. She found herself being marginally emotionally abusive with her son, and highly protective of her daughter. She discovered that she had always had hostile feelings about her son, which she had felt guilty about and had successfully repressed. She did not understand why she had mistreated her son until she was able to see that her feelings about her abusive brother had been displaced to him, and her unresolved feelings about herself had been displaced to her daughter. As I explained to her, feelings experienced in childhood don't disappear; they just seek expression in some other way.

Susan came into a therapy session one day and proudly announced: "Facing those old rancid feelings has set me free." She had been able to hold her son that week and begin to make a new type of bond with him. This feeling of success made her want to confront her brother and her parents at last. I supported her; but at the same time I worried that this new-found confidence might prove brittle. I expressed my hesitation, supported her decision, and discussed timing and preparation.

First, I asked her if there was a friend she could talk with about her childhood—preferably someone with whom she had grown up, and with whom she could do an experimental test run. She said she had a high school friend whom she saw from time to time. This woman had visited her and her family as a teenager and certainly knew all the players. I suggested that she make a date and plan to allow some time in which to discuss her childhood with this woman. Susan agreed to see how she felt about discussing her brother's abuse with someone who knew her brother but who did not know what he had done. She planned to gauge her internal and external responses as the friend listened and gave her own reactions.

Susan came in the following week somewhat discouraged and teary. I asked for an accounting of the meeting. She said that she had been more nervous and anxious than she had expected. She had felt disloyal to her family because she was planning to talk about her past. She couldn't understand why she felt this way, but she immediately began to criticize herself for doing so. When she met with her friend, she had spent an hour and a half avoiding the subject. During this time, she had found herself repeating remonstrances that she thought she had long ago discarded. "Why can't you just do what you're supposed to?" "What is wrong with you?" "You're acting like a stupid girl." "She doesn't even want to hear what you have to say." "You're probably exaggerating the whole thing."

Susan was obviously disappointed in herself. I asked what she imagined my reaction might be. She was mildly irritated. "Oh, I know you're not going to say anything bad. You'll probably tell me I did the best I could. That's not the point. The point is I thought I was over this stuff."

This was a temporary setback, but it showed how easily the old familiar responses could be summoned up. It also showed that Susan was not yet ready to confront her parents and her brother. A confrontation at this point would only frighten and frustrate her more.

We did some more work on the deeper fears of rejection that Susan was harboring; on her inability to believe she was remembering the abuse accurately; and on the fact that she slipped into childlike responses when she was under stress. A month later, she tried again. This time she took specific precautions to reduce her stress. She did not drive anywhere. She did not set a date at a restaurant, where she would have to deal with many distractions. She asked her friend to come to her house; and she told her ahead of time that she wanted to talk to her about some important things that she had on her mind regarding her own childhood. The friend was well aware that Susan was in therapy and asked if this was something that she was working on. When Susan said that it was, the friend made a supportive comment.

This time, Susan began her story shortly after her friend arrived. It turned out that the friend had secretly dated Susan's brother, and she was quite shocked by Susan's revelations. Indeed, at one point she expressed incredulity, saying, "This is so hard to believe." Susan felt a surge of panic. She became withdrawn, and then hostile. The friend was sensitive enough to grasp the impact of what she had said. She told Susan, "When I said it was hard to believe, I didn't mean I didn't believe it happened. I just meant it's hard to believe it could have been happening without my knowing anything about it."

Apparently the friend was warm and receptive, but Susan was disheartened by her own reactions and by her emotional fatigue. She knew that she was not yet ready to confront her family, and we continued to work on this problem for the next few months. During this time Susan continued to make great strides in both her personal and professional goals. She had been unwilling to enter graduate school, afraid that it was too late for her to go to school, and that she would not be accepted in a graduate school. She was accepted, and had began courses. She progressed especially in her relationship with her son, which thrived and became redefined. She no longer projected onto him her feelings about her brother but was able to view him realistically. She was able to be physically affectionate with him, made eye contact and spent more time with him. She was excited about getting to know him.

I asked Susan to do various exercises that were designed to clarify what specifically she wanted to communicate to her brother and family. She wrote a letter (which she did not mail) to each member of her family. She did some introspective drawings. She threw darts at pictures of her brother, and had internal cathartic dialogues with all concerned.

In short, Susan was initially enthusiastic about a confrontation, but she was not quite prepared for one, because she was unaware of her own range of feelings. Practicing the disclosure with a friend allowed her to explore her reactions more deeply and deepen her understanding of the work to be done.

Susan eventually confronted her brother in a therapy session. She called him up and asked him to attend. Her brother wanted to bring his wife along for moral support and Susan agreed to this, seeing the wife as a potential advocate. Her brother had told her that his wife knew everything there was to know about their shared childhood, and Susan thought she would be sympathetic.

Here is a partial transcript of their therapy session:

<u>Family meeting</u>.

Dr.G. (<u>After checking in with each person to ascertain their reactions to being in the room together, and allowing them each a chance to express their nervousness</u>) *Susan, I'd like you to tell your brother why you've asked him to join us here today.*

Susan. *Well . . . it's a long story.* (<u>Smiling nervously</u>)

Dr.G. *Take your time, Susan.*

Susan. *It has to do with when we were kids.*

Richard. *I figured as much.*

Dr.G. *Richard, you had imagined this meeting might be about your childhood?*

Richard. *Yeah.*

Dr.G. *What about your childhood?*

Richard. *I was an asshole.*

Susan. *To put it mildly.*

Dr.G. *So, Richard, you're not so proud of some of the ways you behaved then.*

Richard. *No I'm not.*

Dr.G. *I'm glad to know that you're aware there was a problem in the way you treated Susan. Let's let her be more specific.*

Susan. *I asked you here today because I want to tell you what it was like for me.* (Crying a little)

Dr.G. (Hands tissues to Susan)

Susan. *Damn. I promised myself I wouldn't cry. I feel stupid when I cry.*

Dr.G. *Well, you're not stupid. It's perfectly normal to cry when you're upset. This is difficult for you to tell your brother about.*

Susan. (Looking at her brother) *I had forgotten what you looked like. You look so different than I remember.*

Richard. *Well, it's been fifteen years since we've really looked at each other.*

Susan. *I know . . .* (Crying)

Dr.G. *Susan, what's it like for you to look at your brother right now?*

Susan. (After a minute of silence) *. . . It's really weird. It's like he's somebody else.*

Dr.G. *It's hard to think of him as the same brother you remember—the one who hurt you.*

Susan. *Yeah.*

Dr.G. *Tell Richard some more about your memories.*

Susan. (Looking down at her lap) *I've remembered real well the times you beat me up.* (Pause)

Dr.G. *And how do the memories make you feel?*

Susan. *That's the stupid part. When I think about those times, I feel like it's happening right now. I feel scared, and I feel pain, and I feel a lot of hate. God, how I hated you.*

Dr.G. *So even now you feel afraid?*

Susan. *Oh, yeah.*

Dr.G. *What scares you right now?*

Susan. *I think he's gonna get mad at me.*

Dr.G. *And what would he say or do to let you know he's mad?*

Susan. *He'd probably leap off that chair and jump on top of me.*

Dr.G.   (Turning to Richard) *Can you understand how Susan might feel that way right now?*

Richard.   *Not really.* (Looking at Susan) *I was a kid then. I was all screwed up. I don't do that kind of stuff any more. You can ask Marion.* (Pointing to his wife)

Dr.G.   *You know, Richard, I want you to understand that when Susan talks about her fears, they seem very real to her at the moment. You know you've changed since when you were both kids. She doesn't know that yet. All she has are memories of the way you were.*

Richard.   *Yeah, but I just want her to know I'm not like that anymore.*

Dr.G.   *Maybe you can tell her directly.*

Richard.   (To Susan) *I'm not like that. I'm not going to hurt you. I don't know why I did it then. I was just screwed up.*

Susan.   *I don't care if you were screwed up or not. You screwed me up.*

Dr.G.   *Tell your brother how his hurting you affected you.*

Susan.   *It's not so simple to say this. But all my life I've felt stupid and afraid . . . .*(Sobbing quietly) *I didn't believe in myself . . . .I thought nobody cared about me.*

Richard.   *You know Mom and Dad always cared about you.*

Susan.   *It didn't seem that way . . . .*(Sob) *They used to take your side . . . they wouldn't punish you . . . they told me I must have been bothering you. They told me I was exaggerating . . . .*(Sob)

Richard.   *I didn't know that.*

Susan.   *You didn't want to know. You just didn't give a shit about anybody.*

Richard.   *I think you're right about that. But you were a pest too you know. You weren't some little angel.*

Susan.   (Sobbing . . .) *I know that. I wanted your attention.* (Sobbing) *At least I got you to notice me.*

Dr.G.   *So you wanted his attention. But you didn't want him to hurt you.*

Susan.   *No, I never wanted to get banged around.*

Richard.   *Why didn't you say so?*

Susan.   *What? You couldn't figure that out?*

Richard. *Well, you never cried or anything. You always acted so tough. Why didn't you just tell me?*

Susan. *Don't put this on me. I knew you would do that.*

Dr.G. *Richard, kids can't usually stop someone from hurting them. They don't usually think they have the power to do that.*

Richard. *Well, she just looked OK all the time . . .*

Dr.G. *Why do you think that might have been?*

Susan. (<u>Making a fist</u>) *I wasn't about to give you satisfaction. It was the only thing I could control. I wasn't gonna let you see me cry.*

Dr.G. *Susan, tell Richard what you felt inside–what you couldn't let him see.*

Susan. *I felt small and scared.* (<u>Sobbing</u>) *And I wanted you to like me so much.*

Richard. *I did like you.*

Susan. *I don't believe you.*

Richard. *I always liked you.*

Susan. *Why didn't you show me?*

Richard. *I couldn't. I was really screwed up inside.*

Dr.G. *Richard, you've said that about four times so far, that you were all screwed up inside. What does that mean?*

Richard. *I was having lots of problems. I can't talk about all that stuff now, but I was just angry inside.*

Dr.G. *Were you angry at Susan?*

Richard. *No, not really.*

Dr.G. *Can you tell her that?*

Richard. (<u>Looking at Susan</u>) *It wasn't you. I wasn't mad at you.*

Susan. (<u>Looking at Dr.G.</u>) *I just don't believe him.*

Dr.G. *You don't have to believe him. It's important for you to speak and listen. Your lack of trust isn't going to disappear immediately.*

Susan. *I spent years feeling small because of you.*

Richard. *I don't know what to say.*

Dr.G. *Richard, how do you feel about not having had contact with your sister all these years?*

Richard. *Bad. I feel really bad.*

Dr.G. *Did you know why she has refused to see you all these years?*

Richard. *I had a pretty good idea.*

Dr.G. *And what was that?*

Richard. *That she hated me for all those years.*

Dr.G. *And what is your reaction to that possibility?*

Richard. *I just wanna make it up to her somehow.*

Susan. *That's impossible.*

Richard. *Well, that's what I would want.*

Dr.G. *What kind of a relationship would you like with your sister?*

Richard. *I just want to be able to talk to her. I want to meet her kids, and have her meet mine. Marion and I would like to be a family with Susan and Steve and the kids.*

Dr.G. *Susan, what's it like for you to hear that?*

Susan. *I just don't know.*

Dr.G. *What don't you know?*

Susan. *If I want that.*

Dr.G. *What do you want?*

Susan. *I wanna feel better about me . . .* (Wiping her eyes) *. . . and I guess I don't want to hate him for the rest of my life.*

Dr.G. *I think that's a good goal. Hate can really wear you down.*

Susan. *Tell me about it.*

Dr.G. *So, Susan, it sounds like you're willing to work at getting rid of the hate for Richard.*

Susan. *Yeah . . . .*

Dr.G. *And Richard, it sounds like you're interested in trying to make some connection with your sister and her family.*

Richard. *Yeah . . . we both are* (Squeezing his wife's hand)

Dr.G. *Well, this is going to have to start with you and Susan. The others will follow.*

Richard. *I know.*

Susan, Richard, and I met for four additional sessions. Richard no longer felt that he needed to have Marion present, and Susan preferred the sessions with Richard alone. The last session included Susan, Richard, and both their spouses. There were very tense and angry moments and very tender moments. There were glimpses of reunification and glimpses of permanent alienation. Both Susan and Richard expressed very childlike thoughts about favoritism, rivalry, love, and hate.

Richard claimed that he had a "deep, dark secret," and that this was the reason why he had been so confused and angry. He was never able to talk about this secret, which made Susan furious. She threatened never to speak to him again unless he told her what it was. He could not, and she struggled with her feelings of helplessness. They called a truce, with Richard promising that he would tell her someday, and Susan saying that she would wait, but would continue to ask questions.

Through the therapy, then, they arrived at resolution. They may never be really close; Susan wasn't sure that she really liked him (my guess was that she needed to be punitive for a while), but they both wanted the children to meet one another. We discussed what the children would be told, and how their questions would be answered.

Susan terminated her therapy with me shortly after this. Once she had dealt with her brother directly, she decided that she did not want to confront her parents. She felt that it was not absolutely necessary to do so, and since they were both ill, she chose not to upset them. The decision to not confront directly, if freely made, can be just as empowering as the decision to confront. She wrote them some letters which she did not mail, and got most of her feelings expressed indirectly.

She called a year later to discuss a new pregnancy and her ambivalent feelings about becoming a mother again. She told me that she and her brother had reached an understanding although they were not close. The children were very close and she had developed a warm relationship with her sister-in-law, Marion. She hardly ever thought about the abuse anymore, and had grown to recognize her brother as an adult, not as the abusive adolescent she had remembered. Her children felt close and comfortable with him and his wife. She also told me that he never did tell her his secret, and she guessed he'd made it up to justify his behavior.

Expectations and Motives

Besides assessing your client's readiness, you must also evaluate his or her motives and expectations. Some clients choose to do family work for the wrong reasons. They want to retaliate, to hurt or harass the person who caused them pain. The problem with this vengeful response is that if it is the client's only reason for doing family work, it is likely to create a counterabusive situation, which will usually elicit defensive or angry responses from the family. Taking the aggressor role is also likely to damage the client's self-image. It is important for the client to know exactly what he or she needs from the family in order to feel resolved about the past. Once you both know what the client's goal is, you can work together to develop the means to achieve it.

There is a difference between wanting to hold the abuser accountable and responsible, and wanting to engage in harmful acts of revenge. I will not support or encourage plans for vengeance or retaliation because they can be dangerous to my client, and may inadvertently set the client up to be punished by society. When a client persists in wanting to take harmful revenge, I am direct about the negative consequences. In chapter 18 I discuss a client with clear homicidal intent. In that situation I was obliged to notify the intended victim and police that I believed my client intended to commit a crime. The client initially felt betrayed by my action, but eventually understood I had to protect her from committing a crime that would result in her incarceration. I always support the client's efforts to become empowered by holding the abuser responsible or accountable in well thought-out, rational ways. <u>The more responsible the client sees the abuser for the abuse, the less responsible the client sees him or herself for the abuse.</u>

The desire to retaliate against the abuser is a natural one. When the abuser is a member of the client's family, the desire to retaliate may coexist with an equally strong desire to be reconciled. In addition to anger, which may be an easier or safer emotion to express, the client may feel a longing for love and approval; and a deep sadness, disappointment and pain.

Many clients choose a different goal: they seek to cut themselves off completely from the abuser, from some of the family, or from all of the family. Some of these clients can explain exactly why they chose this goal. In that case, you can assist and support them in their decision. The client who chooses this goal may feel empowered and relieved and may also be surprised by a sense of loss. All reactions are discussed.

The decision to withdraw from, or be reconciled to, the family is a difficult one. It is best if you take a neutral role in this decision, helping your clients to clarify their feelings about both alternatives. It is useful to ask them to envision (and possibly to role-play) their best hopes and worst fears about each alternative. Clients who can accept either alternative are probably ready to decide how to proceed, and whether or not they want to do family work.

The purpose of this type of family therapy is to help the adult survivor break the family homeostasis by breaking silence. The family may react to the disclosure in a variety of ways. Its members may be cold, distant, and uncaring; or warm and supportive; or remorseful. The family may be very dysfunctional, or it may be fairly intact at this time. Disclosure may precipitate an enormous family crisis, or it may have no noticeable effect..

Probably the most common response to disclosure is denial, followed by accusations of mental illness or general wickedness. It is rare for the client's family—and particularly for the abuser—to say, "I'm really glad you brought this up. It's been a tremendous burden to me all my life, and now I know I can make it up to you and we can be a happy family again."

At the same time, I have had parents and siblings who acknowledge that they did abuse the client and ask for forgiveness, clearly feeling shame and guilt for the abuse. I have seen families become close as a result of disclosure, I have seen families cast the abuser out and some families decide on a permanent separation.

Probably the worst outcome is when the disclosure precipitates an illness, a heart attack, a stroke, a suicide, or a homicide. If this happens, the client will probably experience tremendous guilt, and I have always found it somewhat helpful to explore all of these possibilities prior to the confrontation. Once they have weighed the possible consequences, some clients choose to avoid a direct confrontation, and to work on resolution in other ways.

Any and all of these choices, as I mentioned before, are acceptable. The critical factor is that the client should feel free to choose; should feel in control; should feel no longer like a victim.

Goals of Family Work

I have already mentioned one of the most important goals of family work. That is, it gives clients a chance to identify and challenge family rules, and to disengage from their assigned family roles, particularly from the silent role of victim. This new freedom helps the client to control habitual responses, such as learned helplessness, or generalized fear and anger. Even if other family members remain untouched by the family sessions, the fact that the adult survivor did something unexpected, different, and purposeful, is likely to modify the sense of being a powerless victim as I have just explained.

Family work can also offer clients a chance to play an adult role within a family system that can evoke childlike emotions and responses. Many clients are able to express themselves, and make themselves heard, for the first time during family sessions. This can give them a new sense of equality. It is liberating for clients to escape the child role with abusive parents. At the same time, it is frightening, for now the transition to adulthood is made.

Establishing an adult identity within the family system enables the client to live in the present instead of the past. This is a vital task for the adult survivor, since the past cannot be relived, and he or she is no longer a victim. Many of the behaviors that were essential to survival in the past are dysfunctional in the present. New options are available and the client must learn to take advantage of them.

Not all changes are positive, and not all changes are permanent. Clients who sever family ties can experience deep loss; these clients must undergo a period of grieving. Clients who perceive that they have hurt the other members of their family may experience unbearable guilt or shame. Clients who have expressed anger or rage may view themselves as despicable and heartless. All of these new wounds take time to heal.

Sometimes the new wound does not heal. Some clients cannot tolerate the renewal, or the severing, of old ties. These clients may fall back into old patterns of behavior in order to maintain family harmony or to avoid stress. Some clients feel suicidal after a family confrontation. Other clients feel homicidal. It is crucial at this juncture for the therapist to do suicide and homicide assessments. In addition, some clients fear that the abuser, or some other member of the family, will retaliate. Sometimes these fears are realized. Be sure to discuss realistic measures that these clients can take to protect themselves.

On occasion, you yourself may become the target of family retaliation. Holding you responsible for the client's disclosure, the family may harass you, threaten you, or attempt to persuade you to adopt their point of view. State your professional opinion to the family once, and then consult an attorney if the harassment persists.

17.

Self-Help Groups

Thousands of self-help groups and networks, dealing with a broad range of problems, have sprung up across the United States, the most prominent and credible being Alcoholics Anonymous. Based on the premise that individuals can benefit from hearing about, and learning from, others' experiences, the self-help approach unites people who have the same problems, allowing them to seek solutions and establish supportive relationships. One of the unique aspects of these programs is the comradery they offer to those seeking help. These bonds are usually not available in traditional therapy, due to the inherent inequality of the therapist-client relationship.

The self-help concept has been successfully applied in the prevention and treatment of child abuse. Parents Anonymous (PA) was founded in California in 1970. There are approximately 1200 PA chapters across the United States, and this model has been widely recognized as one of the most effective responses to child abuse.

PA is a self-help group for physically abusive parents. It was developed by a formerly abusive parent and a social worker (Jolly K. and Leonard Lieber). They designed the group leadership to include an abusive parent (Chairperson) and a professional (Sponsor). PA has recently developed a new self help group for adult survivors of physical and emotional abuse. This group is called SPEAKS (Survivors of Physical and Emotional Abuse as Kids).

In 1975 Dr. Henry Giaretto established a Child Sexual Abuse Treatment Program (CSATP) for incest families which included a self-help component for parents and children. The self-help component, Parents United (PU), became an integral and autonomous element of the comprehensive child sexual abuse treatment program (Giaretto, 1982). The CSATP staff report that there are currently 135 active Parents United chapters in the United States and Canada. Child abuse professionals have recognized this model as viable and highly effective. Parents United chapters include self-help groups for the incest offender, for the nonoffending spouse, for children (Daughters and Sons United), and since 1975 for adults, Adults Molested as Children, or AMAC.

Parents Anonymous and Parents United are the two best-known self-help programs in the prevention and treatment of child abuse. Other, similar groups are being formed, including Sex and Love Addicts Anonymous and Adult Children of Alcoholics. Most notable is the rapid development of Incest Survivors Anonymous (ISA), based on the twelve-step program for alcohol recovery. Many survivors find these groups extremely helpful.

An Adjunct to Other Services

I believe that self-help programs can be a valuable adjunct to other therapeutic services. Certainly when the problem is child abuse the parties involved will probably need an array of services, including, but not limited to, self-help resources. Many clients will require, and nearly all could benefit from, more in-depth therapy. Depending on the circumstances, individual, marital, family, or group therapy may be required. The mental health practitioner is well advised to know what community resources exist, and to make good use of the self-help programs. However certain safeguards should be observed. I shall discuss the advantages and potential disadvantages of self-help groups presently.

Advantages of Self-Help Groups

Self-help groups offer numerous benefits to their members. The following discussion of benefits is not all inclusive, but does raise many of the known advantages of self-help programs.

Comradery

Members of a self-help group see themselves as being united by a common problem. They feel kinship with others who have had similar backgrounds and experiences. This breaks the stigma many survivors feel, and can offer a sense of being understood and supported.

Support

Members turn to each other for support. They are encouraged to phone each other; to lean on each other; and to spend time together discussing mutual concerns, getting through difficult times, or simply sharing activities. In other words, the boundaries of self-help groups are intended to be permeable.

Understanding

Members feel understood on a deep level by others who have experienced the same problem. They all feel able to put themselves in one another's shoes.

Recognition

Members are able to recognize one another's dysfunctional patterns and denial systems, since they frequently use the same defense mechanisms themselves.

Confrontation

Nonpunitive confrontation is more readily accepted from those who have had similar experiences and similar conflicts.

Availability

Both group members and sponsors are available day or night. Self-help chapters are available in most cities. Potential members can find the nearest one by consulting the telephone directory or by calling or writing the national office of the organization. Some self-help programs have weekly meetings, others have daily meetings with a drop-in policy. Alcoholics Anonymous group members for example, can attend a meeting any time of day or night.

The groups are free of charge. This makes the services available to everybody. It also increases the chances of continued involvement, since clients see the service, and the emotional support, as convenient and available to them. Some clients who pay for therapy services doubt the sincerity of the helper. This does not become an issue with free services. Although, conversely, some clients question the validity of anything that is received at no cost.

Consistency

Because there is an established model, which is duplicated in all the chapters, the procedures and structure are similar in most groups.

Normalization

Many clients who seek help with child abuse problems see themselves as freaks, whose experience will forever separate them from other people. This sense of peculiarity often generates a sense of alienation and an inability to seek help. Membership in the self-help group may help these survivors to create a bridge back to membership in the human race.

Extended Family

Perhaps the most compelling aspect of self-help groups is the potential for the development of surrogate family relationships. Parents United and the Santa Clara Child Sexual Abuse Treatment Program in California renamed their program the Institute for the Community as Extended Family to reflect this concept. Since these groups have permeable boundaries, as I have explained, they make it possible to create long-term relationships within the group. In this respect, they are very unlike the therapist-client relationship, which has distinct, impermeable boundaries.

Disadvantages of Self-Help Groups

Self-help chapters function autonomously. In my experience, they are not routinely monitored by the parent organization. The national organization typically provides training and technical assistance; however, the day-to-day operation, once begun, is left to the local chapter. The quality, therefore, varies from group to group. Never assume that everything that happens in group is beneficial. Consider the following factors when you refer to a self-help group.

Credibility

Make sure that you refer your clients to self-help groups that are credible and stable. If possible, talk with people who attend regularly, or who have referred their own clients to the group. Contact your local child abuse agencies and ask them to verify the group's reputation in the community. If professionals are involved (as, for example, the Sponsor in Parents Anonymous), make sure that they are licensed and experienced in the treatment of child abuse. The national organizations will provide information on local chapters, although from time to time the information may be dated.

Lack of Screening

In many self-help programs, clients are encouraged to drop in at their own convenience. Clients are not necessarily screened; announcements for these groups list the time and place and offer an invitation to attend. Thus the groups attract individuals with a wide range of problems, up to and including severe mental disorders. These people can seem alarming to other group members, and can also elicit and drain the group's concern. Since trained, licensed professionals do not necessarily participate (with the exception of PA groups), a group may be unable to cope with the demands and challenges of disturbed or excessively demanding or manipulative members.

Contamination

If emotionally unstable members begin to dominate the group, more reserved members may be overwhelmed by the things they hear. If these latter members cannot preserve their own integrity, the material may penetrate their personal boundaries and cause great distress. They may even confuse what happened to the unstable members with what happened to them.

Leadership Issues

Some self-help groups have literally collapsed because their leaders did not have the group's best interests at heart, rather they sought leadership to promote their own self-interests or because they prefer positions of power. It has been my experience that the leadership very frequently determines the success of a group.

My advice is to refer to self-help groups that compliment whatever therapy the client may be in. Be aware that groups do differ in quality. Good self-help programs offer countless benefits to members. Ask your clients about group activities and what type of discussions are undertaken in the group work. I frequently ask my clients about their groups so I can learn whether or not the goals of the group are congruent with those of therapy. On occasion, I have dropped in on self-help groups to see how they are run. Many of my clients attend Adult Children of Alcoholic groups. These are frequently very relevant and helpful to adult survivors of childhood abuse.

This critical review of self-help programs should not be interpreted as a broadbrush condemnation. I have worked in self-help programs and understand the advantages and disadvantages. The benefits usually outweigh the potential risks.

18.

Legal Considerations

Various legal issues may surface during the course of treatment. The most common of these issues are reporting suspected child abuse; filing civil and criminal suits; testifying on behalf of a client; giving expert testimony; self-protection; legal implications of the <u>Tarasoff</u> decision; and the issue of sex with a previous therapist.

Two admonitions when reading this section. First, the laws are in a constant state of flux, and what I write today may be obsolete tomorrow. It is always crucial to keep up-to-date on the laws affecting the mental health profession. You should review this subject on a yearly basis, since most legislation is signed into law for implementation the following year. Second, the interpretation of laws varies from state to state and it may become necessary to seek legal advice rather than assuming anything. Lastly, this chapter is limited to a discussion of the clinical approaches to legal issues.

Reporting Suspected Child Abuse

Every state has a law that obliges professionals from specific disciplines (physicians, therapists, educators) to report suspected or known child abuse to the police or child welfare. Some states impose this obligation on nonprofessionals as well.

In most states, child abuse is defined as <u>physical abuse</u>, <u>sexual abuse</u>, or <u>neglect</u>. To these, some states have added one or more of the following: <u>sexual exploitation</u>, (child prostitution and pornography), <u>cruel and inhuman punishment</u>, and <u>emotional or psychological abuse</u>.

All child abuse laws include both protection for reporters and sanctions for failing to report. Thus if you report child abuse as required or authorized by law, you usually cannot be sued for having done so. On the other hand, failure to report as required by law is considered a misdemeanor in most states. In some cases, failure to report can make the mandated reporter liable for damages incurred by the victim due to subsequent abuse. (Landeros vs Flood, 1976).

In California, many services for adult survivors have been introduced in recent years, and the problem of childhood abuse has been widely treated in the popular and educational media.[1] The resulting increase in public awareness has led more adult survivors to seek therapy, and mental health professionals seem more willing and able than they once were to assess for the presence of childhood abuse.

The Office of the Attorney General of the State of California recently reviewed the question of reporting suspected child abuse in cases where the victim is now an adult (Ziskind, 1986). This review resulted in an informal written opinion that reiterated what most professionals had inferred: the intent of the child abuse laws is to protect minors in need of current protection. The opinion further referred this matter for legislative amendment, declaring:

> Therefore, it appears that the express language of the statute is unclear and does not fully serve the intent of the statute. This ambiguity has caused a great deal of confusion and is more appropriately resolved by the legislature. Until it does, we believe the literal wording of the statute should prevail—there is no mandatory duty to report unless the victim, in the terms of section 11166(a), is still a child.

A task force was formed to review this and other matters pertaining to the California Child Abuse Reporting Law. However, the wording proposed to the task force was opposed by professional groups (primarily mental health groups), who believed that the new wording might inadvertently impose investigatory duties on reporters. As of this writing, no legislative amendment has been passed. At present, then, the informal written opinion quoted above provides the best available guideline for the reporting of child abuse. It would appear, therefore, that mandated reporters in California have a reporting responsibility to children in current need of protection because of known or suspected abuse. If an adult survivor, in the course of treatment, discloses information that suggests that a minor is in current danger, the reporting responsibility applies to the minor in question. The adult survivor's identity must be kept confidential, unless he or she is willing to discuss the previous abuse with the authorities. The following examples illustrate this point.

Marianne is now thirty-six years old. She was sexually abused by her father from the age of seven to the age of twelve. Her two sisters were also sexually abused. When Marianne was ten, she told her mother about the incest, but two more years went by before any change occurred. At that point, her parents separated, and Marianne and her mother moved to another area. All contact with the father ceased, and Marianne heard no more about him for over twenty years.

When she was in her twenties, Marianne sought counseling for a sexual dysfunction. Although she loved her boyfriend, she found sexual contact with him repugnant. She wanted to marry him, but she felt that she could not do so until she was able to respond to him sexually.

Marianne's therapist worked with her on the issue of her childhood abuse. Together they examined this issue at length, and Marianne also received sexual therapy. She subsequently married her boyfriend, formed a stable marital relationship, and had two children.

She sought consultation and treatment with me when she learned that her father had remarried and was living again with minor children in his household. Marianne was gravely concerned for the children's welfare, and she had sufficient insight to know that this concern was warranted given her own experiences. Marianne told me that she had both pitied and despised her mother for her inability to protect Marianne and her sisters. Now she herself was in a position to stop her father, if in fact he was abusing his stepchildren.

Marianne and I reviewed a number of options. Marianne thought that perhaps she could call her father and find out whether he was abusing the children simply by asking him. She quickly decided that this was unrealistic, since he had never even admitted to abusing her. She also considered talking to the children directly, but feared that since she did not know them—indeed they might be unaware of her existence—they would not talk to her. She considered talking to the new wife, but again feared that she would be treated like an unwelcome stranger. She had not been able to sleep or eat since she learned of the existence of these children. She felt compelled to take protective action. I gave her support and told her that she was right to be concerned, since it is generally believed that sex offenders tend towards chronic behavior unless there is an appropriate intervention. In other words, the problem doesn't just go away. At the same time, there was always the possibility that her father was no longer sexually abusive or that he had already received treatment. In any event, I told her, a trained professional must have the chance to investigate, to make sure that the children were not being abused.

I told her about the current laws and standard procedures. I told her that in some cases the authorities cannot proceed with protective or legal intervention, either because the children cannot make a definitive statement, or because there is insufficient evidence. I showed her a child abuse reporting form and told her I would help her to file a report. I recommended that she be the one to call the authorities, but I emphasized that I had a legal responsibility to do so when I had suspicion or knowledge; therefore, if she chose not to report, I would. She seemed prepared and willing to make the report herself.

When I asked Marianne if she knew her father's current address, she said that she knew only the county he lived in. I asked her to talk to the friend who had told her about her father's wedding, to see if she could get his address, and she agreed to do this.

She came back one week later, having obtained the information. She was tense and nervous, and we discussed all of her concerns. Uppermost was her fear of being mistaken. She was also afraid that she was right but that her father would deny it. In addition, she expressed an underlying fear of taking a stand against him, accompanied by a desire to try. She had always felt that her healing was incomplete, since she had never faced her father directly.

As a nonprofessional, she had the option of making an anonymous report. I told her that the authorities might be in a position to do more if they were aware of her father's past sexual abuse history. After much consideration, she decided that she could and would speak freely about her own abuse, to make it clear why she suspected that her father might now be abusing his stepchildren.

In my office she called Child Protective Services (CPS) and gave them the information necessary to file a child abuse report. She told CPS that she was consulting with me and gave them my name. She gave me permission to speak with them as needed. She continued in therapy on a weekly basis to process the action she had taken. She felt alternately powerful and guilty, relieved and burdened. She had taken an important step in her own recovery. The report would be therapeutically beneficial to her, no matter what the outcome of the investigation. Two months later, she got a call back from the authorities stating that their investigation was complete, and the matter had been turned over to the district attorney's office for prosecution. She was told that someone from the DA's office would contact her before long. The investigation had resulted in a disclosure from both children that they were having sexual contact with their stepfather. There were positive medical findings. In addition, the children's mother was an alcoholic, who seemed to be incapable of caring for them. The children had been placed in foster care.

Marianne felt a great deal of conflict on this last point. She wondered whether she had done the right thing. I reminded her that, while it is always difficult for children to be in foster care, it was important to remember the children were no longer being abused or neglected and they were living in a safe environment.

Dwight was another adult survivor who came to treatment with current relationship problems. He felt very hostile towards women and had abused them physically. At thirty-eight, he had been married three times, and his third wife had just moved out, unable to tolerate his violence any longer. He felt forlorn and lost. He claimed that he truly loved his estranged wife. As for her, she had said that he would have to get therapy before she would even discuss a reconciliation. However, she had not made any promises.

A thorough history revealed severe physical abuse on the part of Dwight's father, now dead. His mother had died in childbirth, and he had always felt responsible for her death. There was some indication that he had not arrived at that opinion on his own—some of his father's violence may have been inspired by the same belief. In addition, at the very vulnerable and impressionable age of twelve, he had had sexual intercourse with a sixteen-year-old baby-sitter. While he initially minimized this event and referred to it as "every kid's dream," it was clear that this forced sexual contact had elicited feelings of helplessness and humiliation. This, coupled with his father's violence and the absence of a nurturing female figure, had a powerful impact on Dwight.

In the course of therapy, Dwight disclosed that there had been many sexual incidents with the baby-sitter, and that several times she had manipulated him to ejaculation while three of her friends looked on. This and other specific instances of abuse, had caused him great shame and pain. Eventually he had convinced his father that he no longer needed a baby-sitter, and the following year he was left unattended.

As he spoke about this baby-sitter, he trembled. During one session he burst into a raging tirade. The baby-sitter was just like all women, "interested in just one thing." Men had gotten a "bad rap" for being perverted, but it was really women who had the "corner on that market." "Even Marge," he said, "is already in bed with someone else." (This was not the case, but it was definitely his worst fear about his estranged wife.)

While the clinical issues are transparent, the issue of reporting is not. The abuse that Dwight experienced at twelve at the hands of a girl of sixteen involved two minors. The sexual contact was initiated by someone in a position of authority over a child who felt he had to consent. Forced sexual contact is sexual abuse. But that child was now a man of thirty-eight. Obviously, he was no longer in need of protection. The question was, were other children at risk of abuse from the baby-sitter, now a woman in her forties? Sexual abuse can be chronic. The question is further clouded by two facts. First, the victim was a male, and the abuser was a female. Most of the time professionals have been skeptical about a man's victimization viewing a man as incapable of being sexually abused unless he is forcibly raped by another male (Porter 1986). Even in these instances, I have observed and heard reactions such as, "he must have been a little willing," "a real man can get away or fight off the aggressor." The skepticism is heightened if the abuser is a woman because women are not seen as aggressors and certainly men are seen as capable of defending against women. (These attitudes seem to be decreasing in the last few years as the public and professionals alike encounter more cases of boy victims and women offenders.) Second, the abuser was an adolescent at the time of the abuse. By now she might have outgrown her need to force sexual contact, as some adolescents are known to do.

I asked Dwight if he knew the baby-sitter's current whereabouts. He did not. He added that he didn't even remember her last name. The issue of reporting was now moot. If Dwight did know the woman's name, whereabouts, and the woman had access to potential child (current) victims I would have been legally mandated to report this situation as a suspected case of child abuse. It would be the investigator's job, not mine, to determine if in fact the woman is currently abusing any minor children. If Dwight's father had been alive, I would have asked Dwight whether he ever saw him, and whether his father still behaved violently towards children. If he did, and if there were children currently at risk of abuse, I would have been obligated to file a report. If no children were currently at risk, however, a report of the old abuse would have been irrelevant.

If you are uncertain whether to report abuse when working with adult survivors and you are licensed in California, I suggest that you review the California attorney general's informal opinion by Ziskind or telephone your own state attorney general's office. Local child abuse councils, state and national organizations, social welfare agencies, the police, probation and your local district attorney's offices can also give you current information on the reporting laws. Also, you can write the State Capitol and obtain a copy of the legislation regarding child abuse reporting in your state.

Filing Suits

Adult survivors can bring civil or criminal charges against their abusers. Civil suits are filed to obtain financial compensation for emotional damages incurred, and criminal suits are filed to prosecute the abuser for past crimes. In California, a few civil suits have been successful and some have not been. More and more adult survivors are seeking to hold the abuser accountable by asking for a specific sum of money. The question of statute of limitations in these cases is currently under appeal.

Both civil and criminal suits are difficult to win. Criminal suits can only be filed at all if the statute of limitations has not expired. For example, one of my clients had been molested by her father throughout her adolescence. Once she left home, entered therapy, and got support to consider prosecution, she pressed criminal charges. She was twenty-one when she did so, and the last time he had molested her she had been seventeen. But the crime had occurred within the statute of limitations (in California, six years), and thus the District Attorney was able to press criminal charges. Her father was convicted and served a prison term.

I always think long and hard before I encourage a client to pursue criminal prosecution, particularly because the fact that they have not taken action until this time, may be viewed with skepticism. Weigh the advantages carefully against the disadvantages. The process can be gruelling for the victim, and he or she should be aware that criminal cases are not easily won. Defense attorneys are likely to challenge the victim's credibility, and the client must be prepared to undergo a great deal of stress.

Conversely, a client who files a suit, whether it results in winning or losing the financial settlement sought, can find the experience liberating and healing. The clients find great comfort in the fact that they have broken secrecy, and been released from the burden of secrecy. They frequently find an enhanced sense of self-esteem from making an unequivocal statement that the abuse was not their fault or responsibility. This action can provide a tremendous sense of relief and clients can feel energized and motivated to put the past behind them and look ahead to their future. Perhaps the greatest reward is the opportunity to hold the abuser publicly accountable for a very private crime.

Testifying on Behalf of Your Client

If your client does ask the District Attorney to prosecute you will probably be asked to provide your professional opinion regarding his or her current psychological state, and the impact of past abuse on current functioning.

When testifying, state your clinical findings clearly and objectively. The defense attorneys will probably suggest that the client's current psychological problems could have been caused by something other than childhood abuse. For example, suppose that you state, "This client has great difficulty in her relationships with men. She is unable to make appropriate choices, and she is unable to say no." The defense attorney will probably counter by asking, "Isn't it possible for someone to develop problems in their relationships with men without having been abused?" Obviously, the answer is yes. You must clearly state that it is your professional opinion that the current problems are associated with the childhood abuse. You might say, "It is my opinion that this client exhibits this behavior as a result of having been exposed to child sexual abuse." If you are asked to verify the identity of the abuser, you must defer this matter to a court of law. For example, you might state, "I am not able to determine the guilt or innocence of anyone. That is not my job; it is the job of a jury and a judge. The client has stated that the abuser was her father."

Giving expert Testimony

You may also be asked to give expert testimony on a specific subject. The legal definition of <u>expert</u> varies, but generally the individual must provide evidence of substantial training, experience, or knowledge that exceeds general knowledge in a specific field. To qualify as an expert in child abuse (or in the subcategories of sexual abuse, neglect, emotional abuse, and so forth), you must be able to verify that you have received substantial training, have worked for a specific number of years that demonstrates significant experience, and possibly have published in the field. Note that expert in one category of child abuse is not necessarily considered an expert in another category. Thus, for example, you may be qualified as an expert in physical abuse, and disqualified as an expert in child sexual abuse. The exact number of years experience and training required to satisfy a court regarding an expert witness status changes from court to court. You will be expected to be familiar with, and able to explain and discuss, the current research in your field.

Expert testimony is generally solicited on specific questions such as delayed disclosure. You may be asked to render an expert opinion about why victims of child sexual abuse are unable to recall childhood abuse and may remember suddenly, even years after the abuse occurred. Your testimony is based on clinical experience and empirical data. Your job is to educate the jury regarding a specific topic.

Protecting Yourself

Working in the field of child abuse can be risky. You will often incur the hostility of disappointed or angry clients. To take just one example, you may be required to testify on behalf of a child, against an abusive parent. You may have been asked to evaluate the case for foster care placement, or to state whether you believe that the abuser would benefit from treatment. If the Court finds in favor of the child following your specific recommendations, parents may see you as responsible for taking their child away from them. If the parents are volatile, impulsive, substance or drug abusers, or emotionally unstable, they may attempt to harass you, intimidate you, or hurt you. A restraining order may be necessary, or other safeguards such as not working in your office alone, asking security for an escort to your car or any other self protective measures.

The Tarasoff Decision

The Tarasoff decision of 1976, requires mental health professionals to inform the police and the intended victim if an evaluation reveals that a client is in imminent danger of causing bodily harm to a specific, identifiable individual. In working with adult survivors, I have twice been obliged to make a Tarasoff notification. In both cases, the issue arose during the middle phase of treatment, when the client had overcome the need to deny the abuse or to protect the abuser, and the client developed feelings of hostility and rage. In these cases, the rage occurred as a reaction to facing past or current helplessness, and while it is a healthy and necessary reaction, it is also potentially dangerous. The therapist must teach the client harmless methods of expressing anger, do a homicide assessment, and discuss things the client can do to feel more powerful now.

Both clients who obliged me to make a Tarasoff notification had become overwhelmed by their anger, obsessed with lethal thoughts and plans, and remained unresponsive to directives about safe expression of anger.

In one of these cases, I was convinced that the client was in imminent danger of committing murder. She had a gun in her possession, and had taken lessons on the firing range. She had gone out hunting and had become an excellent shot. She had begun to rehearse where and when she would stalk and shoot her intended victim. She seemed unconcerned with the consequences, and it was clear that her judgment was severely impaired. I had no choice but to make a Tarasoff notification to the intended victim and to the police.

The client temporarily transferred her rage to me for betraying her. Eventually I was able to assure her that I had taken this action at least partly to protect her. "The last thing I want is for you to commit a crime and be sent to jail for the rest of your life. It seems to me," I told her, "that you've just begun to take charge of your own life. You have a lot of positive goals you want to accomplish. I want you to have a chance to do that."

She dropped out of treatment for one month. Then she returned, and we repaired what she still considered to have been a breach of trust. It was a year before she was able to tell me that she had come to understand and appreciate why I had done what I did.

Sex with a Previous Therapist

There is a growing literature that describes the incidence and dynamics of sex between clients and therapists. (Milgrom and Schoener 1987; Schoener and Gonsiorek 1984; Pope 1986; Gartrell 1986; Burgess and Hartman 1986.) It was certainly alarming for me to encounter clients who had experienced sexual abuse by previous therapists (see chapter 3). This is a subject that will probably always remain difficult to address. Clients (like most victims) are reticent to report sexual exploitation by therapists, and the therapists who commit these crimes will certainly not incriminate themselves. I find it shocking and frustrating that there are so few mechanisms to protect clients from this form of abuse.

The first few times one of my clients reported sex with a previous therapist, I attempted to report the therapist in question to the regulatory board that oversees the licensing of mental health professionals. I was advised by the board's representative that in California I had "neither a legal nor an ethical responsibility" to do so. Indeed, I was advised not to file a complaint, on the grounds that I would be breaching my client's confidentiality.

I was told to discuss the matter with my client, advising her of her rights to file a complaint or file criminal charges. The clients in question were not able to pursue legal action. I have had very few clients who have been able to file complaints. Most adult survivors lack self-esteem, and have a limited sense of entitlement. They have a history of victimization and learned helplessness, and are likely to tolerate what they perceive as familiar or deserved behavior.2

In 1987, California attempted to pass a law that would impose a reporting responsibility on mental health professionals who learn of a colleague's sexual misconduct, but this legislation was defeated. The compromise bill requires mental health professionals to make written information available to all clients who disclose sex with therapists, notifying them of their rights and options. My personal opinion, for the reasons that I have just stated, is that this will have little or no effect. I am more encouraged by another California reporting law, which mandates or allows—depending on the type of abuse—the reporting of "elder abuse and abuse of the developmentally disabled." This legislation (Papan AB238) has the intent of protecting "individuals whose physical and mental limitations restrict their ability to protect their rights." One potential interpretation of this language encompasses adult survivors, who, due to the nature of their prior victimization have a resultant "mental limitation" that "restricts their ability to protect their rights." To my knowledge this application has not yet been tested.

A word of advice for all therapists who have a primary practice with abuse clients, whether they be victims, offenders, or families: Secure an attorney who is familiar with the rules of confidentiality and the other laws governing the practice of mental health. Consult with your colleagues and if possible, join a professional association, which usually provides the services of an attorney who is available for consultation. Attend seminars on forensic issues and read as much as you can about the legal issues faced by clinicians. Certainly, if you regularly working with child abuse cases, all these actions will be critical to your work.

19.

The Therapist Survivor

Survivors can be drawn to the helping professions. Informal surveys of therapists, nurses, and physicians indicate that many of them have a history of childhood abuse. I myself have met many mental health professionals who were abused as children. For some of these survivors, seeking out a career as a helping professional is a type of displacement. The survivor gives to another as a symbolic representation of the self. Within that displacement, the client's catharsis is the therapist's catharsis. Both therapists who are and are not survivors question, however, whether survivors should do treatment with other survivors.

There are some advantages to being a therapist-survivor. Therapists abused as children may have a greater ability to empathize; they may have a deeper understanding of abuse because they have experienced it. For the same reason, they may tend to believe their clients' descriptions of the abuse, unlike some other therapists, who have told me how incredible some of these reports seem. They are also familiar with the difficulties that survivors face, having experienced these difficulties themselves and (one hopes) having worked them through.

There are also some disadvantages to being a therapist-survivor. Often these therapists have very strong opinions about every aspect of child abuse. They may, for example, believe that abusers must be confronted; that men are inherently violent; that you can-or cannot-completely overcome the effects of abuse; that the system works-or does not work-on behalf of victims; that therapy (or some specific form of therapy) is-or is not-effective. The danger lies in imposing these views on clients, who must work at their own pace, and on their own issues. Although therapist-survivors have a great deal to offer, they must be cautious and deliberate if they are to avoid the many pitfalls that lie hidden in their paths.

There is also the issue of self-disclosure for the therapist-survivor. This is a momentous clinical decision. Clients may yearn to know whether the therapist was abused, and the therapist may want to be honest and tell them. Disclosure can also offer an opportunity for the therapist to increase his or her credibility with a client. One thing is certain. The therapist's disclosure will alter the therapeutic relationship. In my opinion, most clients are best served by allowing transference to occur against a blank slate. In this way, the focus remains on the client, not on the therapist. I feel this way now because many clients have told me about working with other therapists who confided personal information regarding their own childhood abuse. This changed the client's view of the therapist, usually for the worse. Some clients want to know all the details about the abuse in particular and the therapist's life in general. Other clients become cautious and self-protective in their dealings with the therapist. Some clients lose respect for the therapist altogether; others feel less healthy when they make the inevitable comparisons to the therapist.

On the other hand, some clients have told me they responded positively to learning of their therapist's abuse. These survivors say they feel better understood, validated and respected by the therapists. They claim this knowledge makes them feel safer and it is therefore easier to talk about the abuse. Obviously, therapists who were not abused can also create this desired therapeutic climate.

I encourage all therapists who are also survivors to weigh the potential benefits or hazards of discussing their own abuse, taking into account the client's transference, possible impact of the information, and timing of the disclosure. As mentioned earlier, I have found that the hazards of therapist disclosure are significant, and I therefore recommend against it as a general rule. Other therapists strongly disagree with me, stating that secrecy or dishonesty with adult survivors is a violation. This view has its own merit.

When clients ask me specifically whether I was abused as a child, I ask them, "What would it mean to you if I was?" and "What would it mean to you if I was not?" Their ambivalence, fears, and concerns about knowing provide me with valuable insights into these client's own experiences and problems. This approach also keeps the therapy focused on the client's needs. One of the basic dynamics of abusive relationships is the primacy of the abuser's needs. It will be important to demonstrate that the client is the priority in as many ways as possible.

There are reputable mental health professionals who have chosen to make public their identity as adult survivors. This is valuable to many clients who may use the information in deciding whether or not to work with that therapist. In my mind, this is very different from disclosing the information only sometime after therapy has begun.

AFTERWORD

This book is born of knowledge, instinct, and tried-and-true experience.

Although we currently understand some of the long-term consequences of abuse based on research and clinical practice, each client is unique, and great care must be taken to provide each client with what best suits him or her.

Therapy is dynamic. Parts of this book will gradually become outdated as the innovative research that is now underway provides us with new information, and as more and more adult survivors speak out about their own childhood abuse. I offer this book as a set of therapeutic guidelines. I encourage you to use it creatively, constructively, and above all, in a way that respects your clients. There is nothing final in what I have said. I offer it in a spirit of humility. I have learned a tremendous amount from my clients. To watch them grow and develop is very rewarding.

I thank my clients for their trust and their willingness to persevere, even when fear seems overwhelming and conflict is intense.

Finally, I urge you, the helping professional, to take care of your own personal needs and replenish your own emotional resources through friendships, loving relationships, and pleasurable activities. This will allow you to be more available and useful to your clients.

APPENDIX

GROUP THEMES

These themes are not all-inclusive, but serve as helpful guides for the issues that might be discussed in groups for adults abused as children. Please review these questions and think about your responses.

<u>SELF IMAGE</u>

How do you describe yourself?
What are your strengths/weaknesses?
What are phrases that you repeat over and over to yourself?
How do other people see you?
How do your parents/siblings describe you?

<u>SELF ESTEEM</u>

What do you like about yourself?
What do you do well?
What are your best qualities?

<u>TRUST</u>

Who do you trust in your life? Why?
When you begin to trust, what's your reflex reaction?
Are you trustworthy?

<u>ANGER</u>

What role has anger played in your life?
Are you a "walking time bomb" ready to jump on everyone with anger?
Do you "swallow" your anger?
Do you let anger build up over time, until you explode?

Does your anger scare you?
Can you be in control of your anger?
What happens when others get angry at you?

RELATIONSHIPS

Do you have a long list of unhappy relationships?
Do you seem to go so far, then pull away from a deep relationship?
Do you find yourself pursuing only to be rejected by others?
Do other become the focus of your whole life?
Do you find yourself in relationships you know are bad for
 you but can't seem to terminate?

PERSONAL SAFETY
Do you feel unsafe in the world?
Do you expect others will attack you?

ILLNESS

Do you get sick a lot?
When you are sick, do others care for you?
Is it OK to ask for help when you're sick?

TOUCHING

Do you flinch when touched?
Do you long to be touched?
Do you cry when you see others touching?

PARENTS/SIBLINGS

What do you need from your parents now?
Is there something left unsaid? What?
What kind of a relationship do you want now?
What about brothers and sisters - anyone you want to
make contact with?
Is there someone you've avoided or longed for?

ABOUT THE ABUSE

How does the abuse affect your life now?
How did you explain the abuse to yourself as a child?
How do you explain it to yourself now?
How did you cope with the abuse as child?
(What "got you through?")
How do you cope with feeling abused now?
Do you find yourself behaving in the victim, perpetrator or rescuer roles?
What are the benefits of staying the same?
How does being afraid, angry, etc., keep you "stuck" in the past?
How powerful do you think you are?
How do you feel about how powerful you are?
Where do you get warmth in your life?

RESOURCES

Who can you talk to about yourself in an open, free way?
Who can you call on when you're in need?
Who can you share your successes with?

NOTES

Chapter 5.

1. I have spoken informally with directors or personnel at about twenty-five California eating disorders programs. They consistently report that eighty to ninety percent of their clients have a history of childhood abuse. Professionals with expertise in the eating disorders have expressed an interest in doing research regarding this correlation. The research would probably have implications for treatment of survivors who have eating disorders.

2. I have always advocated encouraging consenting adults to choose their own sexual practices freely. However, when the adult has been abused as a child, I find it counterproductive to allow sadomasochistic practices to continue without intervention. The intervention I have found most useful is to assign nonviolent, nondegrading sexual activities. This is more effective, especially initially, than banning the sadomasochistic practices outright which might elicit resistance or defiance.

3. In the last three years, I have become better trained in diagnosing multiple personality disorder and its correlation to early, severe childhood abuse. I recommend that all survivors who present with early, severe, bizarre, ritualistic, and chronic abuse be thoroughly evaluated for MPD, because in these cases MPD has been shown to be a likely diagnosis. A speedy and accurate diagnosis will help the clinician respond to the client's needs.

Chapter 9.

1. Among the most remarkable and disturbing cases I have encountered are those involving human sacrifice and human and animal decapitation or dismemberment in front of children. It is important to note that while some of these practices reportedly occur within satanic cults, there are some satanic cults which do not engage in child abuse or human sacrifices. Other bizarre abuses include depriving children of

sleep, food, and shelter or forcing them to endure physical confinement, or torture, in order to gain control of children and program their responses. The literature on these types of abuse and abusers is beginning to surface (Peck 1983; Hollingsworth 1986).

Chapter 15.

1. Parents Anonymous of California has recently formed groups called SPEAKS (Survivors of Physical and Emotional Abuse as Kids).

2. PLEA (Prevention, Leadership, Education and Assistance) is a non-profit organiation of concerned professionals and nonprofessionals interested in the problem of male sexual, physical and emotional abuse and neglect. PLEA exclusively serves non-offending male survivors.

3. One salient issue in these groups is the members' tendency to engage in splitting. That is, they will usually assign the role of the good (rewarding) parent to one therapist, and the role of the bad (withholding) parent to the other. Splitting will usually occur without any effort on the leaders' part to elicit the reaction. It provides a precious opportunity to work with this basic disparity in perception and response.

4. Adults abused as children suffer from low self-esteem and little sense of entitlement. Often they cannot ask for time, yet they will resent you if you do not make time for them. You must maintain a delicate balance, neither overfunctioning for, nor ignoring, the client.

5. It is critical to review the client's reactions to disclosing childhood abuse. It has been my experience that may children are threatened with harm to themselves or others if they tell. These threats, because they are made to vulnerable children, carry tremendous weight. One client who finally disclosed her abuse believed she was in imminent danger even though the abuser had been dead for several years.

6. I have frequently used the words toxic and cancerous to refer to the negative, critical, abusive thoughts that have grown and fester inside the client's mind. Clients find these graphic descriptions helpful in their recognition that these thoughts, if left uninterrupted, will spread and grow.

Chapter 18.

1. When I refer to services for adult survivors, I am talking about those programs which focus on survivors per se, rather than providing

services to survivors who come to treatment with other presenting problems.

2. It is my experience that people who were abused as children expect and tolerate abuse longer than people who are not accustomed to abusive behavior.

REFERENCES

American Psychiatric Association. (1987). <u>Diagnostic and statistical manual of mental disorders</u> (3rd ed. rev.). Washington, D.C.: Author.

Ayalon, O. (1983). Coping with terrorism. In D. Meichenbaum & M. Jaremko (Eds.), <u>Stress reduction and prevention</u>. New York: Plenum Press.

Bagley, C., & Ramsey, R. (1985, February). <u>Disrupted childhood and vulnerability to sexual assault: Long term sequels with implications for counseling</u>. Paper presented at the Conference on Counseling the Sexual Abuse Survivor, Winnepeg, Canada.

Black, D. (1982). Children and disaster. <u>British Medical Journal</u>, <u>285</u>, 989-990.

Black, J., & Keane, T. (1982). Implosive therapy in the treatment of combat related fears in a World War II veteran. <u>Journal of Behavioral Therapy and Experimental Psychiatry</u>, <u>13</u>(2), 163-165.

Blake-White, J., & Kline, C. M. (1984, September). Treating the dissociative process in adult victims of childhood incest. <u>Social Casework: The Journal of Contemporary Social Work</u>, pp. 394-402.

Bliss, E. (1980). Multiple personalities: A report of 14 cases with implications for schizophrenia and hysteria. <u>Archives of General Psychiatry</u>, <u>37</u>, 1388-1398.

Boor, M. (1982). The multiple personality epidemic. additional cases and references regarding diagnosis, etiology, dynamics and treatment. <u>Journal of Nervous and Mental Disease</u>, <u>170</u>, 302-304.

Braun, B., & Sachs, R. (1985). Development of multiple personality disorder. In R. P. Kluft (Ed.), <u>Childhood antecedents of multiple personality</u> (pp.37-64). Washington, DC: American Psychiatric Press.

Braun, B. G., & Saachs, R. G. (1985). The development of multiple personality disorder: Predisposing, precipitating, and perpetuating factors. In R. P. Kluft (Ed.), <u>Childhood antecedents of</u>

multiple personality, (pp. 38-64). Washington, D.C.: American Psychiatric Press.

Briere, J., & Runtz, M. (1985, August). <u>Symptomology associated with prior sexual abuse in a non-clinical sample</u>. Paper presented at the annual meeting of the American Psychological Association, Los Angeles.

Briere, J. (1984, April). <u>The effects of childhood sexual abuse on later psychological functioning: Defining a post-sexual abuse syndrome</u>. Paper presented at the Third National Conference on Sexual Victimization of Children, Washington, DC.

Briere, J., & Runtz, M. (1986). Suicidal thoughts and behavior in sexual abuse survivors. <u>Canadian Journal of Behavioral Sciences</u>, <u>18</u>, 413-423.

Briere, J. & Runtz, M. (1987). Post sexual abuse trauma, data and implications for clinical practice. <u>Journal of Interpersonal Violence</u>, <u>2</u>, 367-379.

Brown, M. (1979). Teenage prostitution. <u>Adolescence</u>, <u>14</u>, 665-675.

Browne, A., & Finkelhor, D. (1986). The Impact of child sexual abuse: A review of the research. <u>Psychological Bulletin</u>, <u>99</u>, 66-77.

Burgess, A. W., & Hartman, C. (Eds.). (1986). <u>Sexual exploitation of patients by health professionals</u>. New York: Praeger.

Cellucci, A., & Lawrence, P. (1978). The efficacy of systematic desensitization in reducing nightmares. <u>Journal of Behavioral Therapy and Experimental Psychiatry</u>, <u>9</u>, 109-114.

Conte, J. R. (1984, November). <u>The effects of sexual abuse on children: A critique and suggestions for further research</u>. Paper presented at the Third International Institute on Victimology, Lisbon, Portugal.

Conte, J. R., & Schuerman, J. R. (1987). The effects of sexual abuse on children, a multidimensional view. <u>Journal of Interpersonal Violence</u>, <u>2</u>, 381-390.

Courtois, C. (1986, May). <u>Treatment for serious mental health sequelae of child sexual abuse: Post traumatic stress disorder in children and adults</u>. Paper presented at the Fourth National Conference on Sexual Victimization of Children, New Orleans, LA.

Donaldson, M. A., & Gardner, R., Jr. (1985). Diagnosis and treatment of traumatic stress among women after childhood incest. In C. R. Figley (Ed.), <u>Trauma and its wake</u> (pp. 356-357). New York: Brunner/Mazel.

Eth, S., & Pynoos, R. S. (1985). <u>Post traumatic stress disorder in children</u>. Los Angeles: American Psychiatric Association.

Evert,K., & Bijkerk,I. (1987). When you're ready. Walnut Creek, CA: Launch Press.

Fairbank, J., & Keane, T. (1982). Flooding for combat related stress disorders: Assessment of anxiety reduction across traumatic memories. Behavioral Therapy, 13, 499-510.

Finkelhor, D. (1986). A sourcebook on child sexual abuse. Beverly Hills, CA: Sage Publication.

Finkelhor, D. (1979). Sexually victimized children. New York: Free Press.

Frederick, C. J. (1986). Post-traumatic stress disorders and child molestation. In A. Burgess & C. Hartman (Eds.), Sexual exploitation of clients by mental health professionals. New York: Praeger.

Friedrich, W. M. (1987). Behavior problems in sexually abused children: An adaptational perspective. Journal of Interpersonal Violence, 2, 381-390.

Fritz, G., Stoll, K., & Wagner, N. (1981). A comparison of males and females who were sexually molested as children. Journal of Sex and Marital Therapy, 7, 54-59.

Fruchholz, E. J. (1985). The relationship among dissociation, hypnosis, and child abuse in the development of MPD. In R. P. Kluft (Ed.), Childhood antecedents of multiple personality (pp. 99-126). New York: American Psychiatric Press.

Garbarino, J., Guttmann, E., & Seeley, J. W. (1980). The psychologically battered child. San Francisco: Jossey-Bass.

Gartrell, N., Herman, J., Olarte, S., Feldstein, M., & Localio, R. (1986). Psychiatric-patient sexual contact: Results of a national survey, I: Prevalence. American Journal of Psychiatry, 9,(143).

Gelinas, D. (1983). The persisting negative effects of incest. Psychiatry, 6, 312-332.

George, C., & Main, M. (1979). Sexual interactions of young abused children: Approach, avoidance and aggression. Child Development, 50, 306-318.

Giaretto, H. (1982). Integrated treatment of child sexual abuse. Palo Alto, CA: Science and Behavior Books.

Goodwin, J. (1985). Post-traumatic symptoms in incest victims. In S. Eth & R. S. Pynoos (Eds.), Post traumatic stress disorder in children, (pp. 157-168). Los Angeles: American Psychiatric Association.

Goodwin, J. (1985). Credibility problems in multiple personality disorder patients and abused children. In R. P. Kluft (Ed.), Childhood antecedents of multiple personality, (pp. 1-20). Washington, DC: American Psychiatric Press.

Gordy, P. L. (1983). Group work that supports adult victims of childhood incest. Social Casework: The Journal of Contemporary Social Work, 5, 300-307.

Greaves, G. B. (1980). Multiple personality 165 years after Mary Reynolds. Journal of Nervous and Mental Disease, 168, 577-597.

Green, A. (1983). Dimensions of psychological trauma in abused children. Journal of the American Academy of Child Psychiatry, 22, 231-237.

Grinker, R., & Speigel, J. (1945). Men under stress. Philadelphia: Blakiston.

Groth, N. A. (1984). Anatomical drawings. Newton Center, MA: Forensic Mental Health Associates.

Herman, J. (1981). Father-daughter incest. Cambridge: Harvard University.

Hicks, R. E. (1985). Discussion: A clinician's perspective. In R. P. Kluft (Ed.), Childhood antecedents of multiple personality, (pp. 239-258). New York: American Psychiatric Press.

Hollingsworth, J. (1986). Unspeakable acts. New York: Congdon & Weed.

Horowitz, M. & Solomon, G. (1975). A prediction of delayed stress response syndromes in Vietnam veterans. Journal of Social Issues, 31, 67-80.

Horowitz, M. J. (1974). Stress response syndromes. New York: Hason Aronson.

Janoff-Bulman, R. (1985). The aftermath of victimization: Rebuilding shattered assumptions. In C. R. Figley (Ed.), Trauma and its wake, (pp. 15-35). New York: Brunner/Mazel.

Keane, T., & Kaloupek, D. (1982). Imaginal flooding in the treatment of post-traumatic stress disorder. Journal of Consulting and Clinical Psychology, 50, 138-140.

Kent, J. T. (1980). A follow up study of abused children. In G. J. Williams & J. Money (Eds.), Traumatic abuse and neglect of young children at home (pp. 221-233). Baltimore, MD: Johns Hopkins University.

Kluft, R. P. (1985). Childhood antecedents of multiple personality. Washington, D.C.: American Psychiatric Press.

Landeros Vs. Flood (1976). 17C 3d 399, 412 FN9-131 Cal Reporter 69.

Lindberg, F. H., & Distad, L. J. (1985). Post-traumatic stress disorders in women who experienced childhood incest. Child Abuse and Neglect, 9, 329-344.

Maltz, W., & Holman, B. (1987). Incest and sexuality: A guide to understanding and healing. Lexington, MA: Lexington.

Marafiote, R. (1980). Behavioral strategies in group treatment of Vietnam veterans. In T. Williams (Ed.), Post traumatic stress disorders of the Vietnam veteran (pp. 49-70). Cincinnati, OH: Disabled American Veterans.

Martin, H. P. (1976). The abused child. Cambridge, MA: Ballinger.

Martin, H. P., & Rodeheffer, M. A. (1980). The psychological impact of abuse on children. In G. J. Williams & J. Money (Eds.), Traumatic abuse and neglect of children at home (pp. 205-212). Baltimore, MD: Johns Hopkins University.

McCann, L., Pearlman, L. A., Sakheim, D. K., & Abrahamson, D. J. (1988). Assessment and treatment of the adult survivor of childhood sexual abuse within a schema framework. In S. Sgroi (Ed.), Vulnerable populations: Evaluation and treatment of sexually abused children and adult survivors (pp. 77-102). Lexington, MA: Lexington.

Meiselman, K. C. (1978). Incest: A psychological study of caused and effects with treatment recommendations. San Francisco: Jossey-Bass.

Milogrom, J. H., & Schoener, G. R. (1987). Responding to clients who have been sexually exploited by counselors, therapists, & clergy. In M. Pellauer, B. Chester & J. Boyajian (Eds.), Sexual assault and abuse: A handbook for clergy and religious professionals. San Francisco: Harper and Row.

Miniszek, N. (1984, September). Flooding as a supplemental treatment for Vietnam veterans. Paper presented at the Third National Conference on Post Traumatic Stress Disorder, Baltimore, MD.

Newman, C. J., (1976). Children of disaster: Clinical observations at Buffalo Creek. American Journal of Psychiatry, 133, 306-310.

Parson, E. (1984). The reparation of the self clinical and theoretical dimensions in the treatment of Vietnam combat veterans. Journal of Contemporary Psychotherapy, 14(1), 4-56.

Peck, M. S. (1983). People of the lie. New York: Simon & Schuster.

Perry, N. W. (1987). Child and adolescent development: A psychological perspective. In J. Meyers (Ed.), Child witness, law and practice (pp. 459-525). New York: Wiley.

Peters, S. D. (1984). The relationship between childhood sexual victimization and adult depression among Afro-American and white women. Unpublished doctoral dissertation, University of California, Los Angeles.

Polansky, N. A., Chalmers, M. A., Williams, D. P., & Buttenwieser, E. W. (1981). Damaged parents: An anatomy of child neglect. Chicago: University of Chicago.

Pope, K. S. (1986). Research and laws regarding therapist-patient sexual involvement: Implications for therapist. American Journal of Psychotherapy, 4,(XL).

Porter, E. (1986). Treating the young male victim of sexual assault: Issues & intervention strategies. Orwell, VT: Safer Society Press.

Powell, G. J. (1987). The multifaceted aspects of child sexual abuse, summary and conclusions. Journal of Interpersonal Violence, 2, 435-445.

Putnam, F. W. (1985). Dissociation as a response to extreme trauma. In R. P. Kluft (Ed.), Childhood antecedents of multiple personality (pp. 65-98). Washington, DC: American Psychiatric Press.

Putnam, F. W., Post, R. M., & Guroff, J. J. (1983). 100 cases of multiple personality disorder. Presented at the American Psychiatric Association Annual Meeting, (From New Research Abstracts, 77).

Putnam, F. W., & Post, R. M., Guroff, J. J. (1987). One hundred cases of MPD. Paper presented at the annual meeting of the American Psychiatric Association, New York.

Reidy, T. J. (1980). The aggressive characteristics of abused and neglected children. In G. J. Williams & J. Money (Eds.), Traumatic abuse and neglect of children at home (pp. 213-220). Baltimore, MD: Johns Hopkins University.

Russell, D. E. H. (1986). The secret trauma: Incest in the lives of girls and women. New York: Basic Books.

Saltman, V., & Solomon, R. S. (1982). Incest and multiple personality disorder. Psychological Reports, 50, 1127-1141.

Schoener, G. R., Milogrom, J. H., & Gonsiorek, J. (1984). Sexual Exploitation of clients by therapists. New York: Haworth.

Schultz, R., Braun, B. G., & Kluft, R. P. (1985). Creativity and imaginary companion phenomena: Prevalence and phenomenology in MPD. In B. G. Braun (Ed.), Proceedings of the Second International Conference on Multiple Personality Dissociative States. Chicago: Chicago Rush University.

Scurfield, R. M. (1985). Post-trauma stress assessment and treatment: Overview and formulations. In C. R. Figley (Ed.), Trauma and its wake, (pp. 219-256). New York: Brunner/Mazel.

Senior, N., Gladstone, T., & Nurcombe, B. (1982). Child snatching: A case report. Journal of the American Academy of Child Psychiatry, 21, 579-583.

Sgroi, S. M., & Bunk, B. S. (1988). A clinical approach to adult survivors of child sexual abuse. In S. M. Sgroi (Ed.), Vulnerable populations (pp. 137-186). Lexington, MA: Lexington.

Sgroi, S. (1975). Sexual molestation of children: The last frontier in child abuse. Children Today, 4, 18-21.

Sgroi, S. M., Bunk, B. S., & Wabrek, C. J. (1988). Children's sexual behaviors and their relationship to sexual abuse. In S. M. Sgroi (Ed.), Vulnerable populations:Evaluation and treatment of sexually abused children and adult survivors (pp. 1-24). Lexington, MA: Lexington.

Stern, C. R. (1984). The etiology of multiple personalities. Psychiatric Clinics of North America, 7, 149-160.

Steward, M. S., Farquhar, L. C., Dicharry, D. C., Glick, D. R., & Martin, P. W. (1986). Group therapy: A treatment of choice for young victims of child abuse. International Journal of Group Psychotherapy, 36(2).

Summit, R. (1983). The child sexual abuse accommodation syndrome. Child Abuse and Neglect, 7(2), 177-193.

Tarasoff vs. Regents of UC (1976). 551 P. 2d. 33417 Cal. 3rd. 425131 Cal Reporter 14.

Terr, L. (1979). Children of Chowchilla: Study of psychic trauma. Psychoanalytic Study of the Child, 34, 547-623.

Terr, L. (1981). Psychic trauma in children. American Journal of Psychiatry, 138, 14-19.

Terr, L. (1983). Chowchilla revisited: The effects of psychic trauma four years after a school bus kidnapping. American Journal of Psychiatry, 140, 1543-1550.

Trumble, M. R. (1985). Post-traumatic stress disorder: History of a concept. In C. R. Figley (Ed.), Trauma and its wake (pp. 5-14). New York: Brunner/Mazel.

Tsai, M., & Wagner, N. (1978). Therapy groups for women sexually molested as children. Archives of Sexual Behavior, 7, 417-429.

Wilbur C. B. (1985). The effect of child abuse on the psyche. In R. P. Kluft (Ed.), Childhood antecedents of multiple personality (pp 21-36). Washington, DC: American Psychiatric Press.

Wilbur, C. B. (1984). Multiple personality and child abuse. Psychiatric Clinics of North America, 7, 3-8.

Wyatt, G. E. (1985). The sexual abuse of Afro-American women and White-American women in childhood. Child Abuse and Neglect, 9, 507-519.

SUGGESTED READINGS

Bass, E. & Davis, L. (1988). The courage to heal: A guide for women survivors of child sexual abuse. New York: Harper and Row.

Bass, E. (1983). I never told anyone. New York: Harper & Row.

Bass, E. (1990) The courage to heal workbook. New York: Harper and Row.

Bear, E., & Dimock, P. T. (1987). Adults molested as children: A survivors manual for women and men. Orwell, VT: Safer Society Press.

Bear, E. & Dimock, P. T., (1988). Adults molested as children: A survivor's manual for men and women. Orwell, VT: Safer Society Press.

Black, C. (1982). It will never happen to me. Denver, CO: Medical Administration Company.

Braun, B. G., (Ed.), (1986). Treatment of multiple personality disorder. Washington, DC: American Psychiatric Press.

Briere, J. (1989), Therapy for adults molested as children: Beyond survival. New York: Springer.

Butler, S. (1978). Conspiracy of silence: The trauma of incest. San Francisco: New Glide Publications.

Caruso, B. (1986). Healing: A handbook for adult victims of sexual abuse. Minneapolis, MN: Author.

Childhelp USA (1988). Survivor's guide. Hollywood, CA: Los Angeles Child Help Center.

Courtois, C.A., (1988), Healing the incest wound. New York: W.W. Norton.

Daugherty, L. B. (1984). Why me? Help for victims of child sexual abuse (Even if they are adults now). Racine, WI: Mother Courage Press.

Donaforte, L. (1982). I remembered myself: The journal of a survivor of childhood sexual abuse. Ukiah, CA.: Author.

Evert, K. (1987). When you're ready: A woman's healing from physical and sexual abuse by her mother. Walnut Creek, CA: Launch Press.

Figley, C. R. (1985). Trauma and its wake: The study and treatment of post traumatic stress disorder. New York: Brunner/Mazel.

Finkelhor, D. (Ed.). (1986). A sourcebook on child sexual abuse. Beverly Hills, CA: Sage.

Garbarino, J., Gutman, E, & Seeley, J. W. (1986). The psychologically battered child. San Francisco: Josey Bass.

Gelinas, D. J. (1983). The persisting negative effects of incest. Psychiatry, 46, 312-332.

Gil E. (1984). Outgrowing the pain: A book for and about adults abused as children. Walnut Creek, CA: Launch Press.

Gil, E. (1990) United we stand: A book for individuals with multiple personalities. Walnut Creek, CA: Launch Press.

Gravitz, H. L., & Bowden, J. D., (1985). Guide to recovery: A book for adult children of alcoholics. Holmes Beach, FL: Learning Publications.

Helfer, R. E. (1978). Childhood comes first: A crash course in childhood. East Lansing, MI: Helfer.

Kluft, R. P., (Ed.), (1985). Childhood antecedents of multiple personality. Washington, DC: American Psychiatric Press.

Leehan, J., & Wilson, L. P. (1985). Grown-up abused children. Springfield, IL: Charles C. Thomas.

Lew, M. (1990). Victims no longer: Men recovering from incest and other sexual child abuse. New York: Harper & Row.

Lindberg, F. H., & Distad, L. J. (1985). Post traumatic disorder women who experienced childhood incest. Child abuse and neglect, 9(3), 329-334.

Maltz, W. & Holman, B. (1986). Incest and Sexuality: A guide to understanding and healing. Lexington, MA: Lexington.

McConnell, P. (1986). A workbook for healing adult children of alcoholics. San Francisco, CA: Harper & Row.

Miller, A. (1983). For your own good. New York: Farrar Straus Giroux.

Miller, A. (1986). Thou shalt not be aware: Society's betrayal of the child. New York: Meridan.

Montegna, D. (1989), Prisoner of innocence. Walnut Creek, CA: Launch Press.

Morris, M. (1982). If I should die before I wake. New York: J.P. Tarcher.

Putnam, F.W. (1989) Diagnosis and treatment of multiple personality disorder. New York: Guilford Press.

Rush, F. (1980). The best kept secret: Sexual abuse of children. Englewood Cliffs, NJ: Prentice-Hall.

Sgroi, S. (Ed.). (1988). <u>Vulnerable populations: Evaluation and treatment of sexually abused children and adult survivor</u>. Lexington, MA: Lexington.

Sisk, S. L., & Hoffman, C. F., (1987). <u>Inside scars</u>. Gainesville, FL: Pandora Press.

Terr, L. (1990). <u>Too scared to cry.</u> New York: Harper & Row.

Thomas, T. (1989) <u>Men surviving incest: A Male Survivor Shares the Process of Recovery.</u> Walnut Creek, CA: Launch Press.

Van der Kolk, B. A., (Ed.), (1984). <u>Post-traumatic stress disorder: Psychological and biological sequelae.</u>   Washington, DC: American Psychiatric Press.

Van der Kolk, B.A. (1987) <u>Psychological trauma.</u> Washington, DC: American Psychiatric Press.

Wyatt, G.E. & Powell, G.J. (1988) <u>Lasting effects of child sexual abuse.</u> Newbury Park, CA: Sage.

Wynne, C. E. (1986). <u>That looks like a nice house</u>. Walnut Creek, CA: Launch Press.

RESOURCES

The following resources include national organizations that provide information on local referral sources or activities in the prevention and treatment of child abuse and a few selected California programs, mentioned in the book.

National Programs

American Humane Association
  9725 E. Hampden Avenue
  Denver, CO   80231
  (303) 695-0811

AAPSAC
  c/o The University of Chicago
  969 East 60th St. Chicago, IL   60637
  (312) 702-9419

C. Henry Kempe Center
  1205 Oneida Street
  Denver, CO   80220
  (303) 321-3963

Child Help National Child Abuse Hotline
  P.O. Box 630
  Hollywood, CA. 90028
  (800) 422-4453

Incest Survivors Anonymous
  ISA World Office
  P.O. Box 5613
  Long Beach, CA   90805

National Committee for the Prevention of Child Abuse (NCPCA)
  320 S. Michigan Avenue, #950
  Chicago, IL   60604
  (312) 663-3520

National Coalition against Sexual Assault
8787 State Street
East St Louis, IL   62203
(618) 398-7764

National Association for Children of Alcoholics (NACOA)
31706 Coast Highway, #301
So. Laguna, CA 92677
(714) 499-3889

National Self-Help Clearinghouse
City University of New York
33 W. 42nd Street, # 1222
New York, NY   10036
(212) 840-1259

National Center on Child Abuse and Neglect
US Department of Health and Human Services
P.O. Box 1182
Washington, DC 20013
(202) 245-2840

National Organization for Victim Assistance
717 D Street, N. W.
Washington, DC 20004

Parents United International, Inc.
Adults Molested as Children United
P.O.Box 952
San Jose, CA   95108
(408) 280-5055

Survivors of Incest International
P.O. Box 21817
Baltimore, MD   21222-6817
(301) 282-3400

Victims of Incest Can Emerge Survivors (VOICES)
PO Box 148309
Chicago, IL 60614
(312) 327-1500

Voices in Action
P.O. Box 148309
Chicago, IL. 60614
(312) 327-1500

California Programs

California Consortium of Child Abuse Councils
  1401 Third Street
  Sacramento, CA   95678
  (916) 448-9143

California Professional Society on the Abuse of Children
  (CAPSAC)
  1401 Third Street, #13
  Sacramento, CA   95814
  (916) 448-9135

Incest Survivors Anonymous
  PO Box 5613
  Long Beach, CA 90805-0613
  (213) 428-5599

Parents Anonymous
  6733 S. Sepulveda Blvd., #270
  Los Angeles, CA 90045
  (213) 410-9732
  (800) 421-0353

P.L.E.A. (Prevention, Leadership, Education and Assistance for
  Men Abused as Children
  Zia Road—Box 22
  Sante Fe, NM   87505

Survivors of Physical and Emotional Abuse as Kids (SPEAK)
  % Parents Anonymous
  6733 Sepulveda Blvd., #270
  Los Angeles, CA 90045
  (213) 410-9732

Women Molested by Mothers
  CAARE Project
  PO Box 409
  Mendocino, CA 95460